THE GREAT SEAL OF THE STATE OF CALIFORNIA

EUREKA

CALIFORNIA VISTAS

CALIFORNIA COMMUNITIES

James A. Banks, Ph.D.   Walter C. Parker, Ph.D.

Kevin P. Colleary, Ed.D.   James J. Rawls, Ph.D.

Stephen F. Cunha, Ph.D.   Rosalía Salinas

Jana Echevarria, Ph.D.   Emily M. Schell, Ed.D.

Macmillan McGraw-Hill

PROGRAM AUTHORS

James A. Banks, Ph.D.
Russell F. Stark University
Professor and Director,
  Center for Multicultural
  Education
University of Washington
Seattle, Washington

Kevin P. Colleary, Ed.D.
Curriculum and Teaching Department
Graduate School of Education
Fordham University
New York, New York

Stephen F. Cunha, Ph.D.
Professor of Geography
Humboldt State University
Arcata, California

Jana Echevarria, Ph.D.
Professor, College of Education
California State University
Long Beach, California

Walter C. Parker, Ph.D.
Professor of Education and Chair
  of Social Studies Education
University of Washington
Seattle, Washington

James J. Rawls, Ph.D.
Department of History
Diablo Valley College
Pleasant Hill, California

Rosalía Salinas
Senior Director
Learning Resources and Educational
  Technology Division (retired)
San Diego County Office of Education
San Diego, California

Emily M. Schell, Ed.D.
Social Studies Education Director,
City Heights Educational Collaborative
Visiting Professor, Teacher Education
San Diego State University
San Diego, California

 California Geographic Alliance
Humboldt State University
Arcata, California

HISTORIANS/SCHOLARS

Don R. Leet, Ph.D.
Chair, Economics Department
Director of the Center for
Economic Education
California State University
Fresno, California

Karen Nakai, Ed.D.
Professor, College of Education
California State University
Long Beach, California

Curtis C. Roseman, Ph.D.
Professor Emeritus of Geography
University of Southern California
Los Angeles, California

Quintard Taylor, Ph.D.
Scott and Dorothy Bullitt Professor
  of American History
University of Washington
Seattle, Washington

Clifford E. Trafzer, Ph.D.
Professor of American Indian History
University of California
Riverside, California

CONSULTANTS

Primary Sources Research
Library of Congress
Publishing Office
Washington, D.C.

Reading and Writing
Adria F. Klein, Ph.D.
Professor Emeritus
California State University
San Bernardino, California

English Learners
Elizabeth Jimenez
Pomona, California

GRADE LEVEL CONSULTANTS AND REVIEWERS

Stephanie Buttell-Maxin
Third Grade Teacher
Kimball Elementary School
National City, California

Marlene Dane
Third Grade Teacher
Bonita Canyon School
Irvine, California

 Students with print disabilities may be eligible to obtain an accessible, audio version of the pupil edition of this textbook. Please call Recording for the Blind & Dyslexic at 1-800-221-4792 for complete information.

B

The McGraw·Hill Companies

 **Macmillan McGraw-Hill**

Published by Macmillan/McGraw-Hill, of McGraw-Hill Education, a division of The McGraw-Hill Companies, Inc., Two Penn Plaza, New York, New York 10121.

Printed in the United States of America

ISBN 0-02-150511-X

2 3 4 5 6 7 8 079 10 09 08 07 06

ACKNOWLEDGMENTS

Grateful acknowledgment is given to the following authors, composers, and publishers. Every effort has been made to trace the ownership of all copyrighted material and to secure the necessary permissions to reprint these selections. In the case of some selections for which acknowledgment is not given, extensive research has failed to locate the copyright holders.

Walk Lightly, from "A World of Wonders: Geographic Travels in Verse and Rhyme." Text by J. Patrick Lewis. Illustrations by Alison Jay. Text Copyright © 2002 by J. Patrick Lewis. Illustrations Copyright © 2002 by Alison Jay. Published by Dial Books for Young Readers, a division of Penguin Putnam Inc. All Rights Reserved. Used by Permission.

Greg and Carmen Mitre, from "West Coast Shipping Contract Is Set" by William Booth. The Washington Post, November 25, 2002. Used by Permission.

Gary Ulman, from "Going the Distance for a Home" by Mary Lynne Vellinga. The Sacramento Bee, June 29, 2003. Used by Permission.

This Land Is Your Land, Words and Music by Woody Guthrie. TRO - © Copyright 1956 (Renewed), 1958 (Renewed), 1970 (Renewed) and 1972 (Renewed). Ludlow Music, Inc., New York, NY. International Copyright Secured. All Rights Reserved Including Public Performance For Profit. Used by Permission.

Cover permission for **Mojave,** Text by Diane Siebert and Illustrations by Wendell Minor. Text Copyright © 1988 by Diane Siebert. Illustrations Copyright © 1988 by Wendell Minor. Published by HarperCollins. All Rights Reserved.

Cover permission for **City of Angels: In and Around Los Angeles,** Text by Julie Jaskol and Brian Lewis. Illustrations by Elisa Kleven. Text Copyright © 1999 by Julie Jaskol and Brian Lewis. Illustrations Copyright © 1999 by Elisa Kleven. Published by Dutton Children's Books, A Division of Penguin Putnam Books for Young Readers. All Rights Reserved.

Cover permission for **Barrio: José's Neighborhood**, by George Ancona. Copyright © 1998 by George Ancona. Published by Harcourt, Inc. All Rights Reserved.

Coyote Rides A Star, from "Back in the Beforetime: Tales of the California Indians." Retold by Jane Louise Curry. Illustrations by James Watts. Text Copyright © 1987 by Jane Louise Curry. Illustrations Copyright © 1987 by James Watts. Published by Margaret K. McElderry Books – Macmillan Publishing Company. All Rights Reserved. Used by Permission.

Georgiana Valoyce Sanchez, from the California Indian Storytelling Association: <www.cistory.org/index2.html> Used by Permission.

David Laughing Horse Robinson, from Artist Statement: <www.angelfire.com/art2/talk_about > Used by Permission.

Mary Youngblood, from: <www.maryyoungblood.com/biography.htm> Used by Permission.

Mary Youngblood, from "Scene" section by Chris

Macias. The Sacramento Bee, February 26, 2004. Used by Permission.

Stan Rodriguez, from "Kumeyaay Singing" by The Alliance for California Traditional Arts. Copyright © 2000-2004 Alliance for California Traditional Artists. <www.actaonline.org/artists_cultural_heritage/sound%20traditions/cuero.htm> Used by Permission.

Cover permission for **Pueblo Boy: Growing Up in Two Worlds,** by Marcia Keegan. Copyright © 1991 by Marcia Keegan. Published by Dutton Children's Books. All Rights Reserved.

Cover permission for **Powwow,** Photographs and Text by George Ancona. Copyright © 1993 by George Ancona. Published by Harcourt, Inc. All Rights Reserved.

Cover permission for **Weaving A California Tradition: A Native American Basketmaker,** Text by Linda Yamane. Photographs by Dugan Aguilar. Copyright © 1997 by Lerner Publications Company. All Rights Reserved.

My Diary from Here to There (Mi diario de aqui hasta alla), Text by Amada Irma Perez. Illustrations by Maya Christina Gonzalez. Text Copyright © 2002 by Amada Irma Perez. Illustrations Copyright © 2002 by Maya Christina Gonzalez. Published by Children's Book Press. All Rights Reserved. Used by Permission.

(continued on page R57)

★ CONTENTS ★

UNIT 1

Communities and Geography   2

THE BIG IDEA   **How does geography affect communities?**

UNIT 2 Native American Communities 84

THE BIG IDEA How has life changed for people over time?

Communities Change 156

THE BIG IDEA Why do communities change over time?

THIS IS
LAKEWOOD
SALES OFFICE 5327 LAKEWOOD BLVD.
AT THE TOWER

CHARTS, GRAPHS, AND DIAGRAMS

TIME LINES

MAPS

Primary Source Quotes

For full publication information, turn to page iii.

Start with Your
CALIFORNIA STANDARDS

★ ☆ ★

You will see California Standards throughout this book. These standards will help you identify the most important topics in each lesson. These are topics you are required to learn in your social studies class.

The first page of every lesson lists the standards covered in that lesson. At the end of each lesson, the "What You Learned" box summarizes the lesson and its standards. The questions in Lesson Reviews, Chapter Reviews, and Unit Reviews all have standards next to them. You will also find standards next to each chart, graph, and activity.

California standards are listed in blue type on the first page of every lesson.

California standards are explained in black type with page numbers that show where they are taught.

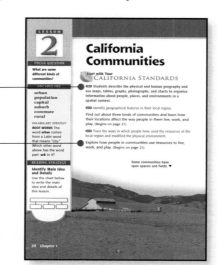

What You Learned reviews the lesson's main ideas and the standards they covered.

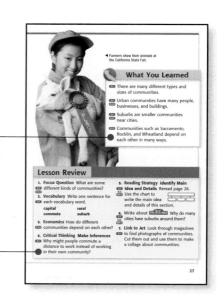

Lesson Review questions list History/Social Science standards and English-Language Arts standards.

ABOUT THE BIG IDEA

The Big Ideas in this book are important ideas about social studies. They will help you understand the information in each unit.

The Big Idea question for each unit appears on its opening pages. At the end of the lessons, look for the "Write about the Big Idea" questions in the Lesson Reviews. These questions will help you answer the Big Idea question for the unit. When you finish the unit, complete the Big Idea activities. They will help you review what you have learned.

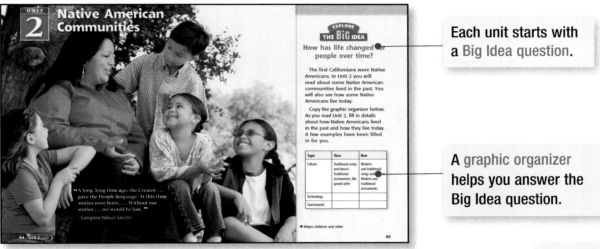

Each unit starts with a Big Idea question.

A graphic organizer helps you answer the Big Idea question.

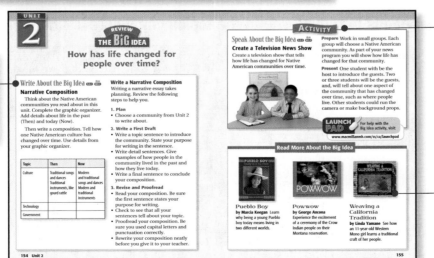

Each unit ends with a Write About the Big Idea.

Big Idea activities help you review what you have learned.

Other books can help you learn more about the Big Idea.

Reading Your Textbook

This book is organized to help you understand and apply social studies content and skills as you read.

■ **Unit Opener** and **Unit Closer** pages help you see the big picture.

The Unit Opener photo and quote capture the excitement of the unit.

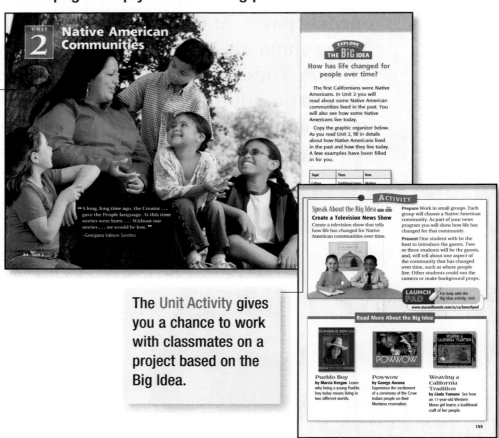

The Unit Activity gives you a chance to work with classmates on a project based on the Big Idea.

■ **Chapter Opener** pages introduce you to the topics you will read about in each lesson.

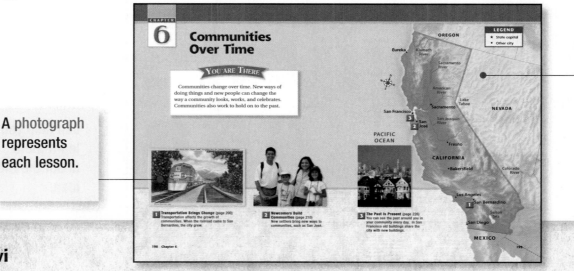

A map helps you see the locations of places from the chapter.

A photograph represents each lesson.

■ **Lesson Opener** pages prepare you to read the lesson.

Focus questions set a purpose for reading.

Graphic organizers help you organize information as you read.

Review questions help you know if you understood the section.

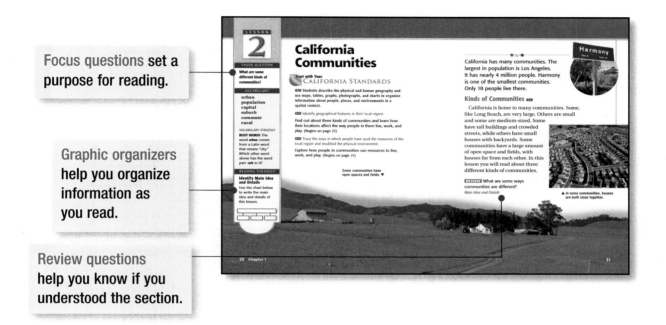

■ **Lesson Review** pages assess your understanding of the lesson.

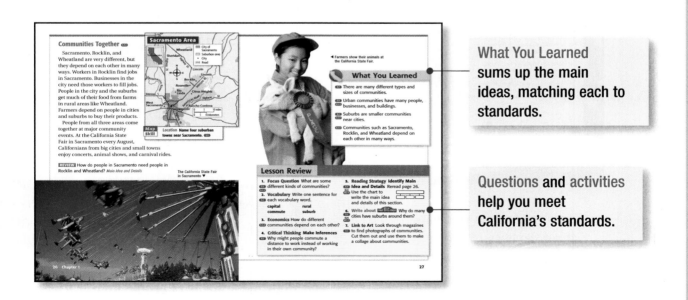

What You Learned sums up the main ideas, matching each to standards.

Questions and activities help you meet California's standards.

Reading Social Studies pages teach reading skills that help you understand social studies content.

Step-by-step instructions **help you learn the skill.**

Graphic organizers **help you apply the skill to the content.**

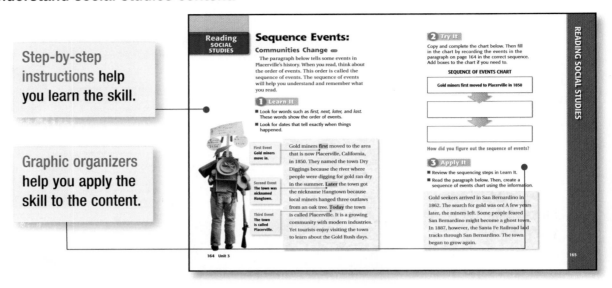

Biographies and **Primary Sources** bring the past to life.

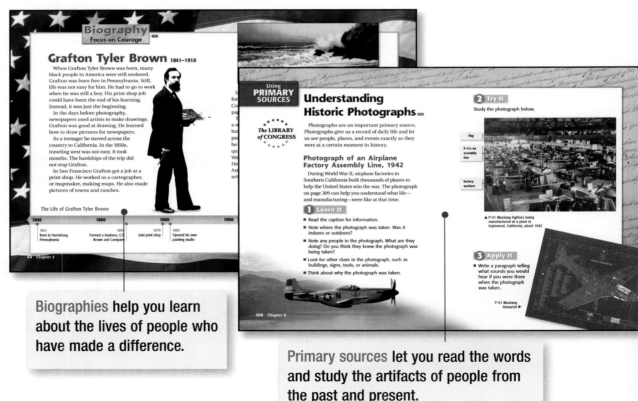

Biographies **help you learn about the lives of people who have made a difference.**

Primary sources **let you read the words and study the artifacts of people from the past and present.**

Readers' Theater plays enrich your reading. **Citizenship** pages show real life participation in democracy.

Readers' Theater plays give you a chance to cover important topics in a fun way.

Third graders explain their views on important topics.

Local Connections helps you learn about your own community.

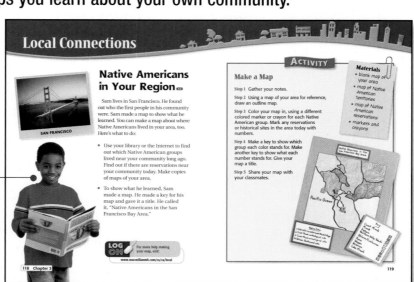

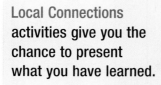

Local Connections activities give you the chance to present what you have learned.

Geography Handbook

A Letter from Steve Cunha

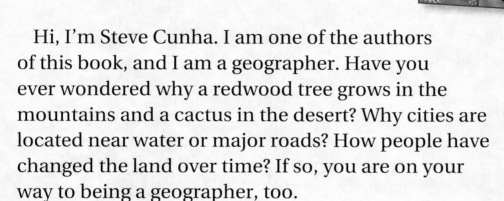

Dear Student:

Hi, I'm Steve Cunha. I am one of the authors of this book, and I am a geographer. Have you ever wondered why a redwood tree grows in the mountains and a cactus in the desert? Why cities are located near water or major roads? How people have changed the land over time? If so, you are on your way to being a geographer, too.

Geographers are people who study Earth. We look at the land and water, the weather and climate, the plants and animals on Earth. We also study people—where they live and how they shape where they live.

Knowing about geography helps you study History and Social Sciences. In the following pages, you will review some important ideas about geography. You will also review some key map skills that will help you as you read about California communities.

Let's get started. From one geographer to another: Enjoy your travels!

Stephen Cunha

Steve Cunha
The California Geographic Alliance

The Five Themes of Geography

Geography is the study of Earth and the way people, plants, and animals live on it. Geographers divide geography into five themes. These themes are location, place, region, movement, and human interaction. They help us to think about the world around us.

Look for these themes as you read the Map Skill questions throughout the book.

■ Location

"Where on Earth are you?" You would know if you knew your location. Location means an exact spot on the planet. Every place on Earth has a location.

A street in San Francisco's Chinatown ▶

■ Place

"What makes one place different from another?" Every place has physical and human features that describe it. Physical features can include mountains and lakes. Human features include things like where people live, how they work, and what languages they speak.

Fog and hills in San Francisco ▶

■ Region

"How are some places more like each other than other places?" A region is an area with common features that set it apart from other areas. For example, one region may have many mountains. A region is bigger than a place or a location.

Satellite photo of the San Francisco Bay Area ▶

■ Movement

"How and why do people move things and themselves from one place to another?" Geographers study why these movements happen. They also look at how people's movement changes an area.

Cable car on the streets of San Francisco ▶

■ Human Interaction

Geographers study how people and places change each other. For example, people wear warm clothes in cold places. People change the environment in order to meet their needs. For example, people build bridges to make travel easier.

San Francisco's Golden Gate Bridge ▶

Dictionary of Geographic Terms

1. **BAY** Body of water partly surrounded by land

2. **BEACH** Land covered with sand or pebbles next to an ocean or lake

3. **CANAL** Waterway dug across the land to connect two bodies of water

4. **CANYON** Deep river valley with steep sides

5. **CLIFF** High steep face of rock

6. **COAST** Land next to an ocean

7. **DESERT** A dry environment with few plants and animals

8. **GULF** Body of water partly surrounded by land; larger than a bay

9. **HARBOR** Protected place by an ocean or river where ships can safely stay

10. **HILL** Rounded, raised landform; not as high as a mountain

11 **ISLAND** Land that is surrounded on all sides by water

12 **LAKE** Body of water completely surrounded by land

13 **MESA** Landform that looks like a high, flat table

14 **MOUNTAIN** High landform with steep sides; higher than a hill

15 **OCEAN** Large body of salt water

16 **PENNISULA** Land that has water on all sides but one

17 **PLAIN** Large area of flat land

18 **PLATEAU** High flat area that rises steeply above the surrounding land

19 **PORT** Place where ships load and unload goods

20 **RIVER** Long stream of water that empties into another body of water

21 **VALLEY** Area of low land between hills or mountains

Reviewing Geography Skills

Looking at Earth

Earth and the Globe

From outer space, Earth looks like a big blue ball with brown areas of land. A globe is a model of Earth. It shows what the land and water look like on Earth.

You can see a line around the widest part of the globe. This is the equator. The equator is an imaginary line that separates the north from the south.

The farthest point north on the globe is called the North Pole. The farthest point south on the globe is called the South Pole.

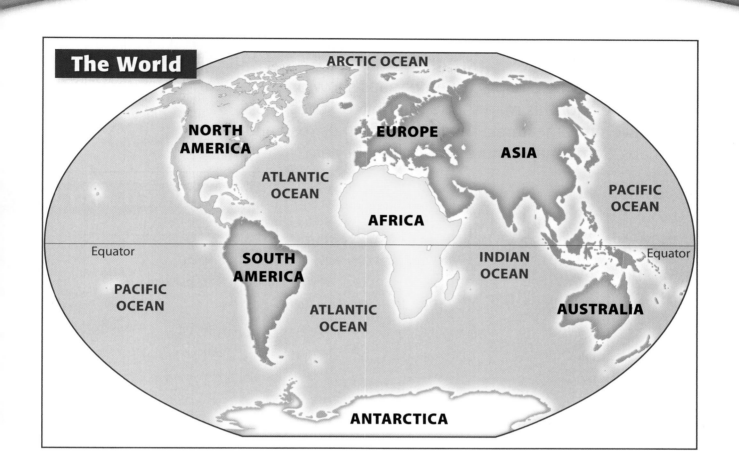

The World

ARCTIC OCEAN

NORTH AMERICA

EUROPE

ASIA

ATLANTIC OCEAN

PACIFIC OCEAN

AFRICA

Equator

SOUTH AMERICA

INDIAN OCEAN

Equator

PACIFIC OCEAN

ATLANTIC OCEAN

AUSTRALIA

ANTARCTICA

A Map of the World

A world map is a flat drawing of Earth. This map shows the continents and the oceans. Unlike a globe, flat maps can be used in books.

The big areas of land on Earth are called continents. The big bodies of water are called oceans.

There are seven continents on Earth. There are four major oceans. The equator divides Earth into the northern half and the southern half.

■ **What are the seven continents of the world?**

■ **What are the four oceans?**

Reading a Map

A map is a drawing of a place. Some maps show only part of the world. This map shows the United States. Most maps have similar features. The features help us read and use maps. Some map features are called out here.

■ What direction would you travel to go from Sacramento, California, to Denver, Colorado? Use the compass rose.

■ About how wide is the state of Utah at its widest? Use the scale rule.

Title

The maps in this book have titles. The title tells the region of the map. It also tells what kind of map it is, such as road map or landform map.

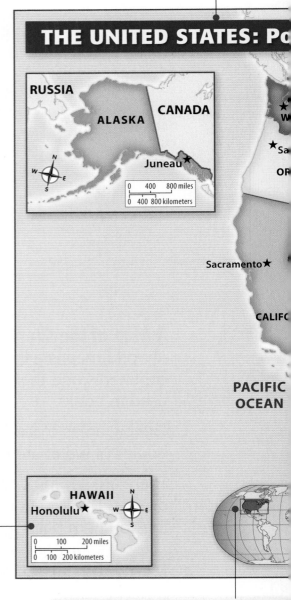

THE UNITED STATES: Po

RUSSIA

CANADA

ALASKA

Juneau

0 400 800 miles
0 400 800 kilometers

Sacramento★

CALIFO

PACIFIC OCEAN

HAWAII

Honolulu★

0 100 200 miles
0 100 200 kilometers

Inset Map

An inset map is a small map. It shows an area that is too large, too small, or too far away to include on the main map.

Locator Map

A locator map is a small map on a bigger map. It shows where the area of the bigger map is located on Earth.

Scale

This is the scale. It shows the real distance covered by the map. Each map has a different scale.

Key

A key, or legend, is the box that explains the symbols on the map.

Compass Rose

A compass rose shows where north, south, east, and west are on the map.

Special Maps

Landform Map

Landforms are different types of land on Earth. For example, mountains, hills, and deserts are all landforms. This map shows the landforms of Pennsylvania. You need to use the map key to understand the different colors on the map.

- **Look at the map key. What color shows mountains?**

- **What other landforms does the map show?**

- **On what kind of landform is Philadelphia located?**

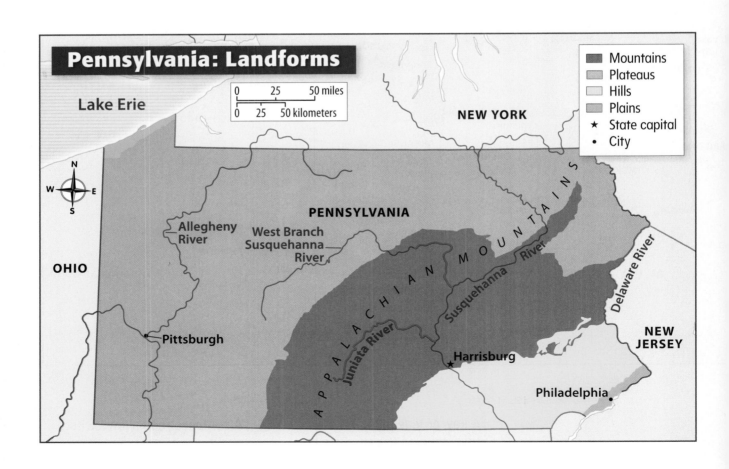

Pennsylvania: Landforms

Key:
- Mountains
- Plateaus
- Hills
- Plains
- ★ State capital
- • City

Lake Erie

NEW YORK

0   25   50 miles
0   25   50 kilometers

PENNSYLVANIA

Allegheny River

West Branch Susquehanna River

OHIO

APPALACHIAN MOUNTAINS

Susquehanna River

Delaware River

Juniata River

•Pittsburgh

★Harrisburg

NEW JERSEY

Philadelphia•

Route Map

A route map shows the streets and features of a city. You would use a route map if you wanted to find your way around a new town.

This map shows a part of Salinas, California. It can help you find a path from one side of town to the other.

■ **What streets are near the train station in Salinas?**

■ **If you wanted to travel from the train station to City Hall, what street would you use?**

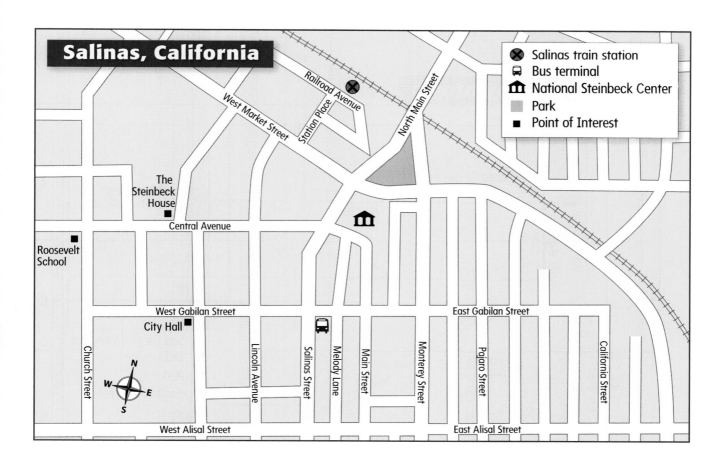

Salinas, California

Legend:
- ⊗ Salinas train station
- 🚌 Bus terminal
- 🏛 National Steinbeck Center
- Park
- ■ Point of Interest

Grid Maps

Grid maps help you locate specific areas. A grid map uses a pattern of lines that form boxes, or a grid. Each box is named for a letter and a number.

Look at the grid on the map of San Diego. Put your finger on City Hall. The number for that square is 3. The letter for that square is A. The grid can help you find places on a crowded map.

Look at the key on the map. The key shows you how to find the trolley line in San Diego.

■ **What is the number and letter of the square for the United States Court House?**

■ **What is found in square B2?**

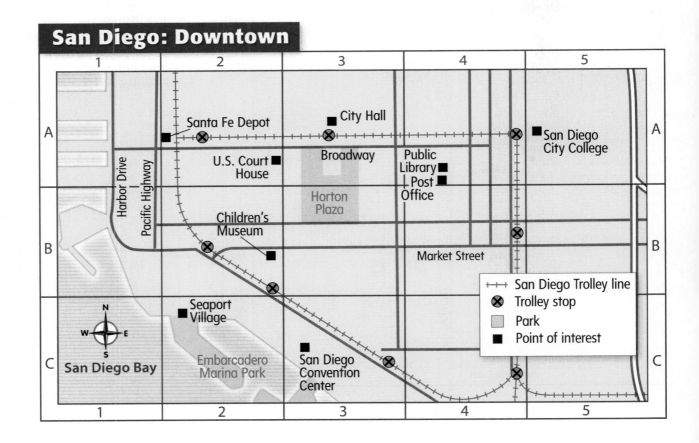

San Diego: Downtown

San Diego Trolley line
⊗ Trolley stop
Park
■ Point of interest

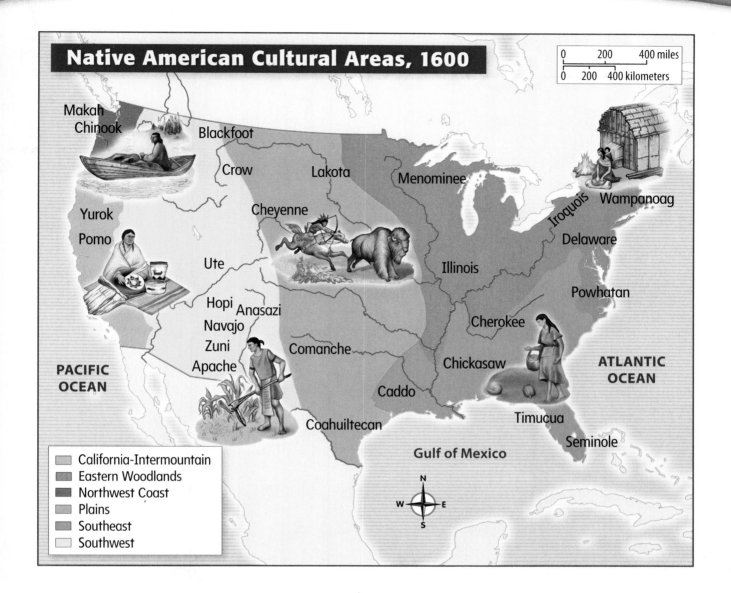

Native American Cultural Areas, 1600

0   200   400 miles
0   200   400 kilometers

Makah
Chinook
Blackfoot
Crow
Lakota
Menominee
Iroquois
Wampanoag
Yurok
Pomo
Delaware
Ute
Illinois
Powhatan
Hopi
Anasazi
Navajo
Cherokee
Zuni
Comanche
Apache
Chickasaw
Caddo
Coahuiltecan
Timucua
Seminole

PACIFIC
OCEAN

ATLANTIC
OCEAN

Gulf of Mexico

N W E S

☐ California-Intermountain
☐ Eastern Woodlands
☐ Northwest Coast
☐ Plains
☐ Southeast
☐ Southwest

Historical Maps

A historical map tells a story about a time in the past. Use the key to understand the story of the map. Sometimes historical maps include art. The art gives details about the time in history.

This map shows where Native American groups lived. The drawings tell how the different groups lived.

■ **In which cultural area did the Timucua live?**

■ **How did the Chinook people travel?**

Communities and Geography

**"It is there I would be
In our land by the sea . . ."**

—"I Love You, California"
by F. B. Silverwood

How does geography affect communities?

California has many different places to live. In Unit 1 you'll read about some places in California where people live and work. You will read about California's land and water, too.

Copy the graphic organizer below. As you read, think about why people choose to live where they do. Think about how land and water play a part in people's choices. Then add more information to the chart. Add information about your community, too.

Community	Location	Resources	Why it is there
Long Beach	Pacific coast	port, two rivers	good port
Sacramento			
Your community			

◀ Santa Catalina Island

3

Walk Lightly

a poem by J. Patrick Lewis
Illustrated by Robert Crawford

Make the Earth your companion.

Walk lightly on it, as other creatures do.

Let the Sky paint her beauty—she is
always watching over you.

Learn from the Sea how to face
harsh forces.

Let the River remind you that everything
will pass.

Let the Lake instruct you in stillness.

Let the Mountain teach you **grandeur**.

Make the Woodland your house of peace.

Make the Rainforest your house of hope.

Meet the Wetland on twilight ground.

Save some small piece of Grassland for
a red kite on a windy day.

Watch the Icecaps glisten with crystal
majesty.

Hear the Desert whisper hush to **eternity**.

Let the Town bring you togetherness.

Make the Earth your companion.

Walk lightly on it, as other creatures do.

---

harsh cruel or severe

grandeur (GRAND jur) greatness; majesty

eternity (ee TUR ni tee) endless time

Write About It! Think of a part of nature that you like, such as the ocean or the mountains. Write your own poem about it.

Identify Main Idea and Details

California Communities 3.1 2.5

The **main idea** is what a paragraph is all about. It is the most important thought in a paragraph. Often the first sentence states the main idea. The other sentences in a paragraph are **details**. Details tell more about the main idea. Finding the main idea and details will help you understand what you read.

1 Learn It

- Read the paragraph. Think about what the paragraph is about. See if there is a sentence which states the main idea.

- Now look for details. Sentences with details give more information about the main idea.

Main Idea
The first sentence states the main idea.

Details
These sentences tell of ways to have fun in Sacramento.

There are many ways to have fun in Sacramento, California. You could visit the California State Railroad Museum. You could go to a baseball game. Many visitors come each year to enjoy the State Fair, too.

2 Try It

Copy and complete the chart below. Write the main idea and the details of the paragraph on page 6 in the boxes.

```
┌─────────────────────────────────────────────────┐
│                                                   │
└─────────────────────────────────────────────────┘
        │                 │                 │
   ┌─────────┐       ┌─────────┐       ┌─────────┐
   │         │       │         │       │         │
   └─────────┘       └─────────┘       └─────────┘
```

3 Apply It

■ Review the steps in Learn It.

■ Read the paragraph below. Then make a main idea and details chart for the paragraph.

   Sacramento is the capital of California and the center of state government. The governor of California lives in Sacramento. State lawmakers meet there at the Capitol Building. Many state government offices are also located there.

Life in Communities

YOU ARE THERE

We all live in communities. Some communities are large, and some are small. However, all communities have certain things in common, and each one is special in its own way. In this chapter you will read about what makes a community.

1 **What Is a Community?** (page 10)
A community is a place where people live, work, and play.

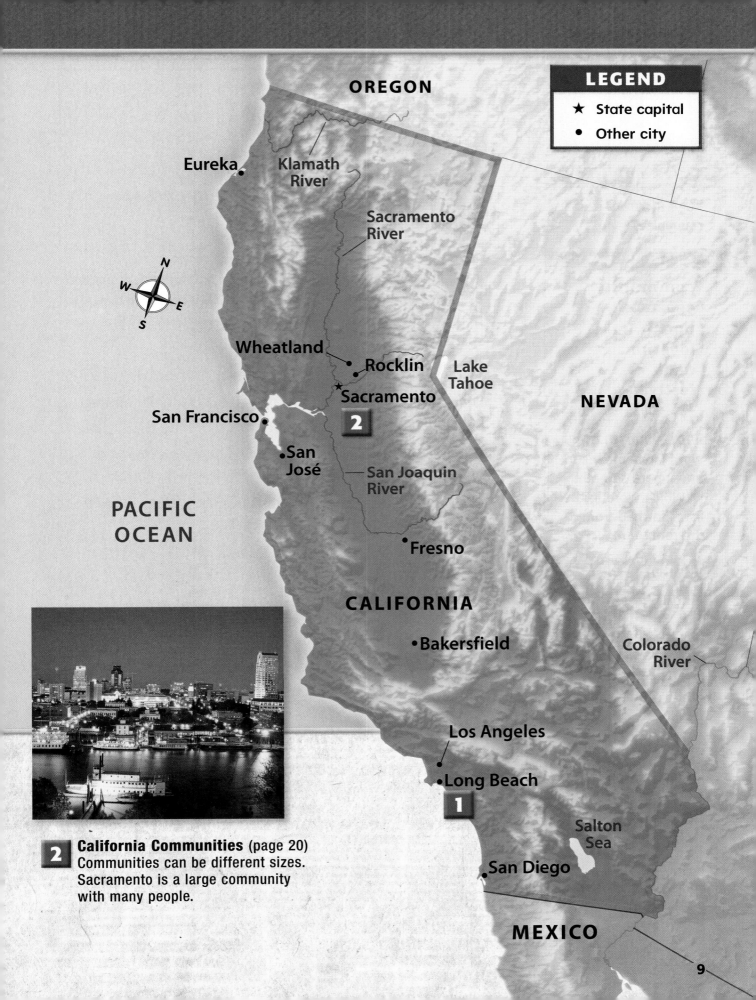

LEGEND
★ State capital
● Other city

OREGON

Eureka

Klamath River

Sacramento River

N
W   E
S

PACIFIC OCEAN

Wheatland

Rocklin

★ Sacramento

2

Lake Tahoe

NEVADA

San Francisco

San José

San Joaquin River

Fresno

CALIFORNIA

Bakersfield

Colorado River

Los Angeles

Long Beach

1

Salton Sea

San Diego

MEXICO

2 **California Communities** (page 20)
Communities can be different sizes.
Sacramento is a large community
with many people.

FOCUS QUESTION

What makes a community?

VOCABULARY

community
coast
port
location
dock
festival

VOCABULARY STRATEGY

ROOT WORDS The word **locate** means to find where something is. Which word in the list is formed from the root word **locate**?

READING STRATEGY

Identify Main Idea and Details

Use the chart below to write the main idea and details of this lesson.

What Is a Community?

Start with Your
CALIFORNIA STANDARDS

3.1 Students describe the physical and human geography and use maps, tables, graphs, photographs, and charts to organize information about people, places, and environments in a spatial context.

3.1.1 Identify geographical features in their local region.

Learn about how geography affects a community on the coast. (Begins on page 11)

3.1.2 Trace the ways in which people have used the resources of the local region and modified the physical environment.

Explore how people use the resources of a community to live, work, and play. (Begins on page 12)

▼ Long Beach, California

More than one hundred ships a week are unloaded in Long Beach. Many are as long as three football fields and as tall as a 15-story building.

People and Communities 3.1.1

Where do you live? No matter where you live in California, you live in a **community**. A community is a place where people live, work, and play. All communities are alike in some ways. They have homes, places for people to work, and places for people to have fun.

Let's take a look at Long Beach. Did you guess from its name that Long Beach is near water? Long Beach is on the **coast**, the land next to an ocean. About 500,000 people live there. You will see how the ocean plays a big part in the way people live, work, and play in Long Beach.

Long Beach

REVIEW What is a community? *Main Idea and Details*

A Community at Work 3.1.2

Long Beach is a **port** city. A port is a place where ships and boats can load and unload safely. Long Beach is a perfect place for a port because of its **location** on the Pacific Coast. A location tells where a place is on Earth. Long Beach's location makes it one of the busiest ports in the United States.

Of course, huge ships cannot just pull up on the beach. So the people of Long Beach built **docks**. A dock is a flat surface where boats or ships are tied up to be loaded or unloaded. The Long Beach docks are a busy place. Greg Mitre unloads ships there. He says, "Most everything you [use], from your coffee to your clothes, the car you drive, and your computer—you name it, we move it across these docks."

REVIEW What makes Long Beach a good place for a port?
Main Idea and Details

▼ Ships from all over the world come to Long Beach.

▲ Sea lions swim at
Long Beach Aquarium.

A Community at Play 3.1.2

Where do people go in Long Beach to have fun?
To the beach, of course! If you visited Long Beach,
you could swim, or you could rollerblade on a path
that runs along the beach. You could go see sharks
and sea lions at the aquarium. You could go to an
auto race. You might visit the *Queen Mary*, a famous
ship that is now a hotel and museum.

You could also hear music. Long Beach holds
many music **festivals** each year. A festival is a
celebration. You can hear all kinds of music—
including rock, jazz, and hip-hop. There is
something for everyone.

REVIEW What are some things that
people do for fun in Long Beach?
Main Idea and Details

Race cars fill city
streets for the Long
Beach Grand Prix. ▲

Helping Hands in a Community 3.1.1

Long Beach's location between two rivers causes a big problem for the community. Lots of trash gets into these rivers. The trash gets carried along by the river water. The rivers dump the trash into the ocean, but the waves push the trash back onto the beach. Look at the map below to see the locations of the rivers.

A man named Justin Rudd decided to do something about the problem. He started the "30-Minute Beach Cleanup." Now, on one Saturday each month, the people of Long Beach get together to help clean up the beach. So far, people have collected thousands of bags of trash. They work together to help improve their community.

REVIEW What is one way Long Beach people help their community? *Summarize*

▲ Justin Rudd got others to help him clean the beach at Long Beach.

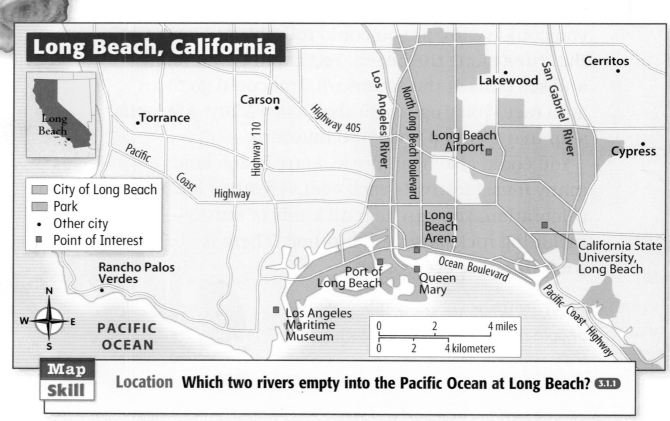

Map Skill

Location Which two rivers empty into the Pacific Ocean at Long Beach? 3.1.1

◀ In many California communities, people enjoy water sports.

What You Learned

3.1.1 A community is a place where people live, work, and have fun.

3.1.2 Long Beach is a community and a port on the Pacific Coast in California.

3.1.2 People in Long Beach make use of its location on the ocean for enjoyment.

3.1.1 The people of Long Beach work together to help their community.

Lesson Review

1. Focus Question What makes a
3.1.1 community?

2. Vocabulary Write one sentence for
3.1 each vocabulary word.

community	**dock**
coast	**location**

3. Economics How do events at the
3.1 port of Long Beach affect you?

4. Critical Thinking Draw Conclusions
3.1.2 What might happen if the people of Long Beach did not clean up their beach?

5. Reading Strategy Identify Main Idea
3.1.2 **and Details** Reread the
ELA
R2.5 first paragraph on page 14. Then use the chart to write the main idea and at least two details for the paragraph.

6. Write about THE BiG IDEA How does
3.1 Long Beach's location affect the
ELA
W2.2 community?

7. Link to Language Arts Write a letter
ELA
W2.3 to a friend in Long Beach about the "30-Minute Beach Cleanup." Tell your friend why it is important to help out.

Use Map Scales 3.1

Maps are drawn using **map scales**. A map scale is a unit of measurement that stands for a real distance on Earth. For example, an inch on a map can stand for a mile on Earth. You can find out a map's scale by looking at the **scale rule** on the map. The scale rule is the line on a map with marks that stand for actual distances.

VOCABULARY

map scale
scale rule

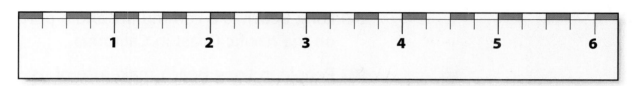

1 Learn It

Copy the scale rule above onto a piece of paper.

- Read the title of Map A. This map shows Oakland and some of its surrounding communities. Like Long Beach, Oakland is a very busy port city in California.

- Look at the map scale rule. It shows that 1 inch equals 4 miles.

2 Try It

Using your scale rule, measure distances on Map A.

- How far is it from City Hall to the Port of Oakland?

- How far is it from the Oakland Airport to Castro Valley?

- How far is it from the Oakland Zoo to McAfee Coliseum and Arena?

3 Apply It

Not all maps have the same scale. That is because different maps show smaller or larger parts of Earth. Some maps show a large area and have few details. Other maps show a smaller area but have more details. Looking at Map B is like "zooming in" on the area of Map A. Use Map B to answer these questions.

- What distance does 1 inch equal on Map B?

- How far is it from Oakland Museum to Mills College?

- Find Lake Merritt on both maps. What differences do you see between maps?

- Which map gives more detail about Oakland?

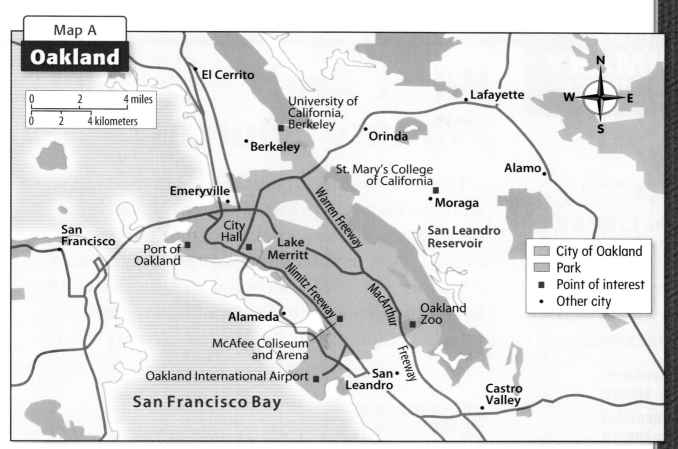

Map A
Oakland

0   2   4 miles
0   2   4 kilometers

N
W   E
S

El Cerrito

Lafayette

University of
California,
Berkeley

Orinda

Berkeley

St. Mary's College
of California

Alamo

Moraga

Emeryville

San Leandro
Reservoir

San
Francisco

City
Hall

Warren Freeway

Lake
Merritt

Port of
Oakland

Nimitz Freeway

MacArthur

Oakland
Zoo

Alameda

Freeway

McAfee Coliseum
and Arena

San
Leandro

Oakland International Airport

Castro
Valley

San Francisco Bay

▨	City of Oakland
▨	Park
■	Point of interest
•	Other city

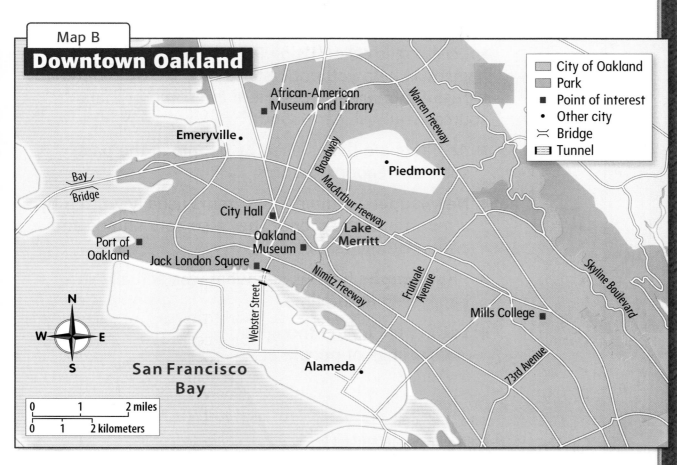

Map B
Downtown Oakland

▨	City of Oakland
▨	Park
■	Point of interest
•	Other city
⋈	Bridge
▤	Tunnel

African-American
Museum and Library

Warren Freeway

Emeryville

Broadway

Piedmont

Bay
Bridge

MacArthur Freeway

City Hall

Lake
Merritt

Oakland
Museum

Port of
Oakland

Jack London Square

Nimitz Freeway

Fruitvale
Avenue

Skyline Boulevard

Webster Street

Mills College

N
W   E
S

Alameda

73rd Avenue

San Francisco
Bay

0   1   2 miles
0   1   2 kilometers

17

What Are Primary Sources?

There are two main kinds of sources used in studying history. A **primary source** is an account from someone who witnessed or took part in an event. Letters or photographs are primary sources. A **secondary source** is an account of the past written by a person who was *not* a witness to an event. Encyclopedias and textbooks are secondary sources.

The LIBRARY *of* CONGRESS

VOCABULARY

primary source

secondary source

1 Learn It

As you read this book, look for quotations and boxes called Primary Sources in the text. Also look for special pages called Using Primary Sources. These pages will help you understand how to use different types of primary sources. Here are some primary sources you will learn about.

- **Artifacts** are things used by people in the past, such as weapons or tools.

- **Newspapers** contain news items usually written by a reporter at the scene. They also contain ads and announcements.

- **Photographs** help us see what was actually happening at the time.

- **Letters** tell us the thoughts and feelings of people at the time.

Native American artifact ▶

This historical photograph is a primary source. It shows an aircraft factory during World War II. ▶

2 Try It

Tell whether each item below is a primary source or a secondary source:

- your textbook
- a letter from your grandmother
- a photograph of your town's main street
- an encyclopedia
- an article from your local newspaper

How were you able to tell?

3 Apply It

- In your classroom, find an example of both a primary source and a secondary source.
- What are some things you use every day that might be artifacts someday?
- Look for the boxes called Primary Sources in the lessons as you read this book.

FOCUS QUESTION

What are some different kinds of communities?

VOCABULARY

urban
population
capital
suburb
commute
rural

VOCABULARY STRATEGY

ROOT WORDS The word **urban** comes from a Latin word that means "city." Which other word above has the word part **-urb** in it?

READING STRATEGY

Identify Main Idea and Details

Use the chart below to write the main idea and details of this lesson.

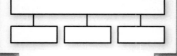

California Communities

Start with Your
CALIFORNIA STANDARDS

3.1 Students describe the physical and human geography and use maps, tables, graphs, photographs, and charts to organize information about people, places, and environments in a spatial context.

3.1.1 Identify geographical features in their local region.

Find out about three kinds of communities and learn how their locations affect the way people in them live, work, and play. (Begins on page 21)

3.1.2 Trace the ways in which people have used the resources of the local region and modified the physical environment.

Explore how people in communities use resources to live, work, and play. (Begins on page 21)

Some communities have open spaces and fields. ▼

California has many communities. The largest in population is Los Angeles. It has nearly 4 million people. Harmony is one of the smallest communities. Only 18 people live there.

Kinds of Communities ⬤3.1

California is home to many communities. Some, like Long Beach, are very large. Others are small and some are medium-sized. Some have tall buildings and crowded streets, while others have small houses with backyards. Some communities have a large amount of open space and fields, with houses far from each other. In this lesson you will read about three different kinds of communities.

REVIEW What are some ways communities are different?
Main Idea and Details

▲ In some communities, houses are built close together.

21

Sacramento is built where two rivers meet. ▼

A City Community 3.1 3.1.2

Close your eyes and picture a city. Did you see many buildings and stores, and crowds of people? Sacramento has all of these. It is an **urban** area. An urban area is a city and its surrounding communities. In an urban area, there are often tall buildings, and the buildings are close together. Except for the parks, almost all the land has something built on it.

▲ People and streetcars share busy K Street in Sacramento.

An urban area has a large **population**. Population is the number of people who live in a place. Sacramento is about the same size as Long Beach. It has about 500,000 people.

Sacramento is located along the Sacramento River and the American River. It is an important city because it is the **capital** of California. A capital is a city where a nation or a state has its government. Many people who live in Sacramento work for the state government.

Work and Enjoyment

Some people in Sacramento work for businesses with offices in the city. People who live outside of the city come to Sacramento to work there, too. People in town travel to work in cars or on buses or streetcars.

There are always many places to have fun in a city like Sacramento. People enjoy going to museums or to the zoo. Others enjoy going to the riverfront. Each year children from all over California visit Sacramento because it is the state capital. People also come from many places to go to the state fair, which is held in Sacramento each year.

REVIEW What is an urban community? *Summarize*

Global Connections

Bangkok, Thailand

Bangkok is a busy city in Thailand, a country in Asia. Like Sacramento, Bangkok is a capital city and was built on a river.

Bangkok has 6 million people, so it is much larger and more crowded than Sacramento. People there work in government offices, banks, schools, computer companies, and shopping malls.

What is one way Bangkok is like Sacramento?

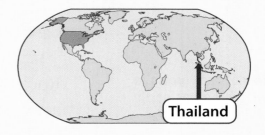

Thailand

Downtown Bangkok ▶

23

Outside Sacramento 3.1 3.1.1

Rocklin is about 35 miles from Sacramento. Here, the houses are not built so close together. There is more open land—land that has not been built on.

Rocklin is one of many **suburbs** of Sacramento. A suburb is a community near a city. Suburbs have houses, stores, and schools, but suburbs have fewer people than cities. Rocklin has about 38,000 people.

▲ Young people in Rocklin play in youth soccer leagues.

Some people who live in Rocklin work in Rocklin, but many of them work in Sacramento. They **commute**, or travel a distance, to work. Most people in Rocklin drive cars to work. In some suburbs people commute by train.

Walnuts are grown in the rural areas north of Sacramento. ▼

Open Spaces

If you keep traveling north from Rocklin, you will see small towns and villages. Wheatland is one of the small towns. It is a **rural** community. A rural community is a place of farms and open land. Rural communities have fewer people than suburbs. Wheatland's population, for example, is about 3,000 people.

Many people who live in Wheatland are farmers. At one time the farmers of Wheatland grew wheat, but now most have switched to rice. Others grow walnuts or peaches, or raise cattle.

However, Wheatland is changing. Many new houses are being built. Houses in Wheatland cost less than houses in Sacramento, so many people who work in Sacramento have bought the new houses in Wheatland. These newcomers commute to work in Sacramento along Highway 65. You can read about the problems this has caused for Wheatland below.

The land near Wheatland is good for growing rice. ▼

Primary Sources

A quote from **Mayor Gary Ulman**

June 29, 2003

The Sacramento Bee

❝From 5:30 to 9 a.m. and from 2:30 in the afternoon to 6:30 at night, it is almost impossible for the citizens of Wheatland to get on or off Highway 65, or even to cross Highway 65.❞

 How do you think people in Wheatland feel about the changes to their town?

REVIEW In what ways are rural areas different from cities or suburbs? *Compare and Contrast*

Communities Together 3.1.1

Sacramento, Rocklin, and Wheatland are very different, but they depend on each other in many ways. Workers in Rocklin find jobs in Sacramento. Businesses in the city need those workers to fill jobs. People in the city and the suburbs get much of their food from farms in rural areas like Wheatland. Farmers depend on people in cities and suburbs to buy their products.

People from all three areas come together at major community events. At the California State Fair in Sacramento every August, Californians from big cities and small towns enjoy concerts, animal shows, and carnival rides.

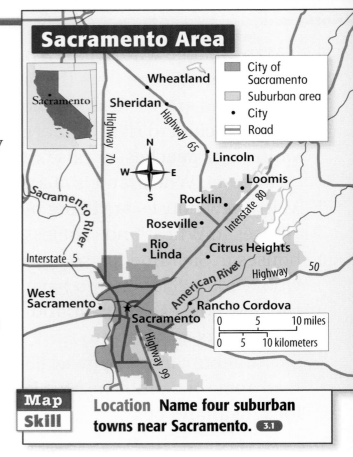

Sacramento Area

Legend:
- City of Sacramento
- Suburban area
- City
- Road

Wheatland
Sheridan
Highway 65
Highway 70
Lincoln
Loomis
Sacramento River
Rocklin
Roseville
Interstate 80
Rio Linda
Citrus Heights
Interstate 5
American River
Highway 50
West Sacramento
Sacramento
Rancho Cordova
Highway 99

0   5   10 miles
0   5   10 kilometers

Map Skill

Location Name four suburban towns near Sacramento. 3.1

REVIEW How do people in Sacramento need people in Rocklin and Wheatland? *Main Idea and Details*

The California State Fair in Sacramento ▼

◀ Farmers show their animals at the California State Fair.

What You Learned

3.1 There are many different types and sizes of communities.

3.1 **3.1.2** Urban communities have many people, businesses, and buildings.

3.1 **3.1.1** Suburbs are smaller communities near cities.

3.1.1 Communities such as Sacramento, Rocklin, and Wheatland depend on each other in many ways.

Lesson Review

1. **Focus Question** What are some **3.1** different kinds of communities?
3.1.2

2. **Vocabulary** Write one sentence for **3.1** each vocabulary word.

   capital   rural
   commute   suburb

3. **Economics** How do different **3.1.2** communities depend on each other?

4. **Critical Thinking** **Make Inferences** **3.1** Why might people commute a distance to work instead of working in their own community?

5. **Reading Strategy** **Identify Main** **3.1** **Idea and Details** Reread page 26. **ELA** **R2.5** Use the chart to write the main idea and details of this section.

6. **Write about THE BiG IDEA** Why do many **3.1** cities have suburbs around them? **ELA** **W2.1**

7. **Link to Art** Look through magazines **3.1** to find photographs of communities. Cut them out and use them to make a collage about communities.

Use the Internet 3.1.2

When you want to find out more about a topic, you can use an Internet search engine to help you. A **search engine** is a computer program that looks for information on the Internet. When you are doing research, ask your teacher, librarian, or another adult which search engine to use.

1 Learn It

- Log on to a computer and go to your search engine. Type in **keywords** about your topic. Keywords are words you use to find other information. For example, if you were interested in redwood trees, your keywords could be redwood, trees, and California.

- Click on *search*. You will see a list of **links** to Web sites. A link is a connection to another Web site. Under each link, there is usually a sample of the information on the site. If one link looks like it has more information on your topic, then click on it.

- Look at the Web site and decide if it will help you.

- If the Web site is not helpful, see if it shows links to other Web sites. If it does, you can click on those to keep looking. Or you can click *back* to return to your list of links and try a different one.

2 Try It

Look at the made-up Web sites on the next page to answer the questions.

- Which links on the search engine page (top) might give you the most facts about California redwoods? Which might not give you facts?

- If you clicked on the "All About Redwoods" link, do you think it would help you to find out about redwood trees? Why?

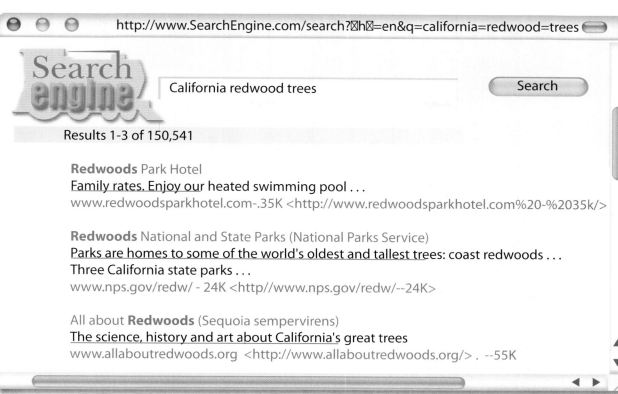

http://www.SearchEngine.com/search?⬛h⬛=en&q=california=redwood=trees

Search engine

California redwood trees

Search

Results 1-3 of 150,541

Redwoods Park Hotel
Family rates. Enjoy our heated swimming pool . . .
www.redwoodsparkhotel.com-.35K <http://www.redwoodsparkhotel.com%20-%2035k/>

Redwoods National and State Parks (National Parks Service)
Parks are homes to some of the world's oldest and tallest trees: coast redwoods . . .
Three California state parks . . .
www.nps.gov/redw/ - 24K <http//www.nps.gov/redw/--24K>

All about **Redwoods** (Sequoia sempervirens)
The science, history and art about California's great trees
www.allaboutredwoods.org <http://www.allaboutredwoods.org/> . --55K

http://www.allaboutredwoods.org

All About Redwoods

The California Redwood tree (*Sequoia sempervirens*) is nature's greatest creation. Standing over 300 feet tall and living over 2,000 years, these mighty trees once covered most of the Pacific Northwest.

Links:
- Science
- History
- Art

For more information:
www.redwoodtreesfacts.org
www.redwoodsforever.org

3 Apply It

In Lesson 2, you read about some of California's natural resources.

- Do an Internet search to find out about the natural resources in your own region.

- What keywords will help you find information?

- Start with more general keywords, such as "California natural resources."

- See if any Web sites offer links to information about counties and their natural resources, or try a new search.
or try a new search.

LONG BEACH

Learn About Your Community `3.1`

Rosa lives in Long Beach. She made a brochure about how people live, work, and play in Long Beach. You can make a brochure about life in your community, too. Here's what to do:

- Go to the library or use the Internet to find maps and photographs of your community. Find information about the population, too.

- Make notes about where most of your friends and family live.

- Ask adults about the places where people work.

- Write down the places where you go to have fun, like parks. Look in the newspaper to see where else people go for fun.

LOG ON

For more help in making your brochure, visit:

www.macmillanmh.com/ss/ca/local

Make a Brochure

Step 1 Gather your notes about your community and decide what to include in your brochure. Copy photos from books, cut them out of newspapers, or make drawings.

Step 2 Make your brochure. Fold a large piece of poster board or stiff paper in half to make four pages. On the front page, give your brochure a title and decorate it.

Step 3 On each page, paste photos or drawings that show people and places in your community. Below the pictures, print clearly your facts about how people live, work, and play there.

Step 4 Share your brochure with classmates.

Materials
- stiff paper or poster board
- markers
- ruler
- map of your community
- your notes
- photographs or your drawings
- paste

Living in Long Beach

More than 460,000 people live in Long Beach.

Working in Long Beach

California State University employs many people.

Chapter Review

Copy the sentences below on a separate sheet of paper. Beside each number, write *C* if the underlined word is used correctly. If it is not, write the word that would correctly complete the sentence.

1. A <u>community</u> is a place where people live, work, and play.
`3.1.2`

2. A <u>commute</u> is the number of people who live in a place.
`3.1.1`

3. A <u>suburb</u> is a community that is near a city.
`3.1.2`

4. <u>Urban</u> areas are places with fewer people than suburbs.
`3.1.2`

5. **Test Preparation** The state government is found in the _____.
`3.1.1`

    A. **coast**   C. **dock**
    B. **capital**   D. **location**

6. Where are many ports located?
`3.1.1`

7. What are some ways people commute to work?
`3.1.1`

8. Why is Sacramento an important city?
`3.1.1`

9. What are three kinds of communities?
`3.1.2`

10. Why is the port of Long Beach important?
`3.1.2`

11. **Critical Thinking** Why do people in the suburbs often work in cities?
`3.1.2`

12. **Critical Thinking** Why do you think some people who work in cities decide to live in suburbs?
`3.1.2`

Write a complete sentence to answer each question.

Use Map Scales

13. About how far is it from
3.1.1 City Hall to the Kern County Fairgrounds?

14. About how many miles is it
3.1.1 from the town of Oildale to Mercy Hospital in Bakersfield?

15. **Test Preparation** A _____ helps
3.1.1 you measure the real distance between places.

16. **Test Preparation** On the map
3.1.1 below, 1 inch equals _____ miles.

Bakersfield

Highway 99
Highway 58
Kern River Parkway
River
Highway 178
Kern
City Hall
California State University Bakersfield
Mercy Hospital
Highway 58
Patriots Park
Highway 99
Highway 204
Kern County Fairgrounds

0   2   4 miles
0   2   4 kilometers

☐ Bakersfield
☐ Oildale
■ Greenacres
■ Park
■ Point of interest

What Are Primary Sources?

17. Name two examples of primary
ELA R2.3 sources.

18. Is this textbook a primary
ELA R2.3 source or a secondary source?

19. **Make a Drawing** Choose
3.1.1 one kind of community in California. Draw a picture that shows an everyday activity in this kind of community.

20. **Descriptive** Write a description
3.1.1 of your community and its
ELA W2.2 geography. Is it urban, rural, or suburban? Where is it located—near the coast, in the mountains, or someplace else? Do people commute from your town to surrounding towns? Be sure to use concrete details in your description.

LOG ON

For help with the process of writing, visit:

www.macmillanmh.com/ss/ca/writing

2

The Geography of Communities

YOU ARE THERE

In this chapter you will read how communities are different places because of their locations. Each community has its own land, water, and weather. People use the land, water, and other resources to live. They also change the land to meet their needs.

1 **California's Geography** (page 36)
The geography of a community affects how people live there. In Laguna Beach people enjoy the beach.

2 **Communities Need Natural Resources** (page 48)
People in communities use things like water, soil, and trees to meet their needs. Long ago people in Bodie had jobs mining for gold. .

OREGON

LEGEND
★ State capital
• Other city

Eureka

Klamath
River

Sacramento
River

American
River

Lake
Tahoe

NEVADA

Sacramento

San Francisco
Oakland

San Joaquin
River

Bodie

San
José

2

PACIFIC
OCEAN

Fresno

CALIFORNIA

Colorado
River

3 Los Angeles

1 Laguna Beach

Salton
Sea

San Diego

3 **People Change the Environment** (page 66)
People change the land to suit their
needs. Almost 100 years ago, Los
Angeles brought water from far away so
the city could grow.

MEXICO

FOCUS QUESTION

How would you describe California's geography?

VOCABULARY

geography
landform
natural
 resource
climate
region
adapt

VOCABULARY STRATEGY

WORD FAMILIES

Geo- comes from the Greek word for Earth. What words do you know that begin with **geo-**?

READING STRATEGY

Identify Main Idea and Details

Use the diagram below to write main idea and details for this lesson.

California's Geography

Start with Your CALIFORNIA STANDARDS

3.1 Students describe the physical and human geography and use maps, tables, graphs, photographs, and charts to organize information about people, places, and environments in a spatial context.

3.1.1 Identify geographical features in their local region.

Name different kinds of land and bodies of water found where you live. (Begins on page 37)

3.1.2 Trace the ways in which people have used the resources of the local region and modified the physical environment.

See how people have used natural resources such as water, minerals, and trees, and have changed the land around them. (page 42)

California has many miles of coastline. ▼

From snow-topped mountains to hot, dry deserts, California has it all! The elf owl makes its home in the deserts of California. This tiny hunter is only 5½ inches tall and lives on insects.

Different Kinds of Land ⬤3.1 ⬤3.1.1

Think about the place where you live. Is it flat or hilly? Is it near the ocean? Is it sunny or cloudy most of the time?

Your answers will depend on where you live. California has many different kinds of land and water. It has high mountains and low, flat land. It has sparkling lakes and long rivers, too.

The study of land and water and the way people, plants, and animals live on them is called **geography**. Geography is important because it affects the way people live.

REVIEW What does the study of geography include?
Main Idea and Details

◀ Some places in California are deserts.

Land and Water 3.1 3.1.2

Have you ever walked up a hill? Walking up a steep hill can be hard work. Walking up a mountain is even harder! California has many hills and mountains. Hills and mountains are two kinds of **landforms**. Landforms are the shapes of Earth's surface.

Landforms can affect where people choose to live. Perhaps your town is on a plain. A plain is a large area of flat or almost flat land. Many of California's communities are built on plains.

Perhaps your community is in a valley. A valley is low land between hills or mountains. Valleys often have rivers flowing through them. California has a large valley called the Central Valley. It runs down the middle of the state. Valleys are good places for farming, because the soil is rich.

Grapevines grow in the rich soil of the Salinas Valley. ▼

▲ Water is a food source for people and animals.

Salt Water, Fresh Water

Water also affects where people live. Why? That is simple. People cannot live without it! Water is one of our most important **natural resources**. A natural resource is something found in nature that can be used. We need water to drink, to wash, and to grow things. Fish and other animals that live in water are sources of food for people. People often use rivers for transportation, too. For these reasons, many communities are located near water.

▼ Pelican

Earth has two kinds of water. Salt water is found in oceans. Fresh water, the kind you need to drink, is found in lakes and rivers. Ponds and streams are fresh water, too. Oceans, lakes, rivers, and streams are all called bodies of water.

REVIEW What are some examples of landforms? *Main Idea and Details*

39

Weather and Land Over Time 3.1 3.1.2

What is the weather like right now? Is it hot and sunny? Is it windy? Is it raining? Weather is another part of geography. California has every kind of weather from very hot to very cold.

The weather can change from day to day. **Climate**, however, is the weather a place has over a long time. Climate tells what the weather is usually like. Is it usually hot in the summer where you live? Is the winter often rainy and foggy? Your answer tells about the climate of your community.

Climate affects how people live, too. People who live in a place with a cold climate need different kinds of clothes and houses than people who live where it is always warm.

▲ People wear warm clothing where it is cold.

California has many climates. Some places (left) are hot and dry while others are cool and foggy. ▼

California Regions

Geographers divide California into eight **regions**. A region is an area with common features that set it apart from other areas. Kinds of landforms, bodies of water, and climate all shape a region. For example, the Sierra Nevada region is known for its snow-capped mountains.

Landforms, climate, and bodies of water affect how people live. Because these things are different from region to region, the way people live varies from region to region. Look at the map on the right. Find the region where you live.

Many artists have celebrated our state's geography. Painters Albert Bierstadt [BEER stat] and Grafton Tyler Brown were two of them. Their art showed the wonder they felt when they looked at California's great natural beauty.

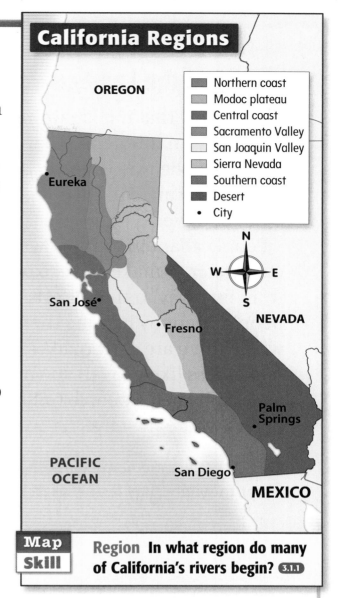

California Regions

Legend:
- Northern coast
- Modoc plateau
- Central coast
- Sacramento Valley
- San Joaquin Valley
- Sierra Nevada
- Southern coast
- Desert
- City

OREGON

Eureka

San José

Fresno

NEVADA

Palm Springs

PACIFIC OCEAN

San Diego

MEXICO

Map Skill

Region In what region do many of California's rivers begin? 3.1.1

REVIEW What are some things a region shares? *Main Idea and Details*

Albert Bierstadt painted this scene in the Sierra Nevada in 1868. ▶

Living on the Land `3.1` `3.1.2`

You know that if it is raining, you wear a raincoat and carry an umbrella. That is one way you **adapt**, or change the way you live. People adapt to the land and climate in their region by changing how they live.

People adapt in many ways. They build bridges over water to make travel easier. They bring water from far away to their farms. In cold climates, people adapt by heating their homes. In places where there are earthquakes, people learn to build homes less likely to fall down. Learning about local geography helps people find ways to adapt to the places where they live.

REVIEW What are some ways that people in a region adapt to where they live? *Main Idea and Details*

▼ The Coronado Bridge in San Diego

▲ People adapt to different kinds of weather and climate.

What You Learned

3.1
3.1.1 Geography is the study of land and water, and the way people, plants, and animals live on it.

3.1
3.1.2 California has every type of body of water and every type of landform.

3.1
3.1.2 Geography and climate affect where people live and how they live. California has eight natural regions with some shared resources.

3.1
3.1.2 People adapt to the area where they live and change the land to fit their needs.

Lesson Review

1. **Focus Question** How would you **3.1** describe California's geography?

2. **Vocabulary** Write one sentence for **3.1** each vocabulary term.

   adapt   landform
   climate   natural resource
   geography   region

3. **Geography** What is a region? What **3.1.1** region do you live in?

4. **Critical Thinking Problem**
   3.1.2 **Solving** Tell how you might adapt if you moved to a place with a very cold climate.

5. **Reading Strategy Identify Main**
   3.1
   ELA
   R2.5 **Idea and Details** Reread the first paragraph on page 39. Use the diagram to list details about why water is needed.

6. **Write about** 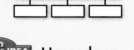 How does **3.1.2** the geography of a place affect how **ELA** **W2.1** people live there?

7. **Link to Art** Look through art books **3.1** to find examples of paintings that show different landforms. Then draw or paint a picture of the landforms in your area.

Grafton Tyler Brown 1841–1918

When Grafton Tyler Brown was born, many black people in America were still enslaved. Grafton was born free in Pennsylvania. Still, life was not easy for him. He had to go to work when he was still a boy. His print shop job could have been the end of his learning. Instead, it was just the beginning.

In the days before photography, newspapers used artists to make drawings. Grafton was good at drawing. He learned how to draw pictures for newspapers.

As a teenager he moved across the country to California. In the 1850s, traveling west was not easy. It took months. The hardships of the trip did not stop Grafton.

In San Francisco Grafton got a job at a print shop. He worked as a cartographer, or mapmaker, making maps. He also made pictures of towns and ranches.

The Life of Grafton Tyler Brown

1840	1860	1880	
1841 Born in Harrisburg, Pennsylvania	1867 Formed a business, G.T. Brown and Company	1879 Sold print shop	1883 Opened his own painting studio

▲ *Cliff House Beach*, 1886

In 1866 Grafton bought the print shop and formed his own business. He called it G.T. Brown and Company. His print shop created advertisements and other papers for businesses like Levi Strauss and Wells Fargo.

The print shop was a success, but after 13 years, Brown had a new dream—to be a painter. It was a risk that took courage, but Brown sold his business. He traveled around the West, painting the places he saw. In 1883 he opened an art studio. People quickly bought his paintings of the West's mountains and waterfalls. He became the first African American to make a living as an artist in the West.

▲ *In the Redwoods*

How did Grafton Tyler Brown show he had courage?

1900   1920

1918
Brown died
in Minnesota

For more about Grafton Tyler Brown, visit:

www.macmillanmh.com/ss/ca/bios

45

MAP and GLOBE Skills

Use a Landform Map [3.1.1]

A **landform map** uses different colors to show where different kinds of landforms are found. You might use a landform map when planning a trip, taking a hike, or just to learn about the geography of your community.

VOCABULARY

landform map

1 Learn It

Follow these steps for using a landform map.

- Read the title of the map to learn what area is shown on the map.

- Look at the map key. Each color stands for a kind of landform.

- Match the colors on the key to areas on the map.

2 Try It

Now, study the landform map at right and answer the questions.

- What is the title of the map?

- Look at the key. Name the different landforms found in California.

- What landform is Los Angeles located on? How do you know?

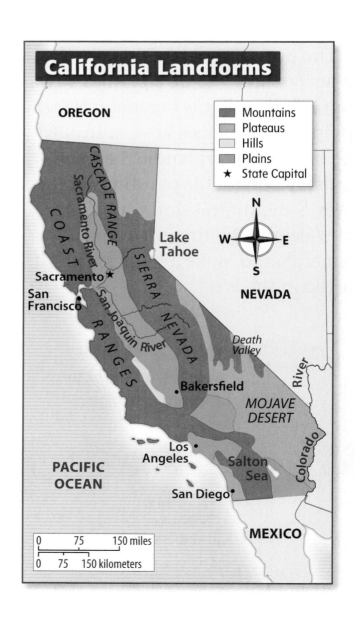

California Landforms

Key:
- Mountains
- Plateaus
- Hills
- Plains
- ★ State Capital

OREGON

CASCADE RANGE

Sacramento River

COAST

Lake Tahoe

SIERRA

Sacramento ★

San Francisco

San Joaquin River

NEVADA

RANGES

Death Valley

Bakersfield

MOJAVE DESERT

Los Angeles

Salton Sea

PACIFIC OCEAN

San Diego

Colorado River

MEXICO

0   75   150 miles
0   75   150 kilometers

 **Apply It**

Look at the landform map of the United States below.

- In which part of the country, the West or the South, are there mountains?

- Is the middle of our country mostly plains or mostly hills?

- Find the Colorado River on both maps. What landforms does it cross?

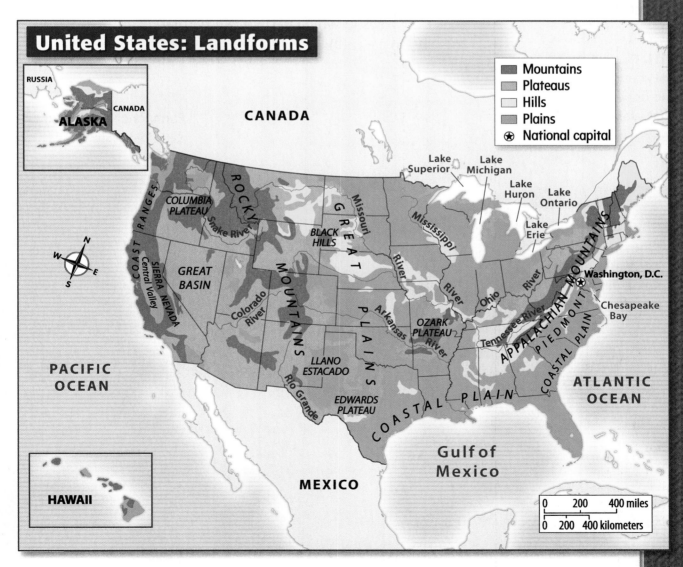

United States: Landforms

Legend:
- Mountains
- Plateaus
- Hills
- Plains
- ⊛ National capital

RUSSIA

ALASKA

CANADA

CANADA

HAWAII

PACIFIC OCEAN

COAST RANGES

COLUMBIA PLATEAU

Snake River

ROCKY

SIERRA NEVADA

Central Valley

GREAT BASIN

Colorado River

MOUNTAINS

LLANO ESTACADO

Rio Grande

EDWARDS PLATEAU

BLACK HILLS

GREAT

Missouri

River

PLAINS

Arkansas River

OZARK PLATEAU

COASTAL PLAIN

MEXICO

Lake Superior

Lake Michigan

Lake Huron

Lake Ontario

Lake Erie

Mississippi

River

Ohio

River

Tennessee River

APPALACHIAN MOUNTAINS

PIEDMONT

COASTAL PLAIN

Washington, D.C.

Chesapeake Bay

ATLANTIC OCEAN

Gulf of Mexico

0 200 400 miles
0 200 400 kilometers

VOCABULARY

renewable
resource
nonrenewable
resource
timber
environment

VOCABULARY STRATEGY

PREFIXES The prefix **non-** means "not" or "the opposite of." What word in the list above has the prefix **non-**?

READING STRATEGY

Summarize
Use the diagram to summarize the lesson.

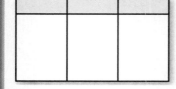

Communities Need Natural Resources

Start with Your
CALIFORNIA STANDARDS

3.1 Students describe the physical and human geography and use maps, tables, graphs, photographs, and charts to organize information about people, places, and environments in a spatial context.

3.1.2 Trace the ways in which people have used the resources of the local region and modified the physical environment.

Discover ways in which people use natural resources.
(Begins on page 49)

Farmers could not grow crops without water. ▼

California strawberry farmers depend on water to grow their berries. How many berries is that? If you laid all the strawberries grown in California each year berry to berry, they would wrap around the world 15 times!

Using Natural Resources 3.1.1 3.1.2

Farmers are not the only ones who depend on resources. We all get everything we need to live from nature—the air we breathe, the food we eat, and the gas to run our cars. As you have learned, natural resources are things found in nature that people can use. They include air, water, land, trees, wildlife, and soil.

Natural resources that can be replaced are called **renewable resources**. Water, wind, sunlight, and trees are all renewable resources.

Some resources cannot be replaced. These are **nonrenewable resources**. When people use them up, they are gone forever. Oil, copper, iron, coal, and gold are all nonrenewable.

REVIEW What is a nonrenewable resource?
Summarize

▲ Oil is an important natural resource.

Renewable Resources 3.1.2

Northern California has rich resources of soil, salmon, and forests. Forests are used to produce **timber**, wood that is used for building. The map on the next page shows the location of California's forests.

As loggers cut trees, they plant new trees to replace them. Since the trees can be replaced in this way, timber is a renewable resource.

However, cutting timber still affects the **environment** [en VIGH ruhn ment], the air, water, land, and other living things around us. When trees are cut down, animals lose their homes and food. Forests help keep soil in place, too. Without forests, rain may wash soil away or cause mud slides. Whenever resources are used, people must think about how using the resources will affect the environment.

REVIEW What are some renewable resources?
Main Idea and Details

New trees are planted to replace those that are cut. ▼

▼ Loggers float cut logs downstream to lumber mills.

California Forests and Timber Production 3.1

The map below shows where forests are located in California. California counties, or sections of a state, use their forests to produce timber.

Read the chart on the right to find out which counties produce the most timber.

Top 5 California Timber Counties, 2002

County	Board feet* of timber	That's enough wood to build...
Humboldt	374 million	🏠🏠🏠🏠🏠
Siskiyou	187 million	🏠🏠🏠
Shasta	152 million	🏠🏠
El Dorado	104 million	🏠
Mendocino	98 million	🏠

🏠 = 5,000 houses

*board foot: a unit of timber equal to a board measuring 12x12x1 inches

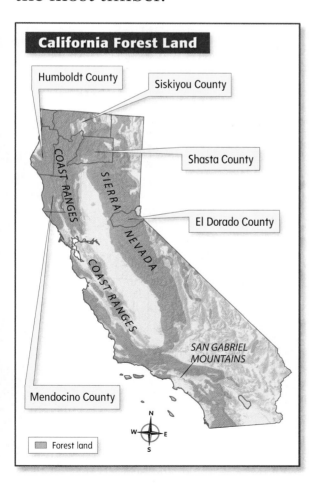

California Forest Land

Humboldt County
Siskiyou County
COAST RANGES
Shasta County
SIERRA NEVADA
El Dorado County
COAST RANGES
SAN GABRIEL MOUNTAINS
Mendocino County
Forest land
N W E S

Think About Forests and Products

1. Which part of California has more forest land—the north or the south?

2. Which California county shown on the chart produces the most timber?

3. Which California county shown on the chart produces the least amount of timber?

51

Nonrenewable Resources 3.1.2

A community cannot last for very long if it depends on a nonrenewable resource. A town called Bodie [BOH dee] depended on a nonrenewable resource. In 1877 Bodie was a small town of about 20 people. Then a large amount of gold was found there. People rushed to Bodie. They hoped to get rich by finding gold themselves.

For a few years, Bodie was a busy town. Over 10,000 people lived there. Then one day all the gold was mined out. Once the gold ran out, the people left town. Soon Bodie became a ghost town, or a deserted town. Today, people visit the empty town to learn what life was like in those days.

REVIEW Why did Bodie become a ghost town? *Cause and Effect*

Bodie in 1906 ▼

Bodie today ▼

Using Resources Wisely 3.1.2

Communities need to use their natural resources wisely. Even renewable resources need to be taken care of. For example, we must keep our water clean and not waste any. Because many places in California do not get much rain, we have to use water wisely.

Nonrenewable resources, such as oil, are a special problem. Oil is made into gasoline to run cars. To save oil, some companies are now making cars that use less gasoline. Others are making cars that run partly on electricity. People can also use other forms of energy besides oil. Some communities use windmills to make electricity.

REVIEW What are some ways to use resources wisely? *Summarize*

▼ Some new cars run partly on gasoline and partly on electricity.

This Land Is Your Land

Words and Music by Woody Guthrie

This land is your land,___ This land is my land,___

from Cal - i - for - nia___ to the New York is - land,___

From the red-wood for - est___ to the Gulf Stream wa - ters;

This land was made for you and me.

What kinds of natural resources does the song describe?

◄ People plant new areas in forests with seedlings.

What You Learned

3.1.1
3.1.2 Natural resources are things from nature that we use.

3.1.2 Renewable resources, like water, can be used again and again.

3.1.2 Nonrenewable resources are resources that can be used up.

3.1.2 Communities must learn to use resources wisely.

Lesson Review

1. Focus Question What are some
3.1 ways people use natural resources?

2. Vocabulary Write one sentence for
3.1 each vocabulary term.

environment
nonrenewable resource
renewable resource
timber

3. Economics What are some jobs
3.1.2 people might have that involve using natural resources?

4. Critical Thinking Problem
3.1.2 **Solving** What is one way to be sure to always have enough trees for timber?

5. Reading Strategy
3.1.2 **Summarize** Copy the
ELA diagram to summarize
R2.3 important information on page 50.

6. Write about THE **BiG** IDEA How do
3.1 natural resources affect where
ELA
W1.0 people decide to build communities?

7. Link to Science Research an animal
3.1.2 that lives in the forests of Northern California. Find out what this animal needs to live. Tell how the animal would be affected if the forest was cut down.

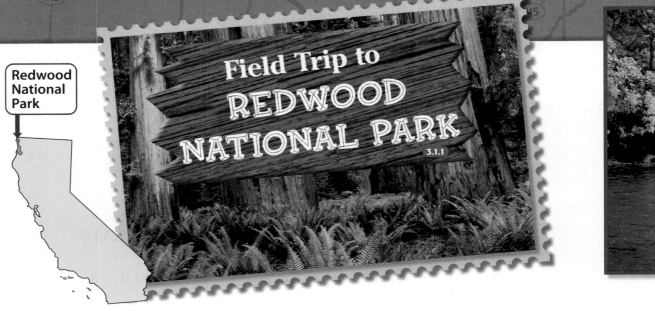
Field Trip to **REDWOOD NATIONAL PARK**
3.1.1

Redwood National Park

The redwood trees of Northern California are among the oldest living things on Earth. Some are more than 2,000 years old. Take a field trip to Redwood National Park and the nearby state parks to see these giant trees.

❶ Tall Trees Grove ▶

As you walk along, stop and look up . . . and up . . . and up! The trees here are some of the tallest in the world. One tree stands 365 feet tall!

❷ Elk Meadow Day Use Area ▲

Have you ever seen an elk? Here's the place to find one. Roosevelt elk are the largest elk in North America. The males can weigh as much as 1,200 pounds.

◄ ❸ Klamath Estuary

Further north in the park is the Klamath Estuary, where the Klamath River meets the Pacific Ocean. An estuary is a great place for plant and animal life. Salmon swim up the river in the fall.

▲ ❹ Enderts Beach

In the north end of the park, wildflowers line quiet Enderts Beach. At morning low tide, you can explore sea life in the beach's tide pools. The cliffs above are great for watching birds and whales.

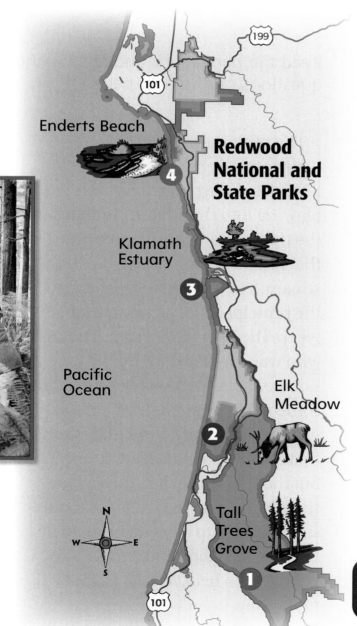

Enderts Beach

Redwood National and State Parks

Klamath Estuary

Pacific Ocean

Elk Meadow

Tall Trees Grove

N
W — E
S

ACTIVITY

Write directions for a drive from Tall Trees Grove to Enderts Beach. Tell what other places you would see on the way.

For more about Redwood National Park visit:

www.macmillanmh.com/ss/ca/fieldtrips

Problem Solving 3.1.2

Problems are part of everyday life. Some problems are small. Other problems can be large. Problem solving is a way to find answers. The following steps show one way you can solve problems.

1 Learn It

- Identify the problem. You need to know what the problem is before you can solve it.

- Gather information. Find out as much as you can about the problem. This will help you solve the problem.

- Identify the options. An option is a possible choice. You can choose to solve most problems in different ways.

- Think about the consequences. Every option has a consequence, or result. Some consequences are better than others. You will want to choose the option with the best consequences.

- Choose a solution. A solution is an answer to a problem. Usually, the best solution has the best results for everyone.

2 Try It

Read the paragraphs and answer the questions on the next page.

The playground at Wilson Elementary School is near a stream. Litter from the playground was blowing into the stream. Students in the third grade class were concerned that litter was bad for wildlife in the stream. They talked to teachers and the principal. They tried to find out where the litter came from. They asked who was supposed to clean it up.

Jorge thought the school should hire someone to clean up the litter, but that would cost money. Kimberley thought that the city should clean up the litter but thought that might take a long time. Miles said the students should start a clean-up day once a month. Parents, teachers, and students could volunteer to help, and it could start right away.

- What problem did the third grade class at Wilson Elementary School identify?

- What steps did they take to learn about the problem?

- What options did the students have?

- What are the consequences of these options?

- What do you think a good solution might be? Why?

3 Apply It

Think about a problem that people in your school or community face. Use the problem-solving steps to tell about this problem. Be sure to include your solution to the problem.

A HOME ON PLANET THEO

3.1.1 3.1.2

Characters

Captain Smith

Will

Judy *(Will and*
  Penny's mother)

Penny

Co-captain Robinson

Explorer 1

Explorer 2

Explorer 3

Gus

—— * ——

Narrator: It's the year 2849. A spacecraft with men, women, and children from Earth is heading to the planet Theo. Earth and planet Theo are very much alike. Theo has air and water, mountains, rivers, and good soil. Planet Theo has two natural resources that Earth doesn't have—Silkcorite trees and a rare mineral called moolamite. The Earthlings have come to farm Theo's Silkcorite trees and to mine its moolamite and send it back to Earth.

Captain Smith: Ladies and gentlemen, this is your captain speaking. Please remain seated until I've turned off the seat belt sign.

Will: Mom, why is this planet called Theo?

Judy: It was named after the nine-year-old boy who discovered it, looking through his telescope on Earth.

Will: I can't wait to get outside.

Captain Smith: Okay, folks, let's exit the spacecraft.

(The passengers exit the spaceship.)

Will: Look at the five moons!

Penny: Look! A Silkcorite tree! Silkcorite is strong and soft enough to make just about anything—clothes, rugs, sheets, pillows.

Will: *(kicking a rock with his foot)* Here's some moolamite. That's enough to power my jet scooter for a week!

Captain Smith: *(raising his voice to be heard)* Everyone, let's gather over here. *(All the passengers gather around.)* We're going to set up some Insta-houses here for now. By spring, though, we'll need permanent houses before the big storms come. So we need to explore.

Co-captain Robinson: *(holding a map)* We have divided Theo into four regions. Each group will take a People Mover to explore one. Look for natural resources. Take pictures with your Toto-Moto-Photos! We'll meet back here tonight.

Narrator: The team went in different directions. At the end of the day, they gathered around a camp fire.

Captain Smith: Well, group one, what did you find today?

Explorer 1: In our region there was a valley between two huge mountains. You can see the river that runs through it on this Toto-Moto-Photo.

Captain Smith: Good. We need water. For drinking and washing, of course, but also for the food we will grow.

Explorer 1: The soil seems good for farming. The climate was comfortable, too.

Captain Smith: What about Silkcorite trees?

Will: *(disappointed)* We saw lots of trees, but not many were Silkcorite. We didn't find too much moolamite, either.

Captain Smith: Group two, what did you find?

Penny: Our region was very hot and dry, a desert. Not a drop of water or a Silkcorite tree in sight.

Explorer 2: We don't want to live there, sir.

Captain Smith: I agree. Group three, you're next.

Judy: Our region had a coast. There's a beautiful beach, and two rivers empty into the ocean. We'd never run out of water, that's for sure.

Penny: I'd like to live near a beach! We could grow Silkcorite.

Co-captain Robinson: *(frowning)* What about moolamite?

Judy: We found some in one spot, but nowhere else.

Captain Smith: Group four, what did you see?

Gus: *(excitedly)* Our region had mountains. Some had snow on top. There were forests of Silkcorite, and our moolamite meter went nuts. The problem is that there's probably not enough water for us to live and farm.

Captain Smith: That could be a problem. Is the soil rich?

Gus: Yes. I brought some back so you could take a look.

Captain Smith: What about the climate? What's it like?

Explorer 3: *(shrugging)* It's in the mountains, so it's cool, but it wasn't freezing, either.

Captain Smith: It sounds like a great place for us. Like region one, it's got a good climate and soil for farming, but it also has more moolamite and Silkcorite than any other region. How do we solve the water problem?

Gus: Captain, we can build a lake to collect and store water from rain and melted snow. Then, we can save the water for when we need it.

Captain Smith: Gus, that's a great idea! I think we just might name our new community "Gusville."

Write About It!

Suppose you lived long ago, before your community was founded. What made it a good place for a community? Write a report, discussing topics such as natural resources, climate, and location.

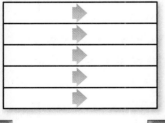

FOCUS QUESTION

How did people change the environment to bring water to Los Angeles?

VOCABULARY

dam
reservoir
aqueduct
conserve

VOCABULARY STRATEGY

WORD FAMILIES

Reserve comes from a Latin word meaning "keep." What does a **reservoir** keep?

READING STRATEGY

Identify Cause and Effect

Use the chart to list causes and effects of building the Los Angeles Aqueduct.

	▶
	▶
	▶
	▶
	▶

People Change the Environment

Start with Your

CALIFORNIA STANDARDS

3.1 Students describe the physical and human geography and use maps, tables, graphs, photographs, and charts to organize information about people, places, and environments in a spatial context.

3.1.2 Trace the ways in which people have used the resources of the local region and modified the physical environment.

Discover how people change the environment by building roads and bridges. Read how the city of Los Angeles changed the environment when it brought water from far away. (Begins on page 67)

Each day the people of Los Angeles use 589 million gallons of water. That is enough to fill more than one thousand Olympic-sized swimming pools! Where does Los Angeles get all that water?

Changing Land and Water 3.1 3.1.2

People adapt to the environment. They also change the environment to meet their needs. One way people change the environment is by building **dams**. A dam is a wall across a river or stream that holds back and controls the water. Dams let people store water for when they need it.

In Northern California people built a dam across the Sacramento River. The water backed up and formed a huge lake called Shasta Lake. People use the lake for fishing and boating, but the most important use of Shasta Lake is as a **reservoir** [REZ urh vwahr]. A reservoir is a place to store water. Water is kept in Shasta Lake until it is needed, and then it is sent south to the Sacramento Valley.

▲ People change the land when they build roads.

REVIEW What is an example of how people change their environment? *Summarize*

◄ The Shasta Dam created Shasta Lake.

Water for Los Angeles 3.1.2

Los Angeles was once a small town. It got its water from the Los Angeles River. At first the river was enough. As the city grew, though, people began to worry that it would need more water.

William Mulholland was in charge of the city's water system. He and other city leaders decided Los Angeles could get water from the Owens River Valley. The city bought the rights to the land and water from the Owens Valley residents. To redirect the water, Mulholland built an **aqueduct** [AK wuh dukt] to bring water from the Owens River. An aqueduct is a long human-made pipe for moving water from one place to another.

The work began in 1908. When the aqueduct was finished in 1913, it was 235 miles long. With more water to use, Los Angeles could grow larger. Today it is California's largest city.

The Los Angeles Aqueduct took five years to build. ▼

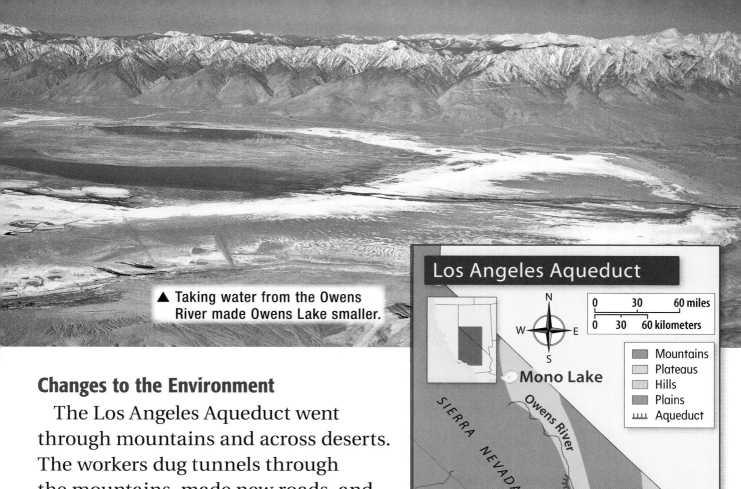

▲ Taking water from the Owens River made Owens Lake smaller.

Changes to the Environment

The Los Angeles Aqueduct went through mountains and across deserts. The workers dug tunnels through the mountains, made new roads, and built railroad tracks to carry supplies as they built. They built power lines and telephone lines. All these things changed the environment.

The biggest change was to the Owens River Valley. Many people there were against the aqueduct. Some farmers wanted to use the water for their own farms and ranches. Instead, with the water going to Los Angeles, there was less water for the people, animals, and plants of the Owens River Valley.

REVIEW How did the Los Angeles Aqueduct change the environment? *Cause and Effect*

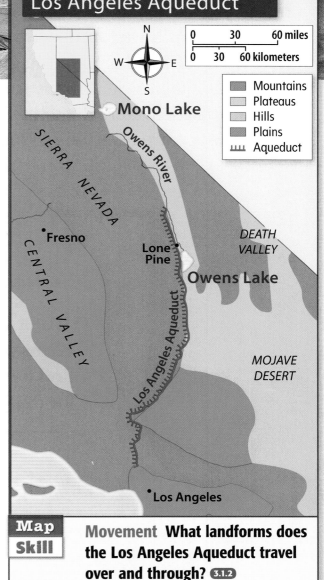

Los Angeles Aqueduct

0   30   60 miles
0   30   60 kilometers

Mountains
Plateaus
Hills
Plains
⊔⊔⊔ Aqueduct

Mono Lake

SIERRA NEVADA

Owens River

CENTRAL VALLEY

Fresno

Lone Pine

DEATH VALLEY

Owens Lake

Los Angeles Aqueduct

MOJAVE DESERT

Los Angeles

Map Skill

Movement What landforms does the Los Angeles Aqueduct travel over and through? 3.1.2

Finding a Balance 3.1.2

Providing enough water is a problem for many California communities, not just Los Angeles. Today people are working to find other ways to provide water. Morro Bay, a town on the central coast, found one solution. In 1991 it built a plant to remove salt from seawater. That makes the seawater drinkable. Building these plants costs a great deal of money, however.

Some towns have found ways to **conserve**, or use less, water. Instead of planting grass in front of public buildings like libraries, many towns now use plants that need little water. Read the interview below. It tells how one area is trying to meet its water needs.

Primary Sources

An interview with **Jeff Becerra,**
Spokesperson for East Bay Municipal Utility District

❝Water use will increase over the years . . . . We have to conserve more water, and also find new ways to store extra water and save it for dry years.❞

Jeff Becerra

Write About It! ➤ **Why do you think Mr. Becerra says that water use will increase in years to come?**

REVIEW What are some ways communities provide for their water needs? *Main Idea and Details*

◄ This garden has plants that need little water.

What You Learned

3.1 3.1.2 People change their environment to make life easier.

3.1.2 The Los Angeles Aqueduct brought water to Los Angeles. It helped the city grow, but it changed the Owens River Valley.

3.1.2 Some towns have found ways to get enough water, such as building plants that remove salt from seawater.

Lesson Review

1. **Focus Question** How did people
3.1 change the environment to bring water to Los Angeles?

2. **Vocabulary** Write one sentence for
3.1 the following vocabulary terms.

   aqueduct   dam
   conserve   reservoir

3. **Environment** What are some
3.1.2 technologies that would make a project like the Los Angeles Aqueduct project possible?

4. **Critical Thinking** **Problem**
3.1.2 **Solving** Do you think that using water from the Owens River Valley for the city of Los Angeles was a good way to solve a problem?

5. **Reading Strategy** **Identify Cause**
3.1.2 **and Effect** Reread
ELA R2.2 paragraph two on page 67. Use the chart to list two causes and effects given in the paragraph.

6. **Write about** THE BiG IDEA How did the
3.1.2 Los Angeles Aqueduct change the
ELA W1.0 lives of people in both Los Angeles and the Owens River Valley?

7. **Link to Science** Do research to find
3.1.2 out where your community gets its water. Present your findings to the class.

How Should We Manage 3.1.2
Our Water Resources?

Californians in cities need water for drinking and cleaning. Farmers need it to grow crops. Others want to protect lakes and rivers. Read below three points of view on how our water resources should be used.

"We need to give water to farms and cities, but if too much water is taken out of our rivers, they can dry up or become polluted."

Arlene Wong
Environmentalist
Moraga, California
From an interview, 2004

"Right now we have enough water for the food we grow, but that could change. Everybody needs to be careful about how they use water."

Bruce Sanbonmatsu
Farmer
El Centro, California
From an interview, 2004

"We need to build more houses . . . but, we should not be covering our rural areas and sides of mountains with too many houses. This puts too big a drain on water resources."

Roger Menard
Home builder
Palo Alto, California
From an interview, 2004

Build Citizenship
Respect

1. Why do you think people sometimes disagree about the best ways to use water?

2. How does sharing water show respect for the needs of others?

3. What are some ways people in your community use water?

Think About It
Points of View

1. Why does Arlene Wong worry about our rivers?

2. What reasons does Roger Menard give for his opinion?

3. What other groups of people might care about this issue?

Write About It!

Choose the point of view you most agree with about how to use water resources. Then, write a short essay about why you think this is a good point of view. Give reasons for your opinion.

Local Connections

Your Community's Land and Resources 3.1.1 3.1.2

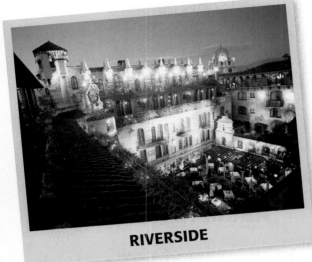

RIVERSIDE

Lee lives in Riverside. He learned about the geography and natural resources near his town. Here's what you can do to learn about the geography of your community.

- At the library, find a map of your community that shows landforms. (This is also called a **topographical** map.) Look for the landforms and bodies of water near your community.

- Use the library, newspapers, or the Internet to find pictures and headlines about your county's natural resources.

- Use the library, newspapers, or the Internet to find examples of ways that people have changed the environment in your community.

LOG ON For more help making your community projects, visit

www.macmillanmh.com/ss/ca/local

ACTIVITY

Make a Clay Landform Model

Materials
- cardboard
- map of your community
- clay of different colors
- paper
- tape
- markers

Step 1 Use a map to learn about the landforms and bodies of water in your area. Then decide what to include on your model.

Step 2 Copy the map onto the cardboard. If you decide to make your model larger than the map, you could use a copy machine to make the map larger.

Step 3 Cover the map with the clay. Build up the features using different colors of clay for different features.

Step 4 Use your paper to make a title, a key, and labels for your model.

Step 5 Share your model with your classmates.

Local Connections

ACTIVITY

Make a Natural Resources Poster

Materials
- Posterboard
- white drawing paper
- pencil
- crayons
- photographs
- markers or colored pencils
- paste

Step 1 Think about what you have learned about the natural resources in your area. Decide which resources you want to show on your poster.

Step 2 Decide whether you will use photos, drawings, or use a combination of both.

Step 3 Make a simple sketch first, to show how your final poster will look. If you are using drawings, make your drawings on separate pieces of paper. Arrange the drawings and photos on the poster board until you find the arrangement that looks best.

Step 4 Paste your drawings or photos to your poster. Print or use a computer to make labels and a title.

Natural Resources Found in Riverside

Water is an important natural resource.

Oranges are grown around Riverside.

Good farmland is important for crops.

Make a Photo Log

Step 1 Think about all of the ways people have changed the environment in your area. Decide which examples to show in your photo log.

Step 2 Decide whether you will take your own photos, print pictures from the Internet, cut them out of newspapers or magazines, or use a combination of all three.

Step 3 Put your photos in the order you think works best. Paste your photos to your paper. Under each photo, print a description of how it shows people changing the environment. Then put your pages in the binder.

Step 4 Share your photo log with your classmates.

Materials
- binder
- photographs
- white paper
- paste
- markers or colored pencils

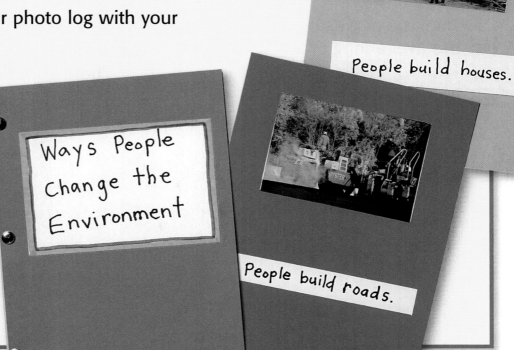

People build houses.

Ways People Change the Environment

People build roads.

Vocabulary Review

Copy the definitions below. Beside each number, write the term from the list that best matches the definition. For 5, write the letter of the correct answer.

aqueduct   geography
climate   renewable resources

1. A large pipe or other channel
3.1.2 that moves water from one place to another

2. Resources from nature that can
3.1.1 be replaced or used again

3. The study of land and water
3.1.1 and the way people, plants, and animals live on them

4. The kind of weather a place
3.1.2 has over a long time

5. Test Preparation The _____ is
3.1.1 the air, water, land, and all the living things around us.

    A. environment   **C. landform**
    B. timber   **D. valley**

Comprehension Check

6. What is the difference between
3.1.1 weather and climate?

7. How does water affect where
3.1.2 people live?

8. Name two regions in California.
3.1.1

9. What are three natural
3.1.2 resources people use? Are they renewable or nonrenewable?

10. How did the Los Angeles
3.1.2 aqueduct solve a problem for Los Angeles?

11. Critical Thinking Why do people
3.1.2 need to be careful with natural resources?

12. Critical Thinking How might a
3.1.2 change to the environment be both good and bad?

Write a complete sentence to answer each question.

Use a Landform Map

13. Is the land near Fresno lower or higher than the land near San José?
`3.1.1`

14. What kind of landform is along the coast from Monterey to San Luis Obispo?
`3.1.1`

15. Test Preparation The _____ shows where north, south, east, and west are on the map.
`3.1.1`

16. Test Preparation On a landform map, the _____ tells which color each landform is on the map.
`3.1`

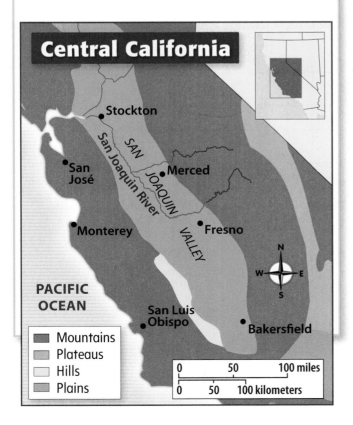

Central California

Stockton

SAN

San Joaquin River

JOAQUIN

San José

Merced

Monterey

VALLEY

Fresno

N
W • E
S

PACIFIC
OCEAN

San Luis
Obispo

Bakersfield

■	Mountains
■	Plateaus
□	Hills
■	Plains

0   50   100 miles
0   50   100 kilometers

Interview

17. What makes the quote from Jeff Becerra (page 70) a primary source?
`3.1.2`

18. What solution does Jeff Becerra suggest for the problem of an increase in the need for water?
`3.1.2`

19. Make a Poster Choose one renewable or nonrenewable resource, and make a poster that shows the steps needed to bring that resource from nature to your community.
`3.1.2`

20. Narrative Write a story about a new nonrenewable resource that is suddenly discovered in your community. Tell what happens to the community as a result of the discovery.
`3.1.2`
ELA
`W2.1`

LOG ON

For help with the process of writing, visit:

www.macmillanmh.com/ca/ss/writing

UNIT 1

Unit Review and Test Prep

Comprehension and Critical Thinking Check

Write one sentence or more to answer each question.

1. What are some features **regions** have
3.1.1 in common?

2. How are all **communities** the same?
3.1.1

3. What kinds of **landforms** are good for
3.1.2 farming? Why?

4. Why do people need **natural resources**?
3.1.1

5. What happens if people use up a
3.2.3 **nonrenewable resource**?

6. Explain what happens when people live
3.1.1 outside the **urban** area where they work.

7. What are some reasons that people
3.1.2 change the **environment**?

8. How did building an **aqueduct** affect
3.1.2 the growth of Los Angeles?

9. Critical Thinking How might people
3.1.2 need to **adapt** to their environment if
they live in a place with lots of rain?

10. Critical Thinking Why is it important
3.1.2 to **conserve** water resources?

Reading Social Studies Check

Identify the Main Idea and Details

**Reread "A Community at Play" on
page 13. Use the chart to show the main
idea and details of the section. Then
answer the questions.** **3.1.2** **R2.5** (ELA)

11. What is the main idea of the section?
ELA
R2.5

12. How did you know what the main
ELA
R2.5 idea was?

13. What are three ways people have fun
ELA
R2.5 in Long Beach?

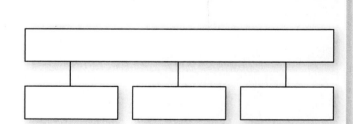

Read the paragraphs. Then, answer the questions.

California has hundreds of miles of coast. Different kinds of fish live in the water along the coast. People like to eat fish from this water. Fish are a natural resource.

Sometimes oil and other things we use flow into the water along the coast and pollute, or dirty, it. Fish can die because the water is polluted. These fish are not safe for people to eat. That means there are fewer fish people can use for food. It is important to keep the water clean, for fish and for us.

14. Which of these is a fact from the
3.1.2 passage?

 A People in California only eat two kinds of fish.

 B California has hundreds of miles of coast.

 C People are not careful with fish.

 D Hundreds of people fish in California.

15. Fish die because—
3.1.2

 A people do not like fish.

 B their environments are safe.

 C people eat too much fish.

 D the water they live in is polluted.

Write About Geography

16. Personal Letter Suppose you live in
3.1.2 a rural community where many new
ELA
W2.3 buildings are going to be constructed. Write a letter to the editor of your local newspaper about why you think this is good or bad for your community.

17. Descriptive Think about being in
3.1.2 Bodie after the gold ran out. Write a
ELA
W2.2 poem about what it would have been like if your family was the last to leave town.

18. Narrative Think about what it would
3.1.2 have been like to live in the Owens River
ELA
W2.1 Valley or Los Angeles soon after the Los Angeles Aqueduct was finished. Write a story set in one of these two places.

For help with the process of writing, visit:

www.macmillanmh.com/ss/ca/writing

How does geography affect communities?

Write About the Big Idea [3.1.2] [ELA W2.2]

Descriptive Paragraph

Think about the places people build communities. Then complete the graphic organizer you started on page 3. Add details about why the communities are there.

Then write a paragraph. Describe the geography and natural resources of your own community. Explain how they affect jobs, transportation, and other ways of life in your community.

Community	Location	Resources	Why it is there
Long Beach	Pacific coast	port, two rivers	good port
Sacramento			
Your community			

Steps for Writing a Descriptive Paragraph

1. Plan
- Plan the topic of your paragraph.
- Identify your purpose and audience.

2. Write a First Draft
- The first sentence of your paragraph should introduce the topic. Describe the place where your own community is located.
- Add a sentence for each new detail. Use adjectives to tell more about each detail.
- Write a final sentence for a conclusion.

3. Revise and Proofread
- Read your paragraph. Does your first sentence tell what you are describing?
- Be sure you used strong adjectives in your detail sentences.
- Proofread your paragraph. Check capitalization and spelling. Rewrite your paragraph neatly before handing it in.

Speak About the Big Idea 3.1.1 ELA LS2.2

Poem

Create a poem about regions in California. Think about what makes each area special.

Prepare As a class, list the geographic regions of California. Then work in small groups. Each group should choose and research one region. Make a list of the things that make the region special. Then write a poem about it. You might decide to make your poem rhyme, or not to rhyme.

Present As a group, recite your poem for your classmates. You could all recite it at the same time, or each person in the group could read a different section.

LAUNCH PAD For help with the Big Idea activity, visit:

www.macmillanmh.com/ss/ca/launchpad

Read More About the Big Idea

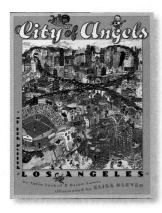

City of Angels
Julie Jaskol and Brian Lewis This is a celebration of Los Angeles's many diverse communities and places of interest.

Barrio
George Ancona Read the story of a young Latino's daily life in the barrio of San Francisco.

Mojave
Diane Siebert The desert tells its story in the form of a poem.

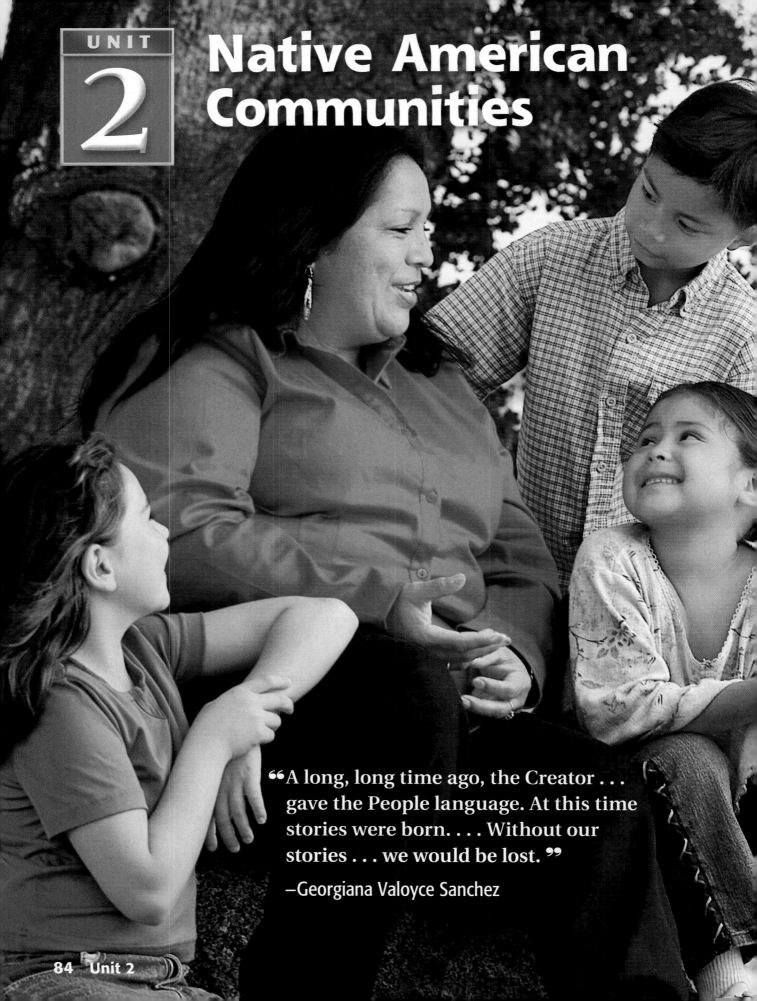

UNIT 2

Native American Communities

"A long, long time ago, the Creator . . . gave the People language. At this time stories were born. . . . Without our stories . . . we would be lost."

–Georgiana Valoyce Sanchez

How has life changed for people over time?

The first Californians were Native Americans. In Unit 2 you will read about some Native American communities that lived in the past. You will also see how some Native Americans live today.

Copy the graphic organizer below. As you read Unit 2, fill in details about how Native Americans lived in the past and how they live today. A few examples have been filled in for you.

Topic	Then	Now
Culture	Traditional songs and dances Traditional instruments, like gourd rattle	Modern and traditional songs and dances Modern and traditional instruments
Technology		
Government		

◀ Viejas children and elder

Coyote Rides a Star

Selection from *Back in the Beforetime, Tales of the California Indians,* retold by Jane Louise Curry

Long ago, according to the old stories, all the animals lived together and were called the animal people. Coyote thought that he was the smartest one of all . . .

The animal people celebrated the return of the salmon with a feast more splendid than any they had ever had before. Though often they thought Coyote a great **nuisance**, they had to admit that he knew how to use his wits. At the feast—after much arguing—they even gave him the place of honor next to Eagle, their chief.

Coyote was full of himself. "Who in the World is more clever than Coyote?" he thought as he made his way home from the feast by starlight. "Who else could have snatched the Sun? Or sniffed out the stolen salmon? With my brains, I should be chief, not Eagle. *I* should have the best seat at the feast, and be served first. I, Kiyoo the Coyote, should be honored above all others!"

Coyote gave a proud toss of his head, and as he did so, he spied the stars glittering in the dark sky above. A shooting star streaked overhead.

"Hai! How beautiful" Coyote exclaimed. And suddenly he knew what he wanted most in the world to do.

"I want to ride on a star," said he. "Even Mouse and Measuring Worm, the least of the animal people, can walk around on the earth. I, Coyote, should have a better way of going. And I shall! I shall take a journey on a star."

So Coyote climbed to the top of the nearest hill, lifted his nose to the sky, and howled up at the Evening Star. "Hai, Bright Star!" he called. "Come down here to me. I am going to take a ride on your back."

But the Evening Star did not obey. It barely blinked as it moved along its sky path.

nuisance (NEW suhns) something that annoys

"Ho! Are you hard of hearing, old Star?" cried Coyote. "I am Coyote—the Great Coyote, Sun-Snatcher and Fish-Finder. I have saved my people from darkness and cold and hunger, and now I wish to see all the World. Come down here so that I may jump onto your back."

The Evening Star smiled, but kept on its way without a word. In a little while it was gone.

But Coyote was not one to give up so easily.

At sundown the next day Coyote climbed to the same hilltop and called as he had called before. "Hai, Bright Star! Come down here to me so that I may jump onto your back."

This time the Evening Star, seeing that Coyote was in earnest, answered in a thin silvery voice. "Be content with your feet, Kiyoo the Coyote," it called. "Your place is on the earth. You may be a Great One among the animal folk, but you could not stand the speed of the stars."

But Coyote would not be put off. Each day at nightfall he returned and howled and yowled and whined and whispered and **blustered** and begged until at last Evening Star grew tired of listening.

"Enough, enough!" it said one night in a voice more sharp than silvery. "Jump on before I change my mind."

Evening Star slid down the sky, barely slowing as it skimmed past the hilltop, and then soared upward once more. Coyote gave a great jump, catching hold with his front paws, and almost slid off. "Hai, yi, yi!" he cried, but the sound whirled away in the star-wind. Evening Star flew so fast that poor Coyote could not haul himself up to crouch upon its back. It took all of his strength just to hold on.

Evening Star flew up and up and up, and then north over lands of ice and snow. The sharp star-wind grew bitter cold. Coyote's paws grew cold, then stiff, then numb, until he could hold on no longer. Letting go, he fell, head over feet over tail, back to earth.

He was a long time falling. Ten snows passed, some say. And when he came at last to earth, his landing was so hard that he was—say some—flattened out as thin as an acorn cake. Certainly, from that day to this he has been thin.

And every day to this day, he climbs at nightfall to the top of the nearest hill and scolds the Evening Star.

---

blustered (BLUS tuhrd) blew loudly

Write About It!

Write your own story explaining why an animal acts the way that it does.

Summarize

Native Americans of California ELA R2.5 3.2

How do you tell a friend about a book or movie? First you remember what happened. Then you retell the story in your own words. Of course, you don't tell every single thing that happened. You tell the important parts. To retell this way is to summarize. Summarizing what you have read can help you remember information in social studies.

1 Learn It

- Read the selection and find the main ideas.
- Use your own words to state the main ideas.
- Find the important details and add them to your summary.

Main Idea
This is a main idea.

Details
These details can be combined.

Main Idea
This is another main idea.

Details
These details can be combined.

California Native Americans often traded with other groups. The tribes of Northern California had obsidian. This black stone was good for making arrowheads. It was traded with other groups for fish, acorns, and other goods.

People near the coast traded shell beads, the way we use money. California shells were traded from one group to another. Some shells even made it east to groups of Native Americans living in the middle of our country.

2 Try It

Now copy the chart below. Reread the passage on page 90. Recall the main points of each paragraph. Use the chart to summarize this information in your own words. The first paragraph is done for you.

Paragraph 1	Paragraph 2
California Native Americans traded with each other. Northern tribes traded obsidian for fish and other goods.	

3 Apply It

Make a chart like the one above. Use it to summarize this passage.

Northwestern California was home to the Yurok people. The Yurok built large houses from redwood planks. To split the giant logs they used elk antlers. They also made canoes from redwood logs.

The Yurok traveled the bays of the Pacific Ocean in their canoes. There they caught their main food, salmon. Each year they held a special ceremony to honor the first salmon.

California's First Peoples

YOU ARE THERE

In this chapter you will read about the people who lived in the first California communities. You will read about how the people of these communities lived long ago and how they live today.

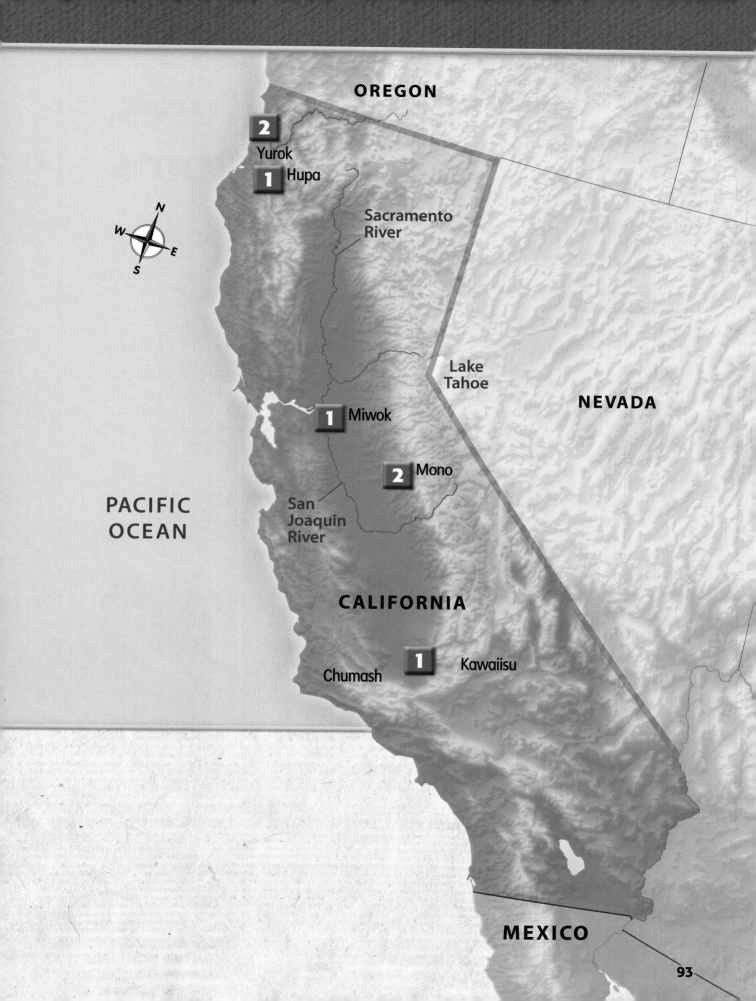

OREGON

2 Yurok

1 Hupa

Sacramento River

Lake Tahoe

NEVADA

N
W · E
S

1 Miwok

2 Mono

PACIFIC OCEAN

San Joaquin River

CALIFORNIA

1 Kawaiisu

Chumash

MEXICO

FOCUS QUESTION

How did California's Native Americans adapt to their environment?

VOCABULARY

culture
technology
homeland
petroglyph

VOCABULARY STRATEGY

WORD ORIGINS The word **petroglyph** comes from two Greek words. **Petro** means "rock" and **glyph** means "carving." What do you think **petroglyph** means?

READING STRATEGY

Summarize
Use the chart below to help you summarize the lesson.

Many Cultures, Many Customs

Start with Your CALIFORNIA STANDARDS

3.2 Students describe the American Indian nations in their local region long ago and in the recent past.

3.2.1 Describe national identities, religious beliefs, customs, and various folklore traditions.

Explore how the first Californians lived and what customs and traditions they followed. (Begins on page 95)

3.2.2 Describe the ways in which physical geography, including climate, influenced how the local Indian nations adapted to their natural environment.

Find out how Native Americans adapted to the land and climate of the places they lived. (Begins on page 95)

This headdress, made by the Hupa people, was used on special occasions. It was made from white deerskin and more than 50 red woodpecker feathers.

The First Californians 3.2 3.2.2

Native Americans were the first people to live in what we now call California. They have lived here for thousands of years. They lived in different groups, each with its own **culture**. Culture is the way of life a people shares. Culture includes language, food, arts, and beliefs.

The way each group of Native Americans lived was shaped by the environment of the region where they lived. Each group adapted to the environment, using the natural resources around them. In addition Native Americans used **technology** [tek NOL uh jee] to provide food, clothing, and shelter. Technology is the use of skills, ideas, and tools to meet peoples' needs.

Hupa dancers in the Jump Dance ▼

In this lesson you will read about how a few of California's Native American groups lived in the past. You will read about their cultures and how they used technology.

REVIEW Who were the first people to live in California? *Summarize*

◀ Yurok Social Dance, Klamath, California

95

Many Cultures 3.2.2

California was home to many groups of Native Americans. Look at the map on the next page. It shows where some California Native American groups lived. Can you find a group that lived close to where you live now?

▲ The Miwok used this stone mortar (bowl) and pestle to grind acorns.

The Miwok [MEE wuk] lived in the Central Valley, an area rich in natural resources. Oak trees that grew there provided acorns which Miwok women used to make bread. The acorn was an important part of Miwok culture. The Miwok even had songs about it. Each year they held a festival to celebrate the acorn and its importance as a food. Miwok people still hold this festival today.

The Chumash were another Native American group. They lived in large villages along the southern coast. They got much of their food from the ocean, so boat building was an important technology for them. They built large canoes called *tomols* [TOH mahls] for fishing. A *tomol* could be 30 feet long, but still light enough that two people could easily carry it.

REVIEW How did the Miwok and the Chumash get their main sources of food? *Main Idea and Details*

A Chumash tomol ▼

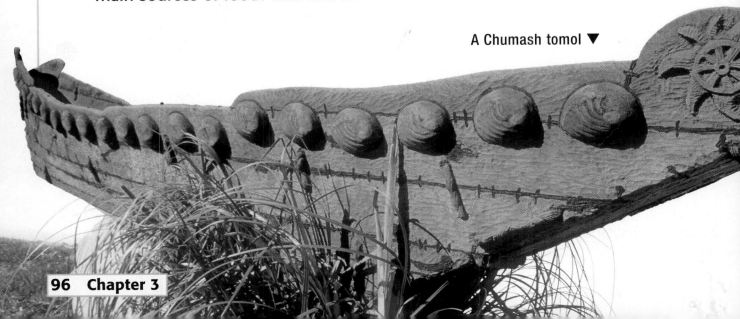

Tolowa
Shasta
Modoc
Yurok
Hupa
Achomawi
Northern Paiute
Yana
Maidu
Sinkyone

N
W E
S

Pomo
Nisenan
Patwin
Washo
Northern Paiute
Coast Miwok
Sierra Miwok
Owens Valley Paiute-Shoshone
Ohlone
Foothill Yokut
Western Shoshone
Esselen
Southern Valley Yokut
Salinan
Chemeheuvi
Kawaiisu
Southern Paiute
Mohave
Chumash
Serrano
Tongva
SONORAN DESERT

PACIFIC OCEAN

Luiseño
Kumeyaay
Quechan

The Kawaiisu 3.2.1 3.2.2

Like the Miwok and the Chumash, the Kawaiisu [kwigh EE soo] used technology to adapt to their environment. They also adapted by moving from one place to another as the seasons changed. In the winter they lived in sunny valleys of the Mojave [mo HAH vay] Desert. There they built waterproof shelters of branches and bark. They warmed these homes at night by using heated rocks from a fire pit where meals had been cooked. In the summer they moved up into the cool Tehachapi [tuh HA chuh pee] Mountains. For shade they built shelters covered with grasses.

The Tehachapi Mountains and the Mojave Desert were the Kawaiisu **homeland**, the land where they had lived as long as anyone could remember. They knew which plants provided food and where animals could be found. Girls and women gathered berries, nuts, and acorns. Boys and men hunted deer. They dried the meat in strips and used it for food when traveling.

▼ Simple shelters gave protection from winter rains.

When a food source was low in one place, the Kawaiisu were careful not to use it up. Instead they moved to another place where food was more plentiful.

▲ Kawaiisu rock carvings

Kawaiisu Rock Art

Rock art was an important part of Kawaiisu culture. The Kawaiisu painted designs of lines and circles on rocks and rock walls. They also made **petroglyphs** (PET roh glifs), or carvings, on the rocks. Some people believe the designs were a kind of road sign that told where the best food and water sources were. Kawaiisu artists today still make art modeled on the petroglyphs. Read below to see what one Kawaiisu artist and Elder says about looking to the culture of the past.

Primary Sources

A quote from
David Laughing Horse Robinson

❝The Kawaiisu Elders said, 'When we look to the past, we will find the best answers to the problems of the future.' My heart speaks that message every day, through the art I feel **compelled** to create.❞

compelled forced

Write About It! Why is the culture of the past important to this artist?

REVIEW How did the Kawaiisu adapt to where they lived?
Main Idea and Details

The Hupa 3.2.2

The Hupa homeland is much different from the Kawaiisu homeland. The climate in the Hoopa Valley along the Trinity River is cooler, and there is more rainfall. The area has many natural resources.

The Hupa were able to find plenty to eat in their environment. The women and girls gathered berries and nuts. Men and boys hunted for deer and elk. They also made nets and built weirs in the river to catch salmon and trout. A weir is a kind of wall with an opening for the water. It forced fish to swim where they could be easily caught.

Because food was plentiful where they lived, the Hupa did not need to move from place to place. Instead they built strong houses from cedar wood and lived in villages close to the river.

REVIEW Why didn't the Hupa move from place to place? *Cause and Effect*

▲ Elk-horn purses were used to store strings of shell beads. The beads were used as money.

▼ The Hupa built houses from cedar wood.

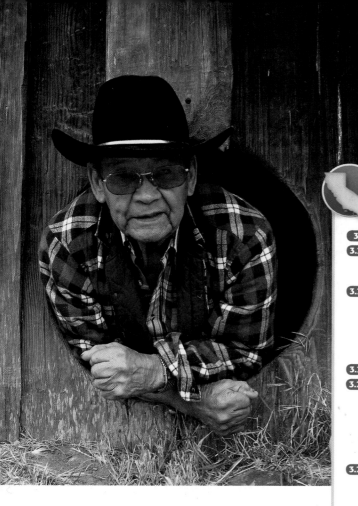

◀ A Hupa elder leans out of an old Hupa house.

What You Learned

3.2
3.2.2 Native American groups have lived in California for thousands of years.

3.2.2 Native American groups used technology to provide food, clothing, and shelter.

3.2.1
3.2.2 The Kawaiisu moved from place to place as the seasons changed. They created rock art paintings and petroglyphs.

3.2.2 The Hupa built villages along the river and did not move with the seasons.

Lesson Review

1. Focus Question How did California's
3.2 Native Americans adapt to their environment?

2. Vocabulary Write one sentence for
3.2 each vocabulary word.

   culture   petroglyph
   homeland   technology

3. Geography How did geography
3.2.2 affect how the Chumash lived?

4. Critical Thinking Problem
3.2.2 **Solving** How did the Kawaiisu solve the problem of living in the desert?

5. Reading Strategy Summarize
3.2.1
ELA
R2.3 Copy the chart. Use it to summarize the section on page 100.

6. Write about 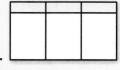 Tell what life
3.2.2 was like for the Kawaiisu and the
ELA
W2.2 Hupa long ago.

7. Link to Art Look back at the rock
3.2.1 art on page 99. Then, think of three things in your life that are important to you. Make designs that stand for those things. Then make some artwork using your designs.

A Native American Child in California 3.2

From an early age, Native American children began learning important skills. Boys learned how to track animals and to hunt and fish. Girls learned which plants were good to eat, how to weave baskets, and to make flour from acorns. Both boys and girls enjoyed stories, singing, and music on special days.

▲ Yurok girls learned to weave baskets from their mothers.

Miwok children used walnuts and sticks in a counting game. ▶

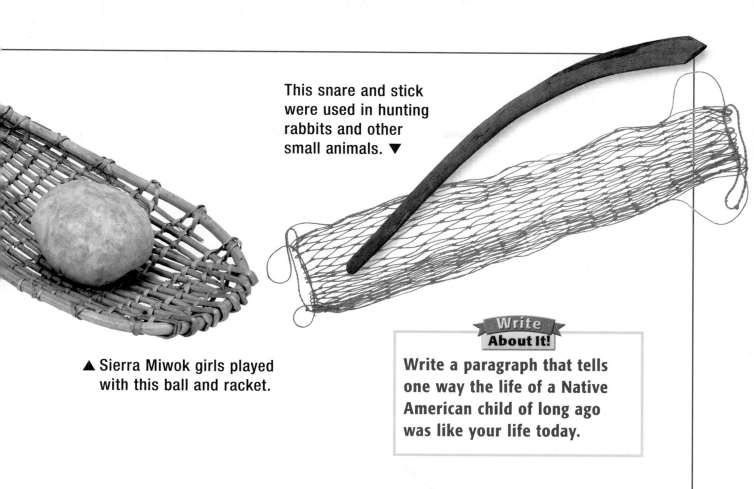

This snare and stick were used in hunting rabbits and other small animals. ▼

▲ Sierra Miwok girls played with this ball and racket.

Write
About It!

Write a paragraph that tells one way the life of a Native American child of long ago was like your life today.

Yurok boys learned dances for special times. ▼

LOG ON

For more about Native American life, visit:

www.macmillanmh.com/ss/ca/dayinthelife

Locate Information 3.1 ELA R2.1

ELA R2.1

A book can be an important source of information. Special parts of books help you find the information you need. Learning how to use these parts of a book will help you find information quickly and easily.

VOCABULARY

table of contents
glossary
index

 Learn It

Three book parts can help you find information.

- The **table of contents** is in the front of a book. It lists chapters and other parts of a book and tells the page number where each part begins.

- A **glossary** is an alphabetical list of words, meanings, and pronunciations in the back of a book.

- An **index** is an alphabetical list of subjects mentioned in a book, with page numbers. It is found in the back of a book.

• Contents •

2 Try It

- Look at the table of contents on page 104. On what page does the section about Hupa basket makers begin?

- Look at the glossary section below. What is a valley?

- Look at the index below. On what pages can you find information about the Jump Dance?

- Which two book parts could help you find information about Hupa ceremonies?

3 Apply It

Choose a Native American group you would like to learn more about. Find a book about Native American groups in your classroom or library. Look at the table of contents and the index. Find the page numbers that tell where you can find information about the group you chose. Then turn to those pages and read about the group.

Index

basket making • Gold Rush

B

C

Glossary

trade • vegetation

trade (trād) The buying and selling of goods and services.

transportation (trans pər ta′ shən) The act or means of carrying or moving something.

U

urban (ûr′bən) A city and its surrounding areas.

V

valley (val′ē) A long lowland surrounded by mountains or hills.

How did life change for California's Native Americans when newcomers came?

explorer
reservation
tradition
powwow

VOCABULARY STRATEGY

WORD FAMILIES
Reserve means "to hold back." Which word in the list above comes from the same word family? What do you think a **reservation** is?

Summarize
Use the chart below to summarize the lesson.

Native Americans Then and Now

Start with Your
CALIFORNIA STANDARDS

3.2 Students describe the American Indian nations in their local region long ago and in the recent past.

3.2.1 Describe the national identities, religious beliefs, customs, and various folklore traditions.

See how Native Americans have worked hard to keep their past alive. (Begins on page 109)

3.2.4 Discuss the interaction of new settlers with the already established Indians of the region.

Discover what happened to Native Americans in California after newcomers arrived. (pages 107–108)

▼ *Mission San Gabriel* Arcángel by Ferdinand Deppe, 1832

When Spanish explorers came to the California coast, Native Americans rowed out in canoes to greet them. It was the beginning of contact that would bring many changes.

Newcomers Bring Change 3.2.4

For thousands of years the Kawaiisu, the Hupa, the Kumeyaay [KOO mee yigh], and other Native American groups lived in California. In 1492 Christopher Columbus sailed to North America. About 50 years later, Spanish **explorers** sailed up what is now the California coast. Explorers are people who go to a place that is new to them to find out about it.

It was about another 250 years before Spanish settlers came to stay, but once they did, life began to change for California Native Americans. One reason that life changed was that the newcomers took their land. Native groups fought back, but the newcomers had better weapons. The newcomers also brought diseases. California's Native American groups had never had diseases like smallpox or measles. When they caught these diseases, many got very sick and thousands died.

REVIEW What happened to Native American groups when Europeans came to California? *Summarize*

Native Americans in a Changed World 3.2 3.2.4

Over the years California was ruled by different countries. In 1850 it became part of the United States. More settlers came here from Europe and Asia. By the early 1900s, most Native American groups had lost their homelands. In some parts of the United States, groups of Native Americans lived on **reservations**. A reservation is land set aside for Native Americans by the United States government. Often reservations were located on land that no one else wanted. However, in California, most Native American groups were not even given reservations.

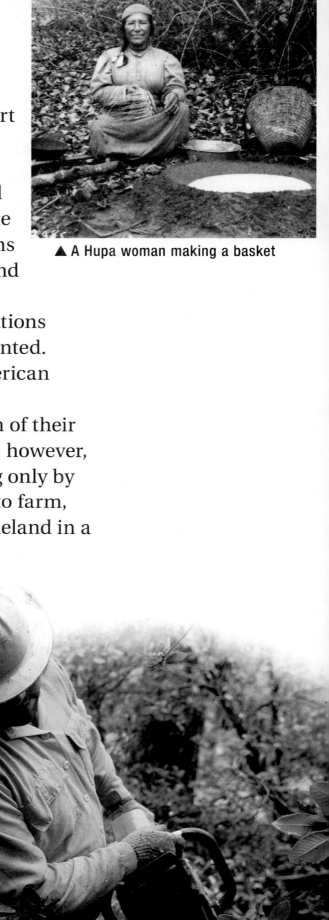

▲ A Hupa woman making a basket

The Hupa were able to hold on to much of their original homeland. The Hupa way of life, however, changed with the times. Instead of living only by hunting and fishing, many Hupa began to farm, too. Today the Hupa use their forest homeland in a new way. They earn money through logging and selling wood that is cut into timber.

The Hupa log on their reservation in Humboldt County. ▼

Western Mono women today carry on the basket-making tradition. ▶

Keeping the Past Alive

Though life has changed much over the years, California's Native Americans work to keep their **traditions** alive. A tradition is a belief or custom handed from parents to children. **Powwows** are one way to keep traditions alive. A powwow is a Native American festival where people share drumming, costumes, dances, and crafts. One of the largest powwows in the United States is held each year in Costa Mesa, California. Everyone is welcome.

Cultural centers, and museums also help Native Americans keep traditions alive. Today many Native Americans are choosing to learn the language of their groups, or tribes, and to learn traditional songs and stories. Some, like musician Mary Youngblood, have learned to play traditional instruments.

REVIEW What are some ways that Native Americans keep their traditions alive today? *Summarize*

109

Living in Two Worlds 3.2

Many Native Americans in California today split their time between cities and their people's reservation. Allyson Bunch is a good example. Allyson is a Yurok, but she lives in Eureka, about 40 miles from the Yurok reservation.

Allyson grew up in San Francisco. Her parents moved there from the Yurok reservation before Allyson was born. They thought they could get better jobs in San Francisco. They also believed the city had more to offer their children.

Allyson found the city exciting. "It was a great place to grow up. I met people from all over. We did fun things, too, all the time."

Even though they lived in San Francisco, the family visited the reservation often. Allyson spent every summer there living with her relatives. "I had the best of both worlds," she says. "I could enjoy all the fun things and excitement about city life. I had my family ties on the reservation. I could learn about my culture and feel a part of the people."

The Yurok still fish for salmon on the Klamath River. ▼

◀ Allyson Bunch with her daughters Taeresia and Tammyce

Taeresia Bunch in her dance costume ▼

Moving Back

A few years ago, Allyson moved from San Francisco to Eureka [yew REE kah]. She wanted her two daughters to be near the reservation. Allyson's parents have returned, too. They live on the reservation. Allyson works for her tribe. She is in charge of a camp where Yurok children can learn about the tribe's culture, language, and dances.

Allyson is helping pass on some traditions to her children. Her daughter Taeresia is in fourth grade. She says, "I like Eureka because we have family nearby. My cousins come over all the time. We go to the reservation to watch ceremonial dances, like the brush dance. I'm not old enough to dance yet, but I am learning about it."

REVIEW Why does Allyson say that she had "the best of both worlds" growing up? *Summarize*

California's Native Americans 3.2

More than four million Native Americans live in the United States today. More live in California than in any other state. The charts below show which states have large Native American populations and which tribes now living in California are the largest.

United States Native American Population, 2000

State	Population
1. California	627,562
2. Oklahoma	391,949
3. Arizona	292,552
4. Texas	215,599
5. New Mexico	191,475

Native American Population in California, 2000

Group	Population
1. Cherokee	97,838
2. Apache	21,599
3. Choctaw	21,011
4. Navajo	14,348
5. Blackfoot	14,310

Think About Population

1. Which state has the highest number of Native Americans?

2. Which is the largest Native American group in California?

An elder leads Kumeyaay children playing a drum. ▶

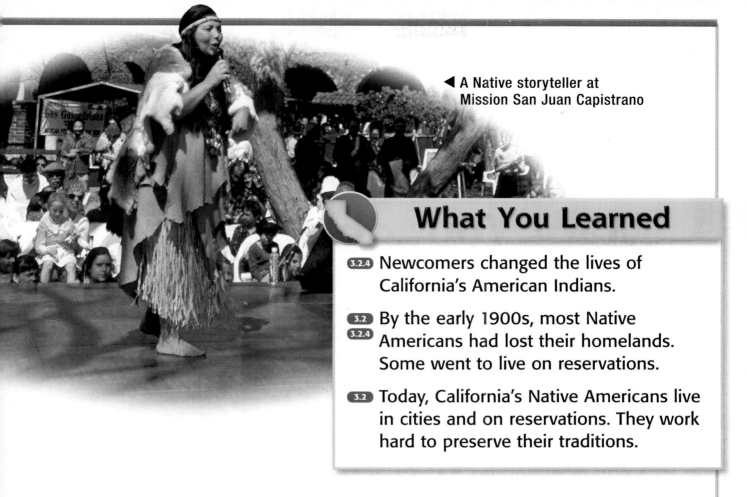

◀ A Native storyteller at Mission San Juan Capistrano

What You Learned

3.2.4 Newcomers changed the lives of California's American Indians.

3.2 **3.2.4** By the early 1900s, most Native Americans had lost their homelands. Some went to live on reservations.

3.2 Today, California's Native Americans live in cities and on reservations. They work hard to preserve their traditions.

Lesson Review

1. Focus Question How did life change **3.2** for California's Native Americans when newcomers came?

2. Vocabulary Write one sentence for **3.2** each vocabulary word.

   explorer   reservation
   powwow   tradition

3. Culture What is one way in which **3.2.1** Native Americans work to keep traditions alive?

4. Critical Thinking Make Inferences **3.2.4** Why do you think some Native **ELA** **R2.3** American groups did not get their homeland back for their reservations?

5. Reading Strategy Summarize **3.2.4** Use the chart to **ELA** **R2.3** summarize the section "Native Americans in a Changed World," on page 108.

6. Write about THE **BiG** IDEA How is **3.2** life different for California's Native **ELA** **W2.2** American groups today from how it was before European settlers arrived?

7. Link to Math Look at the **3.2** Datagraphic on page 112. Which is greater—the number of Navajo living in California, or the number of Cherokee living in California?

113

"These songs came from those who walked before me."

Mary Youngblood 1958–

Mary Youngblood grew up knowing little about her Native American heritage. She was adopted when she was seven months old and grew up in a non-Indian community.

From an early age, Mary had a special talent for music. She learned to play the piano at six years old and the violin at age eight. At ten, she learned classical flute and guitar. In school Mary played in the band and sang in school choirs. However, the flute was always her favorite instrument.

When she grew up, Mary Youngblood decided to find out about her Native American heritage. That was when she tried the Native American flute for the first time.

The Life of Mary Youngblood

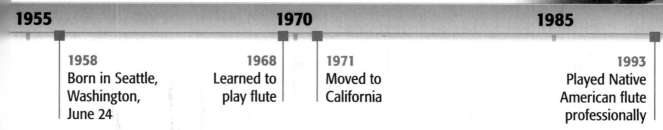

1955	1970	1985
1958 Born in Seattle, Washington, June 24	**1968** Learned to play flute	**1971** Moved to California	**1993** Played Native American flute professionally

Mary has been performing on the Native American flute ever since. Traditionally, the Native American flute has been a man's instrument, and Mary is the first woman to play it professionally. She now owns more than a hundred Native flutes. Each is handcarved and has its own special sound.

Mary has recorded four albums and received many awards and honors. In 2003 she won music's highest award, the Grammy, for Best Native American Music Album. When she accepted her award, she said, "We are working together to show that Native American music and culture are alive and well."

How does Mary Youngblood's music help keep Native American traditions alive?

▼ Mary performs in concert.

2000

1999–2000
Won the
Flutist of
the Year

2003
Won
Grammy
Award

For more about
Mary Youngblood, visit:

www.macmillanmh.com/ss/ca/bios

Cooperation and Compromise 3.4.2

Students at a school in Pasadena had a problem. After school the soccer field was shared by second, third, fourth, and fifth graders. The second and third graders complained that the older students played on the soccer field most of the time. The younger students wanted more time to play there. The students agreed to take the problem to their Student Council. After many meetings, the members of the council voted on a plan that gave older and younger students an equal number of days to play on the soccer field.

These students solved their problem through cooperation and compromise. Read these steps to learn how to make a successful compromise.

Build Citizenship

1. **Identify the problem.** Find out what each group or person thinks is the problem.

2. **Express points of view.** Share the reasons why people disagree. Find out what each person wants.

3. **Look for common goals or interests.** Talk about the ideas or goals that all groups share.

4. **Find ways that everyone can gain from cooperation and compromise.** Look for a way to give each group or person at least part of what they want, so that everyone can reach an agreement.

Think About It

1. What might the younger students say was the problem?

2. What might have been the point of view of the older students?

3. What are some other ways this problem might have been solved?

4. Why is it important to find a solution that everyone agrees to?

Write a paragraph that describes an activity in your own school that requires cooperation. It might be playing on a sports team, performing a play, or having a class party. How do people need to cooperate and compromise to make the activity successful?

SAN FRANCISCO

Native Americans in Your Region 3.2

Sam lives in San Francisco. He found out who the first people in his community were. Sam made a map to show what he learned. You can make a map about where Native Americans lived in your area, too. Here's what to do:

- Use your library or the Internet to find out which Native American groups lived near your community long ago. Find out if there are reservations near your community today. Make copies of maps of your area.

- To show what he learned, Sam made a map. He made a key for his map and gave it a title. He called it, "Native Americans in the San Francisco Bay Area."

LOG ON For more help making your map, visit:

www.macmillanmh.com/ss/ca/local

Make a Map

Step 1 Gather your notes.

Step 2 Using a map of your area for reference, draw an outline map.

Step 3 Color your map in, using a different colored marker or crayon for each Native American group. Mark any reservations or historical sites in the area today with numbers.

Step 4 Make a key to show which group each color stands for. Make another key to show what each number stands for. Give your map a title.

Step 5 Share your map with your classmates.

Materials

- blank map of your area
- map of Native American territories
- map of Native American reservations
- markers and crayons

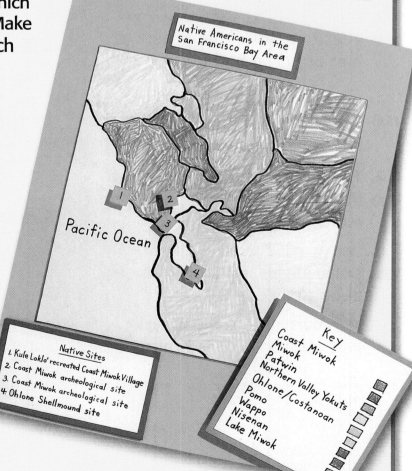

Native Americans in the San Francisco Bay Area

Pacific Ocean

Native Sites
1. Kule Loklo' recreated Coast Miwok Village
2. Coast Miwok archeological site
3. Coast Miwok archeological site
4. Ohlone Shellmound site

Key
Coast Miwok
Miwok
Patwin
Northern Valley Yokuts
Ohlone/Costanoan
Pomo
Wappo
Nisenan
Lake Miwok

Vocabulary Review

Copy the sentences below on a separate sheet of paper. Use the list of vocabulary words below to fill in the blanks.

explorer	petroglyph
homeland	reservation

1. A _____ is a kind of carving
3.2.1 made on rocks.

2. A(n) _____ is someone who
3.2.4 goes to a place that is new to him or her to find out about it.

3. A _____ is land that has been
3.2.4 set aside for Native American groups.

4. The place where a people have
3.2.2 lived for as long as anyone can remember is called their _____ .

5. Test Preparation The use of
3.2.1 skills, ideas, and tools to meet people's needs is _____ .

    A. culture   C. petroglyph
    B. explorer   D. technology

Comprehension Check

6. Which plant and plant product
3.2.2 were very important to the Miwok?

7. How did the Chumash use
3.2.1 technology to help their community?

8. According to some people, why
3.2.1 did the Kawaiisu make their petroglyphs?

9. How did the Kawaiisu adapt to
3.2.2 the changing seasons?

10. Critical Thinking How did the
3.2.1 Kawaiisu show that they knew their homeland well and took good care of their environment?

11. Critical Thinking Why do you
3.2.4 think many Native Americans today study the traditions of long ago?

Write a complete sentence to answer each question.

Locate Information

12. Where in a book would you
3.2.1
ELA
R2.1
look to find out on what page a chapter about the Hupa begins?

13. In what part of a book would
3.2.1
ELA
R2.1
you look to find the definition of the word powwow?

14. Where would you look in a
ELA
3.2.1
book to find out which pages of the book have information about Kawaiisu ceremonies?

15. **Test Preparation** Information in
ELA
R2.1
a glossary is listed in _____ order.

16. **Test Preparation** You would
ELA
R2.1
usually find an index and a glossary in the _____ of a book.

Quote

17. Why did Allyson Bunch
3.2
enjoy living in San Francisco as a child?

18. Why does Taeresia Bunch like
3.2
living in Eureka?

19. **Make a Poster** Think about the
3.2.1
lives of the Hupa and Kawaiisu. Make a poster that shows how both the Hupa and the Kawaiisu used their environment.

20. **Personal Letter** Suppose you
3.2.1
ELA
W2.3
are a performer like Mary Youngblood. Write a letter to a fan telling why you think it's important to preserve your heritage by performing.

For help with the process of writing, visit:

www.macmillanmh.com/ss/ca/writing

The Kumeyaay

YOU ARE THERE

In this chapter you will take a closer look at one Native American group, the Kumeyaay. You will read about their way of life and their leaders in the past. You will also read about how the Kumeyaay have changed over time, yet have kept their traditions alive.

1 **Life in a Kumeyaay Village**
(page 124)
The Kumeyaay lived in villages that were the center of their community life.

2 **Kumeyaay Leaders and Healers**
(page 132)
Leaders and healers were an important part of the Kumeyaay community.

OREGON

LEGEND

Kumeyaay, present-day

Kumeyaay, around 1750

★ State capital
• Other city

Present-day cities are shown

Eureka

Klamath River

Sacramento River

American River

Lake Tahoe

★ Sacramento

NEVADA

San Francisco
Oakland

San José

San Joaquin River

PACIFIC OCEAN

Fresno

CALIFORNIA

Bakersfield

Colorado River

Los Angeles

Anaheim

Salton Sea

San Diego **3**

1 2 3

3 **Kumeyaay Then and Now** (page 140)
The Kumeyaay people have preserved their culture, while changing with the times.

MEXICO

How did the Kumeyaay use knowledge of their environment to meet their needs?

ligament
snare
vegetation
agriculture

VOCABULARY STRATEGY

ROOT WORDS You probably know what a vegetable is. **Vegetable** comes from a Latin word meaning "to grow." Which list word means "things that grow"?

Summarize
Copy the chart below to summarize the lesson.

Life in a Kumeyaay Village

Start with Your
CALIFORNIA STANDARDS

3.2 Students describe the American Indian nations in their local region long ago and in the recent past.

3.2.2 Discuss the ways in which physical geography, including climate, influenced how the local Indian nations adapted to their natural environment.

Learn how the Kumeyaay of long ago used the environment to find the things they needed to live. (Begins on page 125)

The Kumeyaay built winter houses like the one on the left, made from willow branches. Who are the Kumeyaay? How did they live long ago?

The Kumeyaay 3.2 3.2.2

The Kumeyaay have lived in Southern California for thousands of years. Their homeland was the rolling hills and the coast near what is now San Diego and northern Mexico. You can see their homeland on the map.

The climate made this area an ideal place to live. The environment provided food, water, shelter, and even medicine. Every member of the family learned to use natural resources to help the community. In this lesson you will take a closer look at how the Kumeyaay lived long ago.

REVIEW Where is the Kumeyaay homeland? *Summarize*

◄ Kumeyaay house

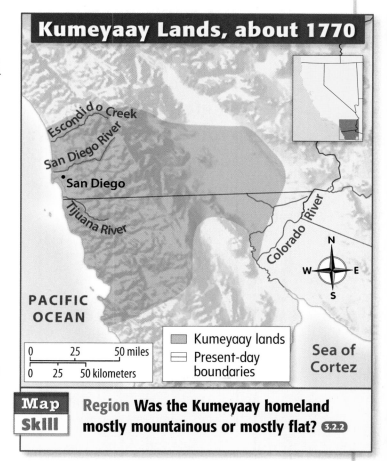

Kumeyaay Lands, about 1770

Escondido Creek

San Diego River

•San Diego

Tijuana River

Colorado River

PACIFIC OCEAN

Sea of Cortez

0 — 25 — 50 miles
0 — 25 — 50 kilometers

Kumeyaay lands
Present-day boundaries

Map Skill Region **Was the Kumeyaay homeland mostly mountainous or mostly flat?** 3.2.2

How the Kumeyaay Lived 3.2.2

The Kumeyaay were skilled hunters. They hunted with bows and arrows made from willow branches. The string of the bow was made from deer **ligaments**, strong bands of stretchy tissue that connect bones. For large animals such as deer or bighorn sheep, the hunters used arrows with stone arrowheads. Women sometimes caught small animals such as rabbits with **snares**, or traps, or hunted them with wooden arrowheads. Animals provided food, and their skins provided clothing, blankets, and rugs.

The Kumeyaay also used the **vegetation**, or plant life, of their homeland. They knew which plants were safe to eat and which, like willows, could be used to make tools. They gathered the food that grew naturally. Agave [ah GAH vay] was an important plant. It was used for both food and medicine.

▲ Rabbits were an important food source.

The agave plant was used to treat cuts and infections. ▼

Kumeyaay bows were made from willow branches. ▶

On the Move

Like the Kawaiisu, the Kumeyaay moved throughout the year, hunting and gathering food. In the winter many Kumeyaay lived along the coast. They fished and gathered clams in the bay. Their winter houses were rounded huts made from willow branches with the leaves left on them. Each house had a small door, which was covered with a mat or basket at night to keep out the cold air.

During the summer the Kumeyaay moved up into the mountains. Summer houses could be simpler shelters, or even caves. In the mountains they gathered wild plums and other fruits.

In the fall they gathered piñon [pin YAWN] nuts and their favorite food, acorns. Women ground the acorns to make meal, which they used to make a sweet bread. The Kumeyaay collected as many nuts and acorns as they could to eat over the winter. When fall ended, they returned to their winter village.

▲ The Kumeyaay used baskets like this to gather acorns.

REVIEW Why do you think the Kumeyaay moved each season? *Draw Conclusions*

Bighorn sheep ▼

Working with Resources 3.2.2

You read how the Kumeyaay gathered foods that grew naturally. They also changed their environment to grow food themselves. Growing food and raising or attracting animals for food is called **agriculture**.

The Kumeyaay knew that after a fire certain plants would grow that were excellent for food and medicine. They would purposely burn parts of their land to get these plants to grow. They also knew that some plants were good food for the animals they wanted to hunt. By helping these plants to grow, the Kumeyaay attracted those animals.

The Kumeyaay built dams with rocks and sticks to guide water to where they wanted plants to grow. They also used dams to slow the flow of water and keep it from washing away their soil. In these ways the Kumeyaay took care of the environment and made it work for them.

REVIEW How did the Kumeyaay make it easier to find animals they wanted to hunt? *Recall Details*

Mule Deer

Skunk

Bobcat

▼ Barrel cacti and brittlebushes grow on this hillside in Kumeyaay country.

◀ Kumeyaay hunters tracked animals by their paw prints.

Coyote

Squirrel

Raccoon

What You Learned

3.2
3.2.2 The Kumeyaay moved from season to season.

3.2.2 The Kumeyaay gathered, hunted, and farmed on their land.

3.2.2 The Kumeyaay changed their environment to meet their needs.

Lesson Review

1. **Focus Question** How did the
3.2
3.2.2 Kumeyaay use knowledge of their environment to meet their needs?

2. **Vocabulary** Write one sentence for
3.2 each vocabulary word.

   agriculture   snare
   ligament   vegetation

3. **Technology** How did the Kumeyaay
3.2.2 use fire to meet their needs?

4. **Critical Thinking Cause and**
3.2.2 **Effect** How do you think that moving each year when the seasons changed affected the way Kumeyaay families set up their homes?

5. **Reading Strategy Summarize**
3.2.2 Use the chart to
ELA summarize the
2.3 information in the
"On the Move" section on page 127.

6. **Write about** THE BIG IDEA Write a
3.2.2 paragraph about how the Kumeyaay
ELA changed the land to meet their
W1.1 needs.

7. **Link to Science** The Kumeyaay
3.2.2 learned how to use certain plants to make medicine. Use your library or the Internet to find other plants that are still used for medicine today.

Use Intermediate Directions 3.1

You have learned that the compass rose on a map shows north, east, south, and west. These are the **cardinal directions**. A compass rose can also show **intermediate directions**. An intermediate direction is halfway between two cardinal directions.

1 Learn It

Follow these steps for using a compass rose to find the cardinal and intermediate directions.

- Find the cardinal directions. The long points of the compass rose show the cardinal directions. The letters **N**, **E**, **S**, and **W** stand for north, east, south, and west.

- Find the intermediate directions. The short points of the compass rose show the intermediate directions, the directions halfway between the cardinal directions. Northeast is halfway between north and east. The abbreviations **NE**, **SE**, **SW**, and **NW** stand for northeast, southeast, southwest, and northwest. Intermediate directions are not always labeled on a compass rose.

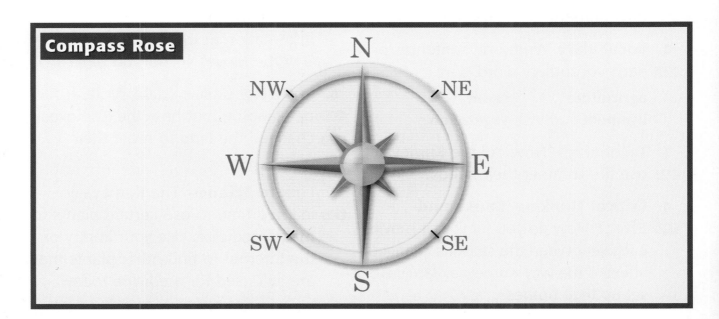

Compass Rose

2 Try It

- Look at the map below to answer the questions. It shows which Native American groups bordered the lands of the Kumeyaay. In what direction would a San Luiseño person go to visit the Yuma?

- If you lived near San Diego Bay, in what direction would you travel to reach the Cahuilla lands?

- Are the Cahuilla lands northeast or southeast of the San Diego River?

3 Apply It

Turn to the map of California counties on page R27. Use the map to answer the questions.

- Find Inyo County. Is it southeast or northeast of Kern County?

- Find Riverside County. Is it south or southeast of San Bernardino County?

- Which county is northeast of Shasta County?

Southern California Native American Lands

Cahuilla

San Luiseño

Cupeño

Colorado River

Yuma

San Diego River

Stonewall Peak

Oakzanita Peak

Cuyamaca Peak

Otay River

San Diego Bay

PACIFIC OCEAN

- Kumeyaay land
- Present-day boundaries
- ▲ Mountain Peak

0   25   50 miles
0   25   50 kilometers

N W E S

FOCUS QUESTION

Who were the leaders of the Kumeyaay people?

VOCABULARY

government
council
ceremony
shaman
astronomy

VOCABULARY STRATEGY

WORD ORIGINS

Astro- comes from the Greek word for **star**. What do you think **astronomy** means?

READING STRATEGY

Summarize
Use the chart below to summarize the important information in this lesson.

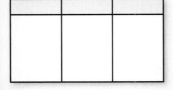

Kumeyaay Leaders and Healers

Start with Your

CALIFORNIA STANDARDS

3.2 Students describe the American Indian nations in their local region long ago and in the recent past.

3.2.1 Describe national identities, religious beliefs, customs, and various folklore traditions.

Learn about leaders and customs of the Kumeyaay. (Begins on page 135)

3.2.3 Describe the economy and systems of government, particularly those with tribal constitutions, and their relationship to federal and state governments.

Discover how the Kumeyaay of long ago governed themselves. (Begins on page 133)

Much of the Kumeyaay homeland was desert. ▼

A Kumeyaay story from long ago explains how the rattlesnake protected acorn meal from being eaten by mice. As a result, the Kumeyaay honor rattlesnakes by weaving their shape into baskets.

Leading the Kumeyaay 3.2 3.2.3

The Kumeyaay nation occupied a large territory. The Kumeyaay people lived in small groups called bands. Each band had its own land and the right to use the natural resources on it. Because they had so many people and such a large territory, the Kumeyaay worked out a plan for **government**. A government is a group of people in charge of leading a community, a state, or a nation. In this lesson you will read about leaders of the Kumeyaay government.

REVIEW Why did the Kumeyaay set up a government? *Summarize*

A Kumeyaay leader wearing a ceremonial headdress ▶

Generals, Captains, and Council 3.2.1 3.2.3

Kumeyaay land was divided into regions. Each region had a general who was in charge of the bands who lived there. A band could have 200 people or as many as 1,000 people. Each band had a leader called a captain. Captains might be born into the position, or they might be chosen because they were good leaders.

Each captain had a **council** [KOWN suhl]. A council is a group of people who work with a leader to make decisions. These leaders made decisions such as when the band should move or how to protect an important food source. They sometimes decided if it was necessary to go to war.

Each band had a central village where the leader and his council lived. Important **ceremonies** were also held there. A ceremony is a special way of doing something to mark an important time.

▲ Plumes of eagle feathers were used for some ceremonies.

◀ Five Kumeyaay Elders leading a ceremony

Religious Leaders and Healers

The **shaman** was an important member of the council. A shaman was a religious leader who led Kumeyaay ceremonies. The Kumeyaay believed being a shaman was something a child was "called to." Children were watched as they grew up to see whether they had this special "calling." If they did, they were carefully taught all they would need to know—the prayers, songs, and knowledge. The council also included healers, who used medicines from plants and herbs, as well as special songs. Jane Dumas, 80, is a Kumeyaay elder. She learned about plants from her mother, a healer. Read what she says about an important plant.

▲ Gourd rattle decorated with sea turtle

Jane Dumas

Primary Sources

Jane Dumas

Kumeyaay elder

❝A lot of plants have . . . meaning to people. The willow gives us clothes to wear, the wood to build our homes, and aspirin comes from the willow.❞

Write About It! Tell about a skill you learned from an older person you know.

REVIEW What were some things the Kumeyaay council decided? *Summarize*

135

Kumeyaay Ceremonies 3.2.1

The Kumeyaay celebrated important events with special ceremonies. Two of the most important Kumeyaay ceremonies celebrated the time when girls became women and boys became men. There were other ceremonies to celebrate marriages, name babies, and to honor the dead. The shaman used his knowledge of **astronomy** to tell people when the ceremony should take place. Astronomy is the science of the changing night sky, the phases of the moon, and the movements of the stars. The shaman would study the stars and decide the best time to hold a ceremony.

Kumeyaay women doing
a ceremonial dance ▼

Ceremonies often involved singing, dancing, drumming, and storytelling. The Kumeyaay also used songs and dances to pray for good hunting and for the health of the people. Everyone, young and old, would sing along.

REVIEW What special times did the Kumeyaay celebrate?
Summarize

▼ Kumeyaay leaders used the stars to tell when the seasons changed.

What You Learned

3.2
3.2.3 Kumeyaay territory was divided into regions, with many bands living in each region.

3.2.1
3.2.3 Kumeyaay government included generals, captains, and a council. The shaman was an important council member.

3.2.1 The Kumeyaay marked important occasions with ceremonies.

Lesson Review

1. **Focus Question** Who were the
3.2.1 leaders of the Kumeyaay people?
3.2.3

2. **Vocabulary** Write one sentence for
3.2 each vocabulary word.

   astronomy   government
   ceremony   shaman

3. **Government** How did the Kumeyaay
3.2.3 share leadership jobs?

4. **Critical Thinking Compare and**
3.2.3 **Contrast** Tell about a special time that your family has celebrated that is like a time the Kumeyaay celebrated.

5. **Reading Strategy Summarize**
3.2.3
ELA
R2.3 Summarize the section "Kumeyaay Ceremonies," on page 136.

6. **Write about** THE BIG IDEA How did the
3.2.3 Kumeyaay people govern themselves?
ELA
W1.1 Explain the jobs of captains, councils, and shamans.

7. **Link to Science** Kumeyaay shamans
3.2.1 used observations of the sky to make important decisions. On a clear night, look up at the night sky. Make a drawing to show what you observe.

137

Understanding Artifacts 3.2.1

An **artifact** is something that was made or used by people in the past. By studying artifacts, we can learn how people lived long ago.

Kumeyaay Rattles

Singing and dancing have always been important to Kumeyaay culture. The Kumeyaay tell stories and remember their history with songs. They use rattles to provide rhythms for the songs.

1 Learn It

At a museum you may have a chance to study actual artifacts. You may be able to touch them. Many times, though, you will be looking at photographs of artifacts. Here are things to think about when studying an artifact.

- Read any information given with the artifact.

- Look at the artifact carefully. What do you think it is made of? If you are able to touch or hold it, what does it feel like?

- What do you think the artifact was used for? Many times there are no written records or people left who remember, so historians must guess what an artifact was used for.

2 Try It

Now study the photograph of a Kumeyaay rattle.

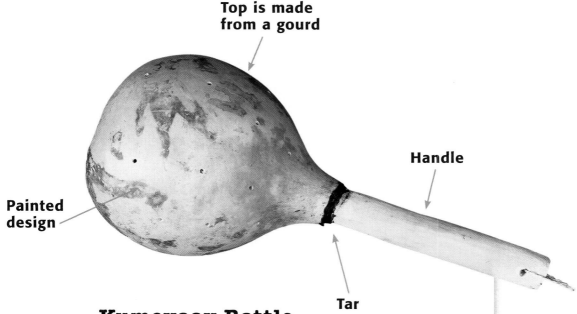

Top is made from a gourd

Handle

Painted design

Tar

Kumeyaay Rattle

Traditional Kumeyaay rattles were filled with seeds from a plant called the date palm. They were decorated with paint made from plants. The handle was made of willow, a light wood, and was attached to the gourd with tar.

3 Apply It

- What natural resources did the Kumeyaay use to make their rattles?

- What is something you cannot tell about the rattle from looking at it?

- Think of something in your house that a historian might find 100 years from now. Tell what the artifact is and what the historian might learn from it.

How did life change for the Kumeyaay after the Spanish came?

VOCABULARY

mission
citizen
sovereign
constitution

VOCABULARY STRATEGY

ROOT WORDS

Citizen comes from the French word for **city**. Today a person may be a **citizen** of a city, a state, or a country.

READING STRATEGY

Identify Main Idea and Details

Use the chart below to write the main idea and details of this lesson.

Kumeyaay Then and Now

Start with Your
CALIFORNIA STANDARDS

3.2 Students describe the American Indian nations in their local region long ago and in the recent past.

3.2.1 Describe national identities, religious beliefs, customs, and various folklore traditions.

Explore how a Kumeyaay tradition is kept alive today. (page 146)

3.2.3 Describe the economy and systems of government, particularly those with tribal constitutions, and their relationship to federal and state governments.

Learn about Kumeyaay government today. (pages 144–145)

3.2.4 Discuss the interaction of new settlers with the already established Indians of the region.

Discover what happened when newcomers came to Kumeyaay land. (Begins on page 141)

Kumeyaay girls pose at an annual powwow. ▼

In 1779 a Spanish soldier named Lt. Colonel Fages said of the Kumeyaay, "Indeed this tribe, which is the most numerous, is also the most restless, stubborn, haughty [proud], warlike,… and full of the spirit of independence."

The Spanish on Kumeyaay Land 3.2.4

In Chapter 3 you read how life changed for the Kawaiisu and the Hupa after the Spanish came to California. Here is what happened where the Kumeyaay lived.

The Spanish sent soldiers and priests. A priest named Father Junípero Serra came to what is now San Diego to build a **mission** [MISH un] on Kumeyaay land. A mission is a settlement built around a church.

Serra wanted the Kumeyaay to live at the mission. He wanted to teach the Kumeyaay a new religion. He thought the Kumeyaays' lives would be better if they were Roman Catholics and learned Spanish ways.

REVIEW Why did the Spanish come to live on Kumeyaay land? *Main Idea and Details*

Inside the mission church of San Diego de Alcalá ▶

Changes for the Kumeyaay 3.2.4

The coming of the Spanish brought many changes to the Kumeyaay. As you read in Chapter 3, the Spanish brought new diseases, such as smallpox, that killed thousands of Kumeyaay. In addition, the Spanish settled on Kumeyaay lands on the coast. The Kumeyaay lost their winter homes and were forced to stay in the mountains all year.

Some Kumeyaay chose to live at the mission. Others were forced to live and work there. Some learned the new religion and decided to follow it. However, most Kumeyaay people wanted to keep their own religion and their own ways.

Most Kumeyaay did not want the Spanish on their land and fought back. From time to time, they attacked the soldiers. In 1775 Kumeyaay warriors attacked and burned Mission San Diego. The Spanish quickly had it rebuilt.

▼ Native workers built the missions.

▲ Mexican ranchers raised cattle.

New Peoples on Kumeyaay Lands

In 1821 Mexico won its independence, or freedom from Spain. Now Mexico ruled California, including Kumeyaay land. The Mexican government closed the missions and turned the land into ranches. Some Kumeyaay worked for the Mexicans on the ranches. Most left to join other Kumeyaay still living in the mountains.

▲ A New York newspaper announced a meeting for those interested in going to California, 1849.

In 1848 Mexico lost a war with the United States. As a result, California became part of the United States. During the war Kumeyaay warriors had helped the United States. They hoped their lives would improve if the United States won. Unfortunately for the Kumeyaay, more and more settlers came to California. The Kumeyaay lost more land. They lost their rights and were treated unfairly.

REVIEW Why did the Kumeyaay help the United States to fight against Mexico? *Cause and Effect*

Citizens of Two Nations 3.2.3

Through the years the Kumeyaay worked to get back their land and rights. Today the Kumeyaay are **citizens** [SIT uh zens] of the United States. A citizen is a community member who has certain rights and duties. The Kumeyaay have the same rights as other United States citizens. They have the right to vote, to speak freely, and to live wherever they choose.

The Kumeyaay are also citizens of the Kumeyaay Nation. The Kumeyaay have 13 reservations in the San Diego area. On the reservations the Kumeyaay are **sovereign** [SAWV uhr uhn], or independent. That means that each group governs itself.

▲ Some Kumeyaay, such as these firefighters, serve the Kumeyaay Nation.

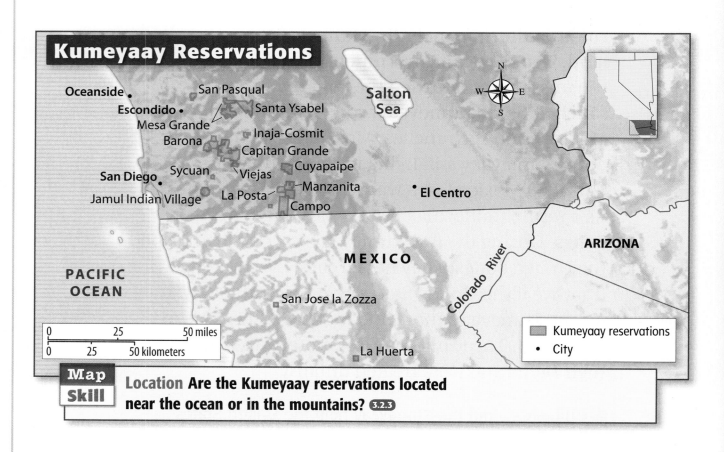

Kumeyaay Reservations

Oceanside
San Pasqual
Escondido
Santa Ysabel
Mesa Grande
Barona
Inaja-Cosmit
Capitan Grande
San Diego
Sycuan
Cuyapaipe
Viejas
Jamul Indian Village
La Posta
Manzanita
Campo
Salton Sea
El Centro

PACIFIC OCEAN

MEXICO

ARIZONA

Colorado River

San Jose la Zozza

La Huerta

0   25   50 miles
0   25   50 kilometers

Kumeyaay reservations
• City

Map Skill **Location Are the Kumeyaay reservations located near the ocean or in the mountains?** 3.2.3

Most groups have their own **constitution**, or written plan of government. Kumeyaay on each reservation elect their own leaders and make their own laws. They have their own schools and newspapers, too.

Today many Kumeyaay work in cities. Some Kumeyaay, such as the Viejas [vee AY has] band, run casinos. Casinos are places where people come for recreation. The Viejas band also owns a bank and a shopping mall. It shares the money it makes from these businesses with other bands.

REVIEW How are the Kumeyaay citizens of two nations? *Summarize*

Global Connections

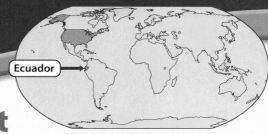

Ecuador

People of the Rain Forest

In the rain forest of Ecuador, in South America, a group of Indians called the Secoya fight for their land and rights. In the 1980s, after oil was discovered on Secoya land, the government of Ecuador gave the land away to oil businesses. Today the Secoya say that their land has been damaged by oil drilling and that much of the vegetation is gone.

Several Indian groups in Ecuador have come together to speak out. They hope that speaking with one voice will help them fight for groups like the Secoya.

What advice might the Kumeyaay give to the Secoya?

Keeping a Tradition Alive 3.2.1

In the past the Kumeyaay did not have a written language. Instead, stories and knowledge were passed on in songs. One group of Kumeyaay songs is called Bird Songs. These songs tell about how different animals came to be. Some of the songs are long and difficult. It takes many years of practice to learn them.

Stan Rodriquez is a Kumeyaay. He started learning the songs when he was 17 years old. That was 24 years ago and Stan knows he still needs to learn much more.

"The need to preserve my people's culture has been very important to me and by learning these songs I will be able to pass this tradition on to others," Stan says. "It is my fear that as the singers get older and pass away, the songs and the stories that are told in the songs will also die out."

REVIEW How can you tell the Bird Songs are important to Stan Rodriquez? *Make Inferences*

▼ Kumeyaay people still perform the Bird Songs.

▲ "Miss Kumeyaay" (left) needs to know Kumeyaay history and language.

What You Learned

3.2.4 Life changed for the Kumeyaay when the Spanish came to build a mission on their land.

3.2.4 When Mexico took over California, the Kumeyaay lost more land and rights.

3.2.3 Today Kumeyaay are citizens of the United States and of the Kumeyaay Nation.

3.2.1 Some Kumeyaay work to keep traditions, such as Bird Songs, alive.

Lesson Review

1. Focus Question How did life
3.2.4 change for the Kumeyaay after the Spanish came?

2. Vocabulary Write one sentence for
3.2 each vocabulary word.

citizen	mission
constitution	sovereign

3. History What three countries have
3.2 ruled Kumeyaay land?

4. Critical Thinking **Problem Solving**
3.2.4 What were some ways the Kumeyaay tried to solve the problem of the newcomers taking their land?

5. Reading Strategy **Identify Main**
3.2.3 **Idea and Details** Reread the
ELA
R2.3 section "Citizens of Two Nations" on pages 144–145. Use the chart to tell the main idea and details of this section.

6. Write about THE **BiG** IDEA Write a
3.2.4 paragraph that tells how life changed
ELA
W1.1 for the Kumeyaay.

7. Link to Music Think of an animal
3.2.1 you like. Write a song about the animal. Try to describe the animal in a way that shows what you like about it.

Culture of Native Americans in Your Region 3.2

Indian Grinding Rock State Park

Ella lives in Ione. She learned about the culture of the Miwok people who lived in her community long ago. To show what she learned, she made artifact information cards. You can do it, too. Here's what to do:

- Use the library, local museums, or the Internet to find out about the Native American groups who lived in your area long ago.

- Find pictures of objects the groups used long ago. Make drawings or photo copies of the objects.

- Look for information that tells what the objects were made of and how they were used.

LOG ON For more help making your artifact cards, visit:

www.macmillanmh.com/ss/ca/local

Make an Artifact Information Card

Materials
- markers
- oaktag
- photographs or your drawings
- paste

Step 1 Gather your notes and drawings. Choose one of the objects you learned about.

Step 2 Cut a piece of oaktag. Paste your photograph or drawing of the artifact on it.

Step 3 Write a short description of the object. Tell which group made it and how it was used.

Step 4 Share your artifact cards with your classmates.

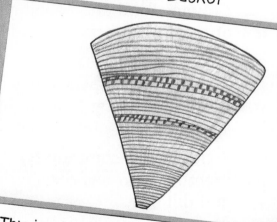

Burden Basket

This is a burden basket. The Sierra Miwok people used it to gather seeds and food.

Acorn Mush Stirrer

This is an acorn mush stirrer. The Sierra Miwok people used it to cook soup.

4 Chapter Review

Vocabulary Review

Copy the sentences below on a separate sheet of paper. Beside each number, write *C* if the underlined word is used correctly. If it is not, write the word that would correctly complete the sentence.

agriculture   government
ceremony   shaman
citizen   vegetation

1. A <u>government</u> is a group of
3.2.3 people in charge of leading a community, a state, or a nation.

2. Growing food and keeping or
3.2.2 attracting animals for food is called <u>vegetation</u>.

3. A <u>shaman</u> is a special way of
3.2.1 doing something to mark a special time.

4. A <u>citizen</u> is a community
3.2.3 member who has certain rights and duties.

5. Test Preparation A written plan
3.2.3 of government is a _____ .

A. sovereign   C. ligament
B. mission   D. constitution

Comprehension Check

6. Give an example of something
3.2.3 the Kumeyaay got from their environment.

7. How did the Kumeyaay select
3.2.1 their shamans?

8. Why did Kumeyaay bands
3.2.1 move each season?

9. Why were songs so important
3.2.1 to the Kumeyaay?

10. What happened to Kumeyaay
3.2.4 land after the United States won a war with Mexico in 1848?

11. Critical Thinking What do singers
3.2.1 like Stan Rodriguez do to keep their culture alive?

12. Critical Thinking How did the
3.2.2 Kumeyaay show that they knew their environment?

Write a complete sentence to answer each question.

Use Intermediate Directions

13. What direction would you travel
3.2.3 if you were going from the Santa Ynez Reservation to the San Manuel Reservation?

14. Which reservation is northeast
3.2.3 of Round Valley Reservation?

15. Test Preparation North, south,
3.2.3 east, and west are the _____ directions.

16. Test Preparation The direction
3.2.3 halfway between east and south is _____.

Some California Reservations

IDAHO

Cedarville

0   100   200 miles
0   100   200 kilometers

■ Reservation

Round Valley

Manchester

Sheep Ranch

Bridgeport

NEVADA   UTAH

Tuolumne   Benton Paiute

CALIFORNIA

N
W   E
S

Tule River

ARIZONA

Santa Ynez   San Manuel

PACIFIC OCEAN

Using Primary Sources

Artifacts

17. What are some things we can
3.2.1 learn from artifacts?

18. Can we be sure about how
3.2.1 people used artifacts long ago? Explain why or why not.

Hands-on Activity

19. Make an Artifact You have learned
3.2.1 that artifacts can tell us about ancient cultures. Make a drawing or painting that tells something about the way people in your community live today.

Write About History

20. Narrative Think about what
3.2.1 life was like for the Kumeyaay
ELA before and after Europeans
W2.1 came to California. Write a story about the experience.

LOG ON For help with the process of writing, visit:

www.macmillanmh.com/ss/ca/writing

Unit Review and Test Prep

Comprehension and Critical Thinking Check

Write a sentence or more to answer each question.

1. What are some ways Native American (3.2.2) groups used **vegetation**?

2. How did **explorers** affect Native (3.2.4) American groups?

3. How did Kumeyaay **agriculture** (3.2.2) use dams?

4. How is the Hupa **homeland** different (3.2.2) from the Kawaiisu homeland?

5. Where did the Kumeyaay hold their (3.2.1) **ceremonies**?

6. How do Native American groups share (3.2.1) their **traditions**?

7. Who governs Kumeyaay **reservations** (3.2.3) today?

8. How did the Kumeyaay use **astronomy** (3.2.1) long ago?

9. **Critical Thinking** How did the (3.2.3) Kumeyaay **government** work long ago?

10. **Critical Thinking** Compare how the (3.2.2) Hupa, Kawaiisu, and Kumeyaay used **technology** and resources. How were they the same and different?

Reading Social Studies Check

Summarize

Reread the section "Changes for the Kumeyaay" on page 142. Use the chart to summarize the section. Then answer the questions below. (3.2.4) (ELA R2.3)

11. What are the main ideas of the section?
(ELA R2.3)

12. Why did the Kumeyaay sometimes fight (ELA R2.3) with the Spanish?

13. Why did many Kumeyaay stay in the (ELA R2.3) mountains all year?

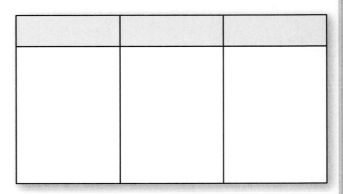

Read the paragraphs. Then answer the questions.

At first Native Americans got along with the newcomers. However, as more people arrived, they needed more land. Native Americans fought to keep their land. The United States government wanted to stop the fighting, and it also wanted to get land for the settlers.

The government signed treaties with the tribes. The tribes had to give up much of their land. In return, Native Americans were also told they would be safe from harm. However, settlers kept coming. Settlers often took the land set aside for Native American groups. The government did not stop the settlers or honor the treaties.

14. **What is the main idea of this passage?**
3.2.4

  A The settlers and Native Americans were friendly.

  B The government wanted to help Native Americans.

  C Native Americans lost their land because of the newcomers.

  D Treaties were good for the Native Americans.

15. **Why did the government make treaties with the tribes?**
3.2.4

  A It wanted to get land for the settlers and stop the fighting.

  B It wanted to return land to the tribes.

  C It wanted to stop the settlers from taking land.

  D It wanted the newcomers and Native Americans to share land.

Write About History

16. **Narrative** Think about what happened to the Native Americans in California after the explorers came. Write a paragraph that explains the sequence of events.
3.2.4 ELA W2.1

17. **Descriptive** Think about the ways in which Native Americans used natural resources. Write a poem that describes their use of resources.
3.2.1 ELA W2.2

18. **Personal Letter** Suppose you are a Native American at the time the United States government took control of California. Write a letter to a government official telling why you should be able to stay on your land.
ELA W2.3

For help with the process of writing, visit:

www.macmillanmh.com/ss/ca/writing

How has life changed for people over time?

Write About the Big Idea ☆3.2.1 ELA W2.1

Narrative Composition

Think about the Native American communities you read about in this unit. Complete the graphic organizer. Add details about life in the past (Then) and today (Now).

Then write a composition. Tell how one Native American culture has changed over time. Use details from your graphic organizer.

Topic	Then	Now
Culture	Traditional songs and dances Traditional instruments, like gourd rattle	Modern and traditional songs and dances Modern and traditional instruments
Technology		
Government		

Write a Narrative Composition

Writing a narrative essay takes planning. Review the following steps to help you.

1. Plan

• Choose a community from Unit 2 to write about.

2. Write a First Draft

• Write a topic sentence to introduce the community. State your purpose for writing in the sentence.

• Write detail sentences. Give examples of how people in the community lived in the past and how they live today.

• Write a final sentence to conclude your composition.

3. Revise and Proofread

• Read your composition. Be sure the first sentence states your purpose for writing.

• Check to see that all your sentences tell about your topic.

• Proofread your composition. Be sure you used capital letters and punctuation correctly.

• Rewrite your composition neatly before you give it to your teacher.

Speak About the Big Idea 3.3.3 ELA LS2.3

Create a Television News Show

Create a television show that tells how life has changed for Native American communities over time.

The Story of Pomo Indians

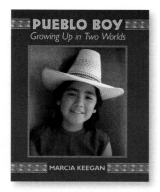

Prepare Work in small groups. Each group will choose a Native American community. As part of your news program you will show how life has changed for that community.

Present One student will be the host to introduce the guests. Two or three students will be the guests, and each will tell about one aspect of the community that has changed over time. Other students could run the camera or make background props.

LAUNCH PAD For help with the Big Idea activity, visit:

www.macmillanmh.com/ss/ca/launchpad

Read More About the Big Idea

PUEBLO BOY
Growing Up in Two Worlds

MARCIA KEEGAN

Pueblo Boy

by Marcia Keegan Learn why being a young Pueblo boy today means living in two different worlds.

POWWOW
Photographs and text by GEORGE ANCONA

Powwow

by George Ancona
Experience the excitement of a ceremony of the Crow Indian people on their Montana reservation.

WEAVING A CALIFORNIA TRADITION
A Native American Basketmaker

by Linda Yamane/Photographs by Dugan Aguilar

Weaving a California Tradition

by Linda Yamane See how an 11-year-old Western Mono girl learns a traditional craft of her people.

UNIT 3

Communities Change

"...yesterday is but a preview of tomorrow."

— Ronald Reagan,
40th President of
the United States

Santa Fe

EXPLORE THE BiG IDEA

Why do communities change over time?

Many communities are a mixture of old and new. In Unit 3 you will read how and why some communities have changed over time.

Copy the graphic organizer below. As you read the chapters in this unit, note the different ways these communities have changed.

Then fill in the graphic organizer with the reasons you find. A few reasons have already been filled in for you.

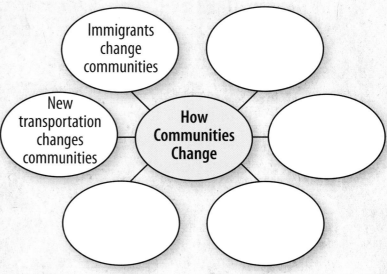

◄ Downtown San Diego

My Diary from Here to There

by Amada Irma Pérez
Illustrated by Maya Christina Gonzalez

Amada is happy and nervous when she learns that her family will leave their home in Juárez, Mexico, to live in California. Her father goes on ahead to get a job and to make arrangements for the family to come later. Then, at long last, Amada and her family set out to rejoin Papá in Los Angeles.

I miss Papá so much—it feels like he left ages ago. It's been tough to stay hopeful. So far we've had to live in three different houses with some of Mamá's sisters. First, the boys broke Tia Tuca's jewelry box and were so noisy she kicked us out. Then at Nana's house, they kept trying on Tia Nena's high heels and purses. Even Nana herself got mad when they used her pots and pans to make "music." And they kept trying to read what I've written here, and to hide my special rock. Tia Lupe finally took us in, but where will we go if she decides she's had enough of us?

Finally! Papá sent our **green cards**—we're going to cross the border at last! He can't come for us but will meet us in Los Angeles.

The whole family is making a big farewell dinner for us tonight. Even after all the trouble the boys have caused, I think everyone is sad to see us go. Nana even gave me a new journal to write in for when I finish this one. She said, "Never forget who you are and where you are from. Keep your language and culture alive in your diary and in your heart."

green cards special cards that allow people from other countries to work in the United States

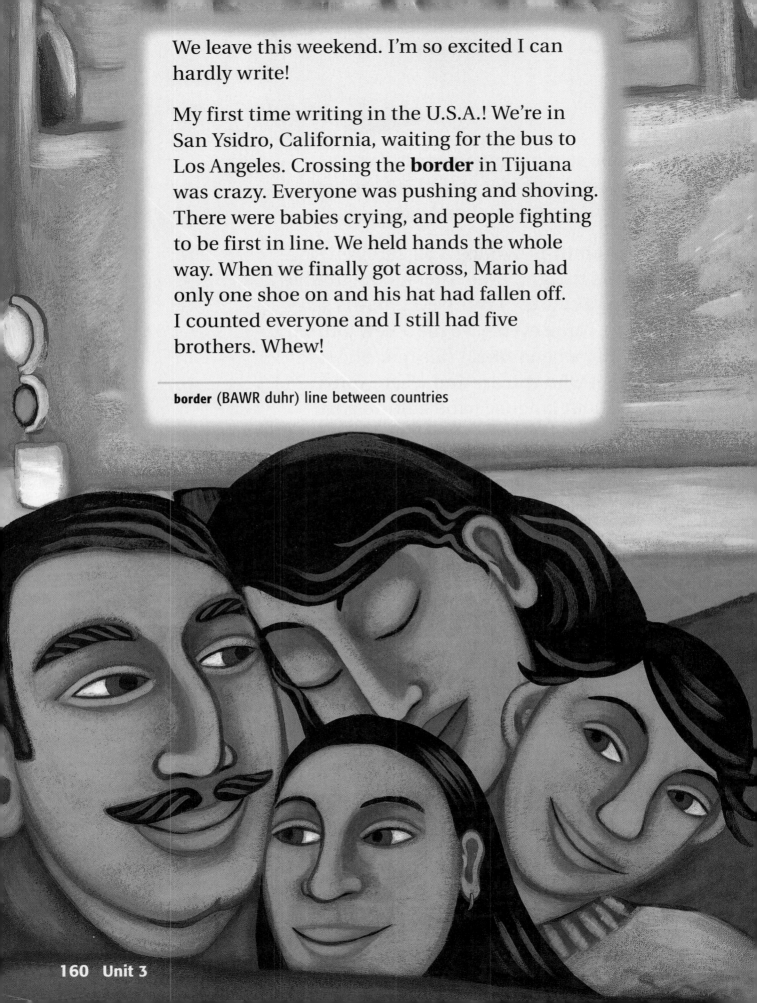

We leave this weekend. I'm so excited I can hardly write!

My first time writing in the U.S.A.! We're in San Ysidro, California, waiting for the bus to Los Angeles. Crossing the **border** in Tijuana was crazy. Everyone was pushing and shoving. There were babies crying, and people fighting to be first in line. We held hands the whole way. When we finally got across, Mario had only one shoe on and his hat had fallen off. I counted everyone and I still had five brothers. Whew!

---

border (BAWR duhr) line between countries

Papá is meeting us at the bus station in Los Angeles. It's been so long—I hope he recognizes us!

What a long ride! One woman and her children got kicked off the bus when the **immigration patrol** boarded to check everyone's papers. Mamá held Mario and our green cards close to her heart.

Papá was waiting at the station, just like he promised. We all jumped into his arms and laughed, and Mamá even cried a little. Papa's hugs felt so much better than when he left us in Mexicali!

---

immigration patrol (im i GRAY shun puh TROHL) police who watch the border

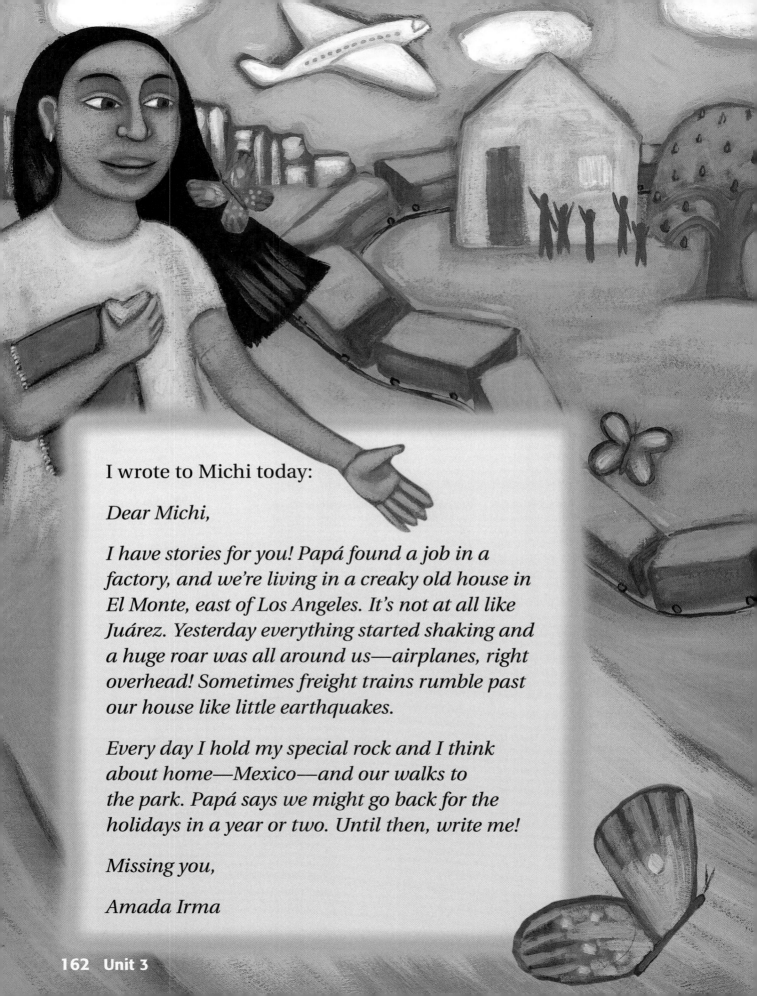

I wrote to Michi today:

Dear Michi,

I have stories for you! Papá found a job in a factory, and we're living in a creaky old house in El Monte, east of Los Angeles. It's not at all like Juárez. Yesterday everything started shaking and a huge roar was all around us—airplanes, right overhead! Sometimes freight trains rumble past our house like little earthquakes.

Every day I hold my special rock and I think about home—Mexico—and our walks to the park. Papá says we might go back for the holidays in a year or two. Until then, write me!

Missing you,

Amada Irma

Well, Diary, I finally found a place where I can sit and think and write. It may not be the little park in Juárez, but it's pretty. You know, just because I'm far away from Juárez and Michi and my family in Mexicali, it doesn't mean they're not here with me. They're inside my little rock, they're here in your pages and in the language that I speak, and they're in my memories and my heart. Papá was right. I AM stronger than I think—in Mexico, in the States, anywhere.

P.S. I've almost filled this whole journal and can't wait to start my new one. Maybe someday I'll even write a book about our journey!

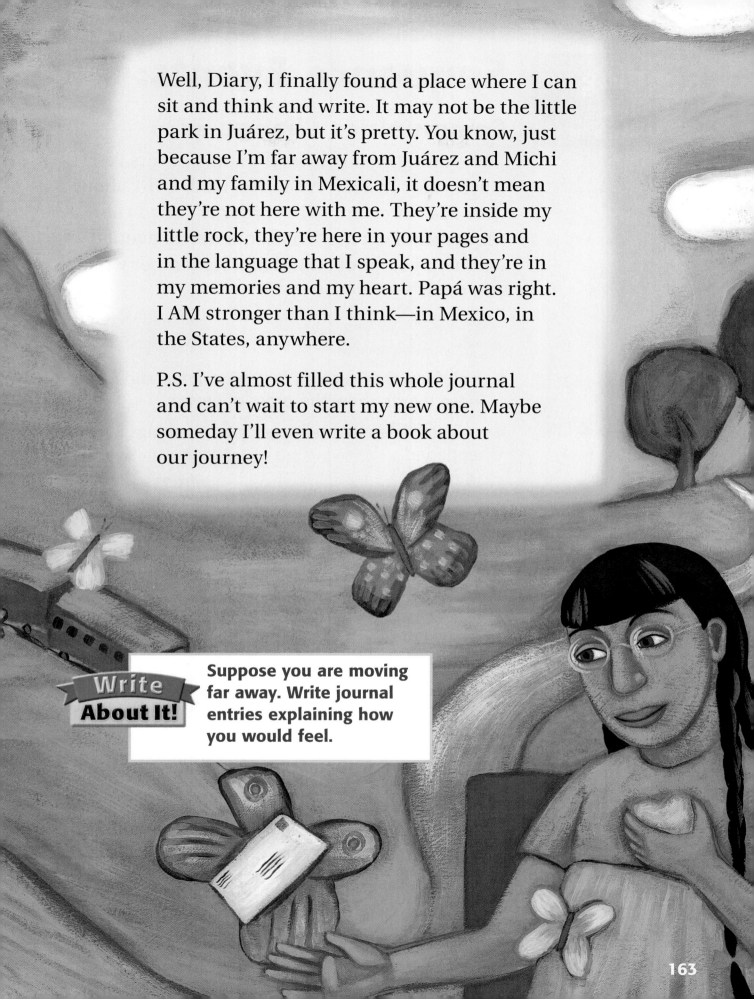

Write About It!

Suppose you are moving far away. Write journal entries explaining how you would feel.

Sequence Events:

Communities Change (3.3.3) ^ELA R2.6

The paragraph below tells some events in Placerville's history. When you read, think about the order of events. This order is called the sequence of events. The sequence of events will help you understand and remember what you read.

1 Learn It

■ Look for words such as *first, next, later,* and *last.* These words show the order of events.

■ Look for dates that tell exactly when things happened.

First Event
Gold miners move in.

Second Event
The town was nicknamed Hangtown.

Third Event
The town is called Placerville.

Gold miners **first** moved to the area that is now Placerville, California, in 1850. They named the town Dry Diggings because the river where people were digging for gold ran dry in the summer. **Later** the town got the nickname Hangtown because local miners hanged three outlaws from an oak tree. **Today** the town is called Placerville. It is a growing community with modern industries. Yet tourists enjoy visiting the town to learn about the Gold Rush days.

Copy and complete the chart below. Then fill in the chart by recording the events in the paragraph on page 164 in the correct sequence. Add boxes to the chart if you need to.

SEQUENCE OF EVENTS CHART

Gold miners first moved to Placerville in 1850

⬇

⬇

How did you figure out the sequence of events?

3 **Apply It**

- Review the sequencing steps in Learn It.
- Read the paragraph below. Then, create a sequence of events chart using the information.

Gold seekers arrived in San Bernardino in 1862. The search for gold was on! A few years later, the miners left. Some people feared San Bernardino might become a ghost town. In 1887, however, the Santa Fe Railroad laid tracks through San Bernardino. The town began to grow again.

Newcomers Leave Their Mark

YOU ARE THERE

Over the years newcomers to California have built new communities. Some came for a new life. Some came for gold. Some came for a job and a new place to live. Whatever their reasons for coming, they have all left their mark on California's many communities.

AN ACCOUNT OF

CALIFORNIA,
AND THE
WONDERFUL GOLD REGIONS.

A New Arrival at the Gold Diggings.

WITH A DESCRIPTION OF
The Different Routes to California;
Information about the Country, and the Ancient and
Modern Discoveries of Gold;
How to Test Precious Metals; Accounts of Gold Hunters;
TOGETHER WITH MUCH OTHER
Useful Reading for those going to Cali-
fornia, or having **Friends** there.
ILLUSTRATED WITH MAPS AND ENGRAVINGS.

BOSTON:
PUBLISHED BY J. B. HALL, 66 CORNHILL.
For Sale at Skinner's Publication Rooms, 60½ Cornhill.

Price, 12½ cents.

1 **The Spanish in California** (page 168)
People from Spain started many California communities, including Santa Barbara.

2 **New Settlers, New Towns** (page 176)
Many California communities, including Placerville, began during the Gold Rush.

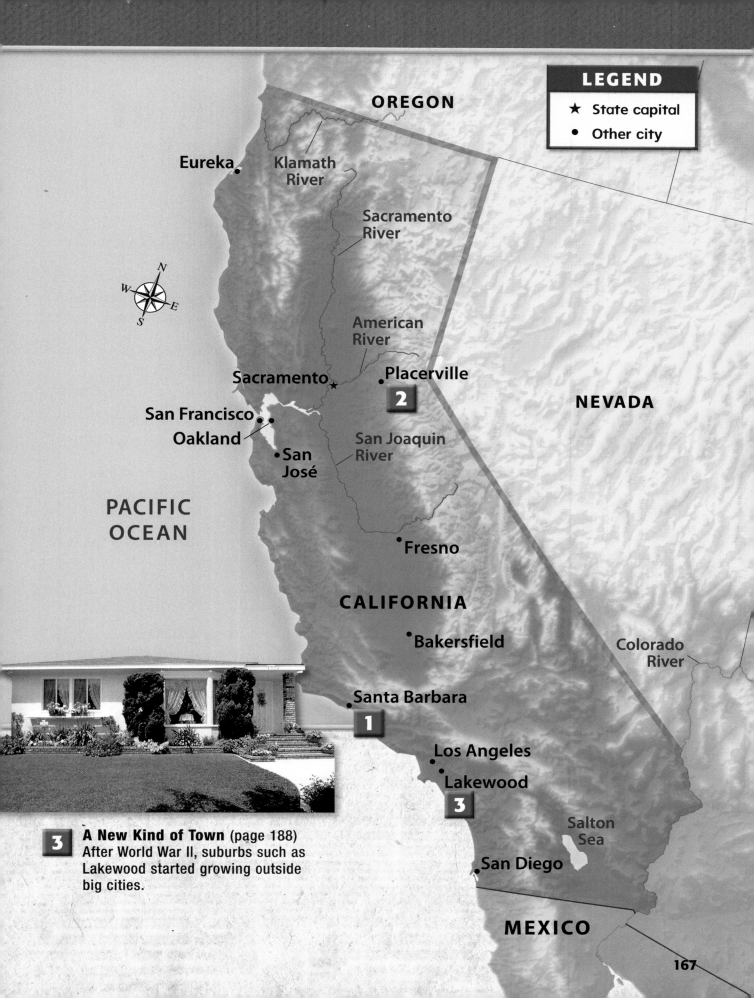

LEGEND
★ State capital
● Other city

OREGON

Eureka

Klamath River

Sacramento River

American River

Placerville
2

NEVADA

Sacramento

San Francisco
Oakland

San José

San Joaquin River

PACIFIC OCEAN

Fresno

CALIFORNIA

Bakersfield

Colorado River

Santa Barbara
1

Los Angeles

Lakewood
3

Salton Sea

San Diego

3 **A New Kind of Town** (page 188)
After World War II, suburbs such as
Lakewood started growing outside
big cities.

MEXICO

FOCUS QUESTION

How does Santa Barbara remember its Spanish background?

VOCABULARY

heritage
rancho
private property
adobe

VOCABULARY STRATEGY

WORD ORIGINS Many words in English have come from other languages. Two words in the list that come from Spanish are **adobe** and **rancho**.

READING STRATEGY

Sequence Events
Use the chart to sequence events in Santa Barbara's history.

The Spanish in California

Start with Your
CALIFORNIA STANDARDS

3.3 Students draw from historical and community resources to organize the sequence of local historical events and describe how each period of settlement left its mark on the land.

3.3.1 Research the explorers who visited here, the newcomers who settled here, and the people who continue to come to the region, including their cultural and religious traditions and contributions.

Learn how the Spanish settled in California and built communities that are still here today. (Begins on page 169)

3.3.2 Describe the economies established by settlers and their influence on the present-day economy, with emphasis on the importance of private property and entrepreneurship.

Discover how Spanish and Mexican settlers changed the way people made a living in California. (pages 170–171)

Mission Santa Barbara, 1852 ▼

Santa Barbara. Los Angeles. Sierra Madre. Did you know that these place names are Spanish words? How did it happen that California places have Spanish names?

Towns with a Spanish Background 3.3.1

How did your community begin? If your town is one of the many places in California whose name begins with *San* or *Santa*, then it may have been settled by the Spanish. *San* and *Santa* are Spanish words for *saint*. A saint is a person that a religious group thinks is very holy.

You have read that explorers claimed California for Spain. Later, Spanish priests came to build missions and settlements here. Today you can find many places in California with a Spanish **heritage**. Heritage means something handed down from the past, such as a special way of doing things.

REVIEW Who came from Spain to California after the explorers? *Sequence Events*

◄ Spanish Days festival in Santa Barbara

169

Explorers Come to California 3.3.1 3.3.2

Santa Barbara is one California community with a Spanish heritage. The first person from Spain to see the area was Juan Rodriguez Cabrillo (kah BREE yoh). Cabrillo was a sea captain exploring the California coast in 1542. The Chumash Indians lived there already. In fact, Cabrillo wrote in his journal about seeing Chumash in their large canoes, or tomols. Still, Cabrillo claimed the land for Spain.

Sixty years later, in 1602, another Spanish sea captain explored California's coast. His name was Sebastián Vizcaíno (viz cah EE no). One day a terrible storm almost sank his ships. Just in time, he sailed his ships to safety in what is now Santa Barbara Channel. Vizcaíno was so thankful to be alive he named the area "Santa Barbara" in honor of the saint. That is how the city of Santa Barbara got its name.

Santa Barbara

▼ Mission Santa Barbara today

◄ The chapel and bell tower of El Presidio de Santa Barbara

The rooms in the Presidio had simple furniture. ►

Spanish and Mexican Heritage

In 1786 Spanish settlers came to the area. They founded Mission Santa Barbara. The Spanish used skilled Chumash workers to build the church and other buildings. The buildings were made in the Spanish style, with red tile roofs. Chumash workers planted orange and olive trees, grew barley and wheat, and raised sheep and cattle on mission lands.

During this time California was part of Mexico. Mexico was ruled by Spain. Then, in 1821, Mexico won a war with Spain and became independent. The Mexican government closed the missions and divided up the mission lands into large **ranchos**, or cattle ranches. The ranchos were owned by a handful of powerful ranchers. The land became **private property**, property that belongs to individual people, not the government or church.

REVIEW What happened to the Spanish missions after Mexico took over California? *Sequence Events*

Signs of the Past 3.3.1

People in Santa Barbara today are proud of their community's Spanish heritage. They work to keep the past alive.

When Mission Santa Barbara was damaged by an earthquake in 1925, the people of Santa Barbara carefully rebuilt it. In addition, many wooden buildings in Santa Barbara have been replaced with new Spanish-style **adobe** (uh DOH bee) buildings. Adobe is a kind of brick made from clay and straw. These buildings often have beautiful courtyards, balconies, and red tile roofs like the Spanish buildings of the past.

Another community project is the rebuilding of the Presidio. The Presidio is a fort built by the Spanish in 1782. Earthquakes almost destroyed the fort and the newer buildings nearby. Now the area surrounding the Presidio, called El Pueblo Viejo (the Old Town), is being protected. In addition, all new buildings in the area must be built in the old Spanish style. Today Santa Barbara is a mix of old and new.

▲ The beautiful tiles and lion's head fountain show Santa Barbara's Spanish heritage.

REVIEW How is Santa Barbara today a mix of the old and the new? *Summarize*

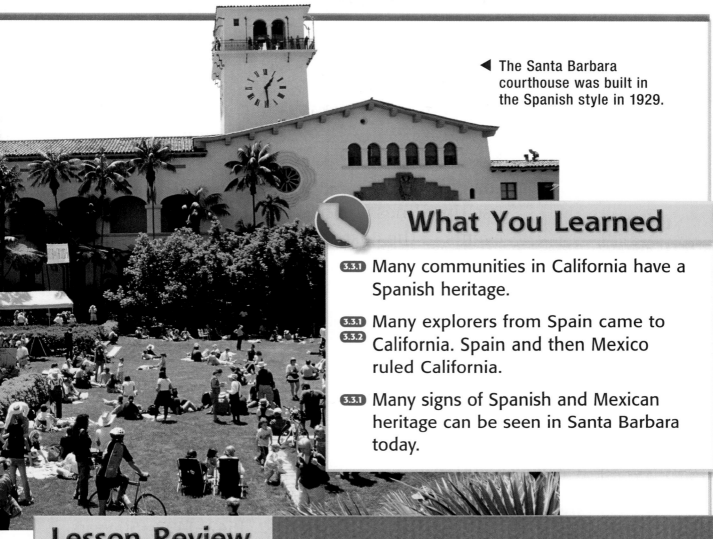

◀ The Santa Barbara courthouse was built in the Spanish style in 1929.

What You Learned

3.3.1 Many communities in California have a Spanish heritage.

3.3.1 **3.3.2** Many explorers from Spain came to California. Spain and then Mexico ruled California.

3.3.1 Many signs of Spanish and Mexican heritage can be seen in Santa Barbara today.

Lesson Review

1. **Focus Question** How does Santa **3.3** Barbara remember its Spanish background?

2. **Vocabulary** Write one sentence for **3.3** each vocabulary term.

   adobe   heritage   private property

3. **History Summarize** How did **3.3.1** Santa Barbara get its name?

4. **Critical Thinking Problem** **3.3.1** **Solving** Why do you think Santa Barbara's Spanish heritage has helped it become a popular place for people to visit?

5. **Reading Strategy** **3.3.1** **Sequence Events** **ELA** **R2.3** Copy the sequence of events chart and use it to show how the 1821 war between Spain and Mexico affected Santa Barbara.

6. **Write about THE BIG IDEA** How has **3.3.3** your own community changed **W.2.1** over time?

7. **Link to Art** Look on the Internet or **3.3.3** in books to find a building in Santa Barbara that shows the city's Spanish heritage. Draw the building and label the parts of your drawing.

Use Time Lines 3.3

You have read about events in California's past. It is not always easy to remember what happened first, next, and last. A **time line** tells the order of important events. Learning to use time lines will help you better understand events in the past.

VOCABULARY

time line
century

1 Learn It

Follow these steps, and look at the time line below as you read.

- Look at the dates on the time line. Time lines are divided to show time periods, such as years or **centuries**. A century is 100 years. This time line covers the centuries between 1400 and 1800.

- Look at the order of events. Events are listed in time order from left to right. An event to the *left* of another event took place earlier.

The earliest event on this time line is Columbus's arrival in 1492.

- Use the dates to tell the number of years between events. Subtract the date of the earlier event from the date of the later event.

For example, Columbus reached the Americas in 1492. Cabrillo explored the California coastline in 1542. 1542−1492=50 years. Cabrillo's exploration was 50 years after Columbus reached the Americas.

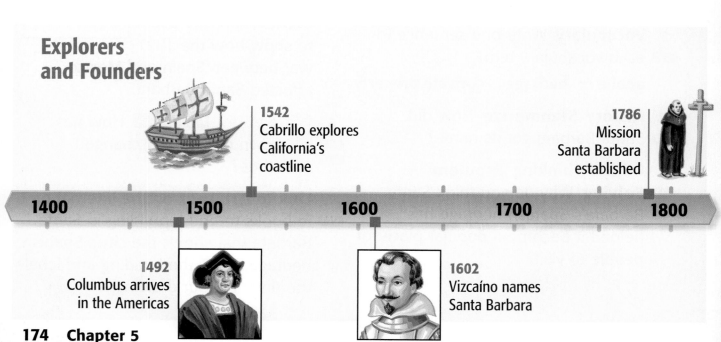

Explorers and Founders

1542
Cabrillo explores California's coastline

1786
Mission Santa Barbara established

1400   1500   1600   1700   1800

1492
Columbus arrives in the Americas

1602
Vizcaíno names Santa Barbara

2 Try It

Use the time line below to answer the questions.

- What period of time does this time line cover?

- How many years does this time line cover?

- What happened to the mission in 1846?

- Which happened first—the mission was sold or the mission was established?

3 Apply It

- Make a time line of your own life.

- Divide your time line into years.

- Decide on five important events to include in your time line.

Mission Santa Barbara

1820
The mission is rebuilt after an earthquake

| 1750 | 1800 | 1850 | 1900 | 1950 |

1786
Mission Santa Barbara is established

1846
The mission is sold under Mexican rule

1925
Another earthquake causes damage

VOCABULARY

mine
claim
tourist

VOCABULARY STRATEGY

SUFFIXES The suffix -ist means someone who does something. Which list word has this suffix? What do you think the word means?

READING STRATEGY

Sequence Events
Copy the chart. Use it to sequence events in the history of the Gold Rush in Placerville.

New Settlers, New Towns

Start with Your
CALIFORNIA STANDARDS

3.3 Students draw from historical and community resources to organize the sequence of local historical events and describe how each period of settlement left its mark on the land.

3.3.1 Research the explorers who visited here, the newcomers who settled here, and the people who continue to come to the region, including their cultural and religious traditions and contributions.

Learn how miners who rushed here to find gold brought change to California. (Begins on page 177)

3.3.2 Describe the economies established by settlers and their influence on the present-day economy, with emphasis on the importance of private property and entrepreneurship.

Find out how Placerville became a modern community instead of a ghost town after the Gold Rush. (page 180)

Mining for gold in the
Calaveres River ▼

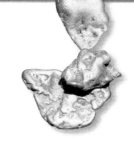

In 1848 James Marshall made an important discovery at the American River. "I reached my hand down," he said, "and picked it up; it made my heart thump, for I was certain it was gold."

Gold Brings Newcomers 3.3.1

You have read how some California communities were founded by Spanish settlers. Other towns were founded as a result of James Marshall's discovery. In fact, once word got out that gold had been discovered in California, people rushed here from all over the world. Most of these people hoped to get rich by finding gold. That is why we call that time the Gold Rush.

Guide to the gold fields printed in Boston, 1849 ▼

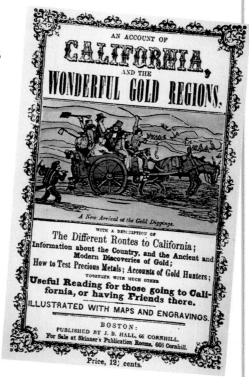

Soon hundreds of new mining camps and towns sprang up. Most of the new towns were near the gold **mines**, the areas where minerals were dug. When the gold was gone, most people left the towns. Many of the boom towns became ghost towns. Some towns, however, hung on. One such community is Placerville. Let's take a look at Placerville, then and now.

REVIEW Why was 1848 an important year in California's history? *Sequence Events*

A Gold Rush Town 3.3.2

When gold was discovered, miners rushed into the area we now call Placerville. They began mining for gold. Of course, miners needed all sorts of equipment, from clothing to shovels. They needed to eat and to get their laundry done, too. So instead of digging for gold, some people started businesses.

They sold hardware, or ran hotels or restaurants. During the rush for gold, some people got rich from gold, but more people got rich by selling goods and services to miners. Soon the supply center became a town. People called it "Dry Diggings."

California Gold Country, 1850s

- • City
- ▢ Mining areas
- — California Trail
- ■ Marshall Gold Discovery site

Rough and Ready
Coloma
Placerville
Sacramento
Jackson
Stockton
Columbia
Sonora
San Francisco
Chinese Camp
San José

Sacramento River
Feather River
American R.
Stanislaus R.
San Joaquin River
Merced River

PACIFIC OCEAN

0   30   60 miles
0   30   60 kilometers

Map Skill Location **Is Placerville east or west of Sacramento?** 3.3.3

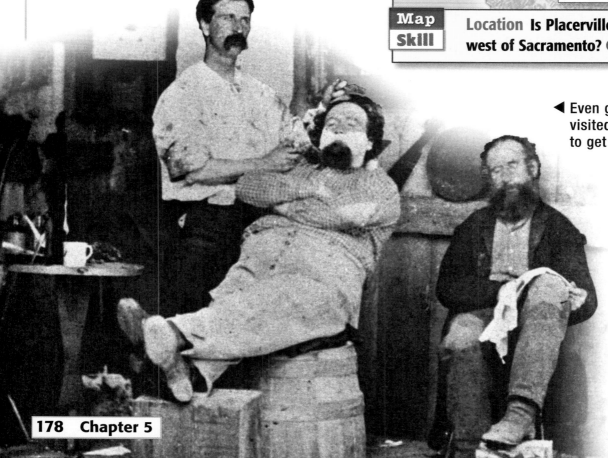

◀ Even gold miners visited barber shops to get a shave.

◀ Miners used pans like this one to look for gold.

Life in "Hangtown"

Dry Diggings had no law and no government. It had no police or fire departments. Miners made up their own rules to protect their **claims**. A claim is a legal right to mine on certain land.

One day local miners caught five outlaws from the Owls Gang robbing a local store. The miners hanged three of the robbers from an oak tree. For a while, the little town had a nickname, "Hangtown." Later, people changed the name to Placerville. Placer comes from a Spanish word for a place near a sandy stream bank where gold could be found.

▼ Miners usually lived in camps near their diggings.

Fire was a problem in Placerville's early days. Most of the buildings were made of wood. In 1856 alone there were three fires. The town was almost destroyed. Townspeople worked together to rebuild. They built a bell tower as a fire alarm. The Old Bell Tower still watches over Placerville.

REVIEW What were some of the problems in Gold Rush towns? *Summarize*

Placerville Today ⬤3.3.2

Placerville today is no longer a Gold Rush town. Modern businesses such as computer companies and banks provide jobs for people. **Tourists**, people who visit a place for fun, also come to Placerville. Many businesses make money providing things tourists need and want. Visitors come to Placerville because it has a good climate and because they enjoy learning about its colorful Gold Rush history. The City Hall is one of the historic buildings in the downtown business section that people can see when they come to Placerville.

REVIEW What are some jobs that people in Placerville have today? *Main Idea and Details*

Global Connections

Australia

The Australian Gold Rush ⬤3.3.2

Like Placerville, Ballarat, Australia, was born because of a gold rush. In 1851 gold was found in southeastern Australia. People from England, China, and even California, came to find gold. Ballarat grew into a large town. Today, 80,000 people live in the city. Some still work in mines. Most people have other jobs. Tourists visit Ballarat to learn about the Australian gold rush, and enjoy the town's museums and theaters.

▲ Ballarat, Australia

Why do you think someone might have left California to look for gold in Australia?

▲ The City Hall shown above was the firehouse until 1902.

What You Learned

3.3.1 Many communities in California started during the Gold Rush.

3.3.2 Crime and fire were problems in boom towns like Placerville, but mining communities worked together to solve these problems.

3.3.2 Placerville is an active community because of its location, its climate, and the new businesses it attracts.

Lesson Review

1. Focus Question How did Placerville
3.3.3 grow and change through the years?

2. Vocabulary Write one sentence for
3.3 each vocabulary term.

   claim   mine   tourist

3. Economics What were the major
3.3.2 businesses in Placerville during the Gold Rush and today?

4. Critical Thinking Draw
3.3.2 **Conclusions** Why do you think more people got rich by selling goods to miners than by digging for gold themselves?

5. Reading Strategy Sequence Events
3.3.1 Copy the chart. Use it to
ELA
R2.3 sequence the events in the 1856 fire that changed the town of Placerville.

6. Write about THE **BiG** IDEA Would you
3.3 have enjoyed living in Placerville
ELA
W2.2 during the Gold Rush?

7. Link to Music These words are from
W2.2 the Gold Rush song "Sweet Betsy from Pike." Write your own lyrics to help you remember the history of the Gold Rush.

   At length they arrived on a very
      high hill,
   With wonder looked down upon
      old Placerville.
   Ike sighed, and he said, when he
      cast his eyes down,
   'Betsy, my darling, we've got to
      Hangtown.'

Field Trip to...

COLUMBIA State Historic Park 3.3.3

Columbia State Historic Park

Columbia, California, was a boom town like Placerville. While Placerville changed with the times, Columbia found a way to survive by not changing. Today Columbia is a state park. Take a field trip and see how people worked and lived during the Gold Rush.

❷ Wells Fargo

A Wells Fargo stagecoach driver will give you a ride around town. There were no cars in California during the Gold Rush era. ▼

❶ Pan for Gold ▲

A miner will teach you how to pan for gold. Swish the water to wash the dirt out of your pan. Gold is heavy. It will shine in the bottom of your pan when the dirt washes out.

4 Main Street Firehouse

Fires burned in Columbia in 1854 and 1857. Finally, in 1859, the town bought a fire engine called Papeete. In 1911 they tore down the old wooden firehouse and built this one. ▼

3 Chinese Apothecary Shop ▲

Do you have a toothache? You might want to stop in at the Chinese apothecary shop, or drug store. People from China settled in Columbia and other gold towns to mine for gold and to start businesses.

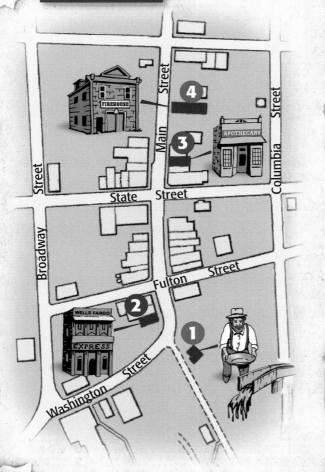

Columbia

ACTIVITY

Suppose you had lived in Columbia during the Gold Rush days. Write a diary entry for one day.

LOG ON

For more about Columbia State Historic Park, visit:

socialstudies.macmillanmh.com/fieldtrips

Understanding Newspapers 3.3.2

Newspapers are an important primary source. In the past newspapers were the main way for people to find out what was happening in their communities and in other places. By looking at newspapers from the past, we can see information exactly as it was available to people at the time.

Newspapers in the Gold Rush

Gold was discovered in California on January 24, 1848. It took time for word to travel across the country. The section of the newspaper shown on page 185 was published on December 26, 1848.

1 Learn It

Read the steps below to help you find information in newspapers.

- Identify the parts of the article. An article usually has one or more **headlines** that sum up the main idea of the story. Headlines are printed in larger letters at the top of the article. The **byline** tells who wrote the story. Not all articles have a byline.

- Read the article to see what information is given.

- A news article usually answers five questions. Who? What? When? Where? Why? Newspapers do not always answer all five questions.

- Look up the meanings of any unfamiliar words.

2 Try It

Read the newspaper article below.

Headline

What took place?

Where did it happen?

The Extensive Preparations
TO
MIGRATE TO THE GOLD REGION,
&c, &c, &c,

The great discovery of gold, in dust, scales, and lumps . . . on the shores of the Pacific has thrown the American people into a state of the wildest excitement. The **intelligence** from California, that gold can be picked up in lumps, weighing six or seven ounces, and scooped up in tin pans at the rate of a pound of the pure dust a scoop. . . .

intelligence information

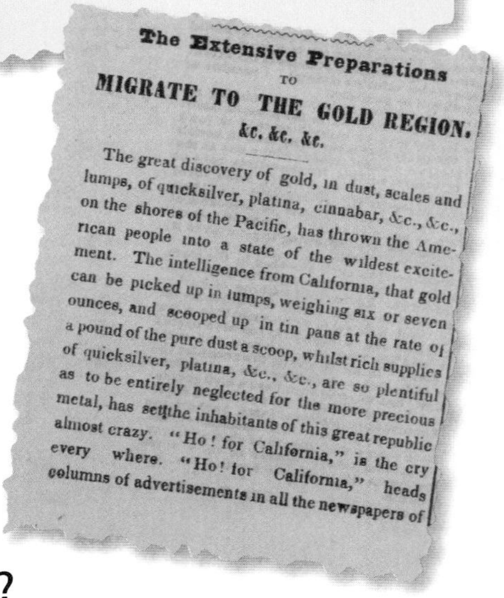

The Extensive Preparations
TO
MIGRATE TO THE GOLD REGION.
&c. &c. &c.

The great discovery of gold, in dust, scales and lumps, of quicksilver, platina, cinnabar, &c., &c., on the shores of the Pacific, has thrown the American people into a state of the wildest excitement. The intelligence from California, that gold can be picked up in lumps, weighing six or seven ounces, and scooped up in tin pans at the rate of a pound of the pure dust a scoop, whilst rich supplies of quicksilver, platina, &c., &c., are so plentiful as to be entirely neglected for the more precious metal, has set the inhabitants of this great republic almost crazy. "Ho! for California," is the cry every where. "Ho! for California," heads columns of advertisements in all the newspapers of

3 Apply It

- What information is given in this article? What information is not given?
- Read a news article from your local paper. In what ways is the article different from this article in the paper of long ago?

MAP and GLOBE Skills

Use Road Maps 3.3.3

Suppose you and your family wanted to drive to Placerville today. How would you find which road to take? A **road map** could tell you. Road maps show the roads you can use to get from one place to another.

1 Learn It

Look at the map on page 187 as you follow the steps for reading a road map.

- Read the map title. This map shows California Gold Country and the many kinds of roads there today.

- Look at the map key to understand the symbols. An **interstate highway** connects two or more states. A **state highway** begins and finishes inside a state.

- Highways have numbers that are the "names" of the roads. On the map, the numbers are in a special symbol. What kind of road is Highway 49?

- Identify directions. Most even-numbered roads usually run east and west. Odd-numbered roads usually run north and south. This can help lost drivers figure out where they are going.

2 Try It

Use the map on page 187 to answer the following questions.

- Which interstate connects Sacramento and Stockton?

- Which U.S. highway connects Sacramento and Placerville?

- In which direction does Interstate 5 run?

3 Apply It

Find a road map that shows your community, or look on the Internet to find a map. Locate your community on the map. What state and interstate highways are near your community?

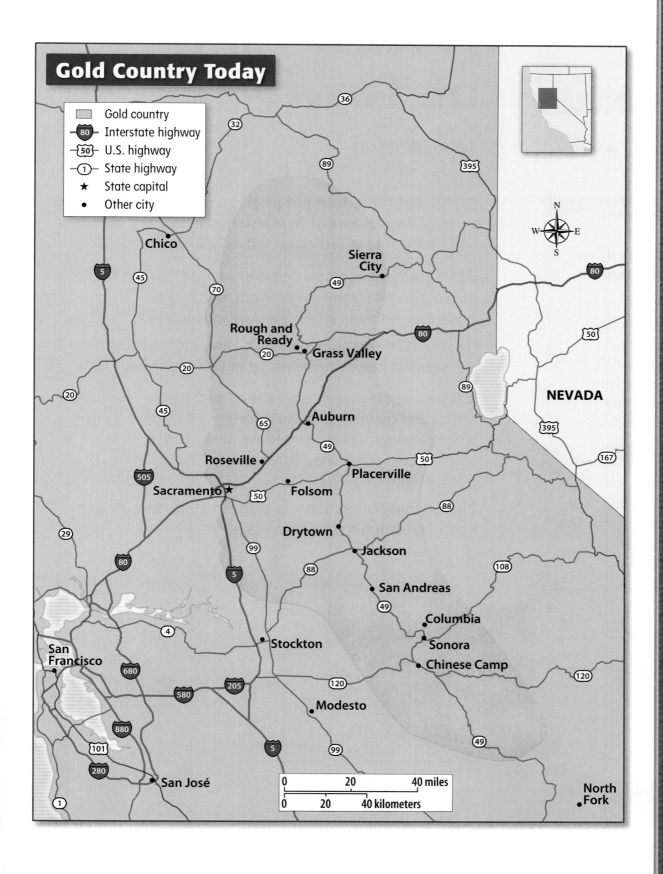

Gold Country Today

Gold country

🛣 80 Interstate highway

🛣 50 U.S. highway

🛣 1 State highway

★ State capital

● Other city

Chico

Sierra City

Rough and Ready

Grass Valley

Auburn

Roseville

Sacramento ★

Folsom

Placerville

Drytown

Jackson

San Andreas

Columbia

Sonora

Chinese Camp

Stockton

Modesto

San Francisco

San José

North Fork

NEVADA

36

32

89

395

45

70

49

20

20

45

65

49

50

88

99

88

49

108

49

120

120

99

4

205

580

680

880

101

280

1

505

29

80

5

5

0   20   40 miles

0   20   40 kilometers

What makes
Lakewood a different
kind of community?

migrate
entrepreneur
development

VOCABULARY STRATEGY

SUFFIXES Develop
means "to put to
use." The suffix **-ment**
means "the act of."
What do you think a
development is?

Sequence Events
Copy the chart. Use
it to sequence events
in the growth of
Lakewood.

A New Kind of Town

Start with Your
CALIFORNIA STANDARDS

3.3 Students draw from historical and community resources to organize the sequence of local historical events and describe how each period of settlement left its mark on the land.

3.3.2 Describe the economies established by settlers and their influence on the present-day economy, with emphasis on the importance of private property and entrepreneurship.

Find out how certain people built Lakewood quickly to meet the needs of newcomers arriving in California. (page 190)

3.3.3 Trace why their community was established, how individuals and families contributed to its founding and development, and how the community has changed over time, drawing on maps, photographs, oral histories, letters, newspapers, and other primary sources.

Discover how Lakewood was planned in advance as a new kind of community. (Begins on page 189)

Lakewood, California ▼

In 1950, when the new houses in Lakewood went on sale, they cost only $43 a month! On the first day, 25,000 people lined up at the sales office.

A Different Kind of Town ⬤3.3 ⬤3.3.3

Most communities start out small and grow slowly. Sometimes a village grows up around a bay where ships can dock. Another community might grow around a stop on a railroad. In the last two lessons, you read about one community that grew up around a mission and another that grew quickly when gold was discovered.

Lakewood, California, is a different kind of community. It was planned in advance. All of its houses were built at the same time. Today we are used to this way of building. Many California communities started this way. When Lakewood was built, however, this was a new idea. Let's take a closer look to see how Lakewood came to be.

Lakewood

REVIEW What are some of the ways communities grow?

Main Idea and Details

On March 9, 1954, Lakewood became a city. ▶

▲ In less than three years, Lakewood went from empty fields to a town of 17,500 houses.

A Need For Houses 3.3.2 3.3.3

During the 1940s, large numbers of people began to **migrate**, or move, to California from other parts of the United States. There were not enough houses for all these new Californians. Three **entrepreneurs** (ahn truh PRUH nurz), Louis Boyar, Mark Taper, and Ben Weingart, had an idea. An entrepreneur is a person who starts and runs a business. Boyar, Taper, and Weingart decided to buy land close to Los Angeles and build houses as fast as possible. They would sell the houses to the newcomers.

Building Lakewood

At this time, Lakewood was a small village in a rural part of Los Angeles County. The area around it was farmland. Boyar, Taper, and Weingart thought the flat farmland would be easy to build on. So they began to plan the **development**. A development is a group of houses planned and built together. They hired architects to design the houses and builders to build them. About 4,000 workers put up as many as 100 houses a day.

A New City

Ruth Smith, one of the first people to live in Lakewood, remembers how it looked. "All these little houses had sprung up like mushrooms. . . . You just couldn't believe it went up that fast."

Some people had laughed at the plan. They said no one would buy the houses. Advertisements like the one below helped convince people to buy. In fact, people bought houses as fast as workers could build them. On one day in 1950, people bought 107 houses in one hour!

In just three years, more than 70,000 people were living in Lakewood. Lakewood began to call itself "The City as New as Tomorrow." Everything was new. There were new streets, new houses, new neighbors, and even newly planted trees.

Primary Sources

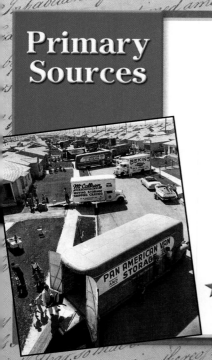

excerpt from a
Lakewood Newspaper Advertisement,
early 1950s

❝Dreaming of the good life? Living in beautiful Lakewood is more than just owning a home. It's a new and better way of living.❞

 How did ads convince so many people to move to Lakewood?

REVIEW How was Lakewood built so quickly? *Summarize*

Lakewood Today 3.3 3.3.3

Gina Marie Juarez has lived in Lakewood a long time. She says living there is like "big-city living with that small-town feeling." She likes being close to Los Angeles. Look at the map. How far is Lakewood from Los Angeles?

Some things in Lakewood have changed. New families from Latin America and Asia have moved in, bringing their cultures to Lakewood. Houses have changed over time, too. People have built extra rooms and second stories.

One thing that has not changed is how people feel. "It's a great town!" says Ruth Smith. She raised two sons there. She says she will never leave.

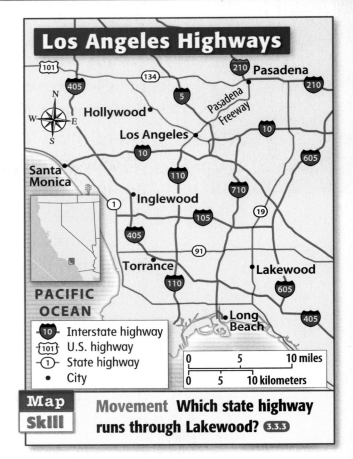

Los Angeles Highways

Legend:
- 10 — Interstate highway
- 101 — U.S. highway
- 1 — State highway
- • City

0   5   10 miles
0   5   10 kilometers

Map Skill Movement **Which state highway runs through Lakewood?** 3.3.3

REVIEW How has Lakewood changed?
Main Idea and Details

A Lakewood house today ▼

Lakewood History

1950	1975	2000

1950 Lakewood founded

1954 Lakewood becomes a city

1990 First Hispanic council member elected

2004 Lakewood celebrates its 50th birthday as a city

◄ The fighter jet in this Lakewood park was built at a factory nearby.

What You Learned

3.3
3.3.3 Lakewood was one of the country's first planned communities.

3.3.2
3.3.3 Entrepreneurs sold thousands of Lakewood houses to families migrating to California, and to soldiers returning from World War II.

3.3
3.3.3 New arrivals from Latin America and Asia have made the population of Lakewood more diverse today.

Lesson Review

1. **Focus Question** What makes
3.3.3 Lakewood a different kind of community?

2. **Vocabulary** Write one sentence for
3.3 each vocabulary word.

   development   **migrate**
   entrepreneur

3. **Economics** Why did so many
3.3.2 families decide to buy homes in Lakewood?

4. **Critical Thinking Draw**
3.3.3 **Conclusions** Why was Lakewood called "The City as New as Tomorrow"?

5. **Reading Strategy**
3.3.3
ELA
R2.3 **Sequence Events** Reread page 190. Use the chart to show the sequence of steps taken by the builders of Lakewood.

6. **Write about THE BIG IDEA** Would you
3.3.3 rather live in a brand-new community,
ELA
W1.1 such as Lakewood in the 1950s, or in a 50-year-old community, such as Lakewood today?

7. **Link to Language Arts** Write a
3.3.3 journal entry as a third-grader moving
ELA
W2.1 to Lakewood in the 1950s. Describe what you like best about the town.

EUREKA

Early Leaders in 3.3.3 Your Community

Christina lives in Eureka. She learned about an important person in her community's history. To show what she learned, Christina made an information card. You can make an information card about someone who was important to your community, too. Here's what to do:

- Look in your school or local library, or on the Internet, for information about your community's history.

- Choose one person who was important to your community's history.

- Make a list of key events in that person's life and the dates they happened. Choose four to six events from your list to use on your card.

LOG ON For more help in making your information cards, visit:

www.macmillanmh.com/ca/ss/local

ACTIVITY

Make a Community Leader Biography Card

Step 1 Use a marker to write the name of the historical leader on top of your oaktag or poster board.

Step 2 Below your title, on the left side of the card, draw a picture of the person, or a place or object important to that person, such as their home or something they invented. You can also paste or tape a photograph on the card.

Step 3 On the right side of the card print your list of key events and dates.

Step 4 Share your information card with your classmates.

Materials
- oaktag or poster board
- markers
- photographs or your drawings
- paste or tape

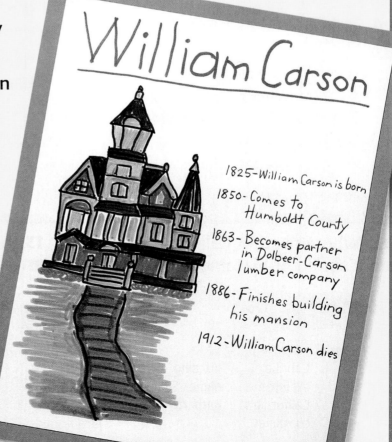

William Carson

1825 - William Carson is born

1850 - Comes to Humboldt County

1863 - Becomes partner in Dolbeer-Carson lumber company

1886 - Finishes building his mansion

1912 - William Carson dies

5 Chapter Review

Vocabulary Review

Copy the sentences below on a separate sheet of paper. Beside each number write the word from the list that best matches the description.

migrate   tourist
mine

1. An area where minerals are
(3.3.1) dug.

2. Someone who travels for fun.
(3.3.3)

3. To move from one part of the
(3.3.2) country to another.

4. Test Preparation Someone who
(3.3.2) starts his or her own business
is a(n) _____ .

    A. **entrepreneur**   C. **tourist**
    B. **presidio**   D. **resident**

Comprehension Check

5. How did many people make
(3.3.2) money in Gold Rush towns?

6. Why is 1821 an important year
(3.3.1) in Mexican history?

7. Why was Lakewood a good
(3.3.2) place for a development?

8. Why was new housing needed
(3.3.2) after the 1940s?

9. What is a planned community?
(3.3.3)

10. Critical Thinking Why does Santa
(3.3.2) Barbara have laws to protect
the area around El Presidio?

11. Critical Thinking What has made
(3.3.2) Placerville different from other
Gold Rush towns?

Use the Time Line

12. Who arrived in California first,
(3.3.1) Cabrillo or Vizcaíno?

13. How many years after the mission
(3.3.1) was established was it sold?

1500	1600	1700	1800	1900	2000

1542 Cabrillo explores California's coastline

1602 Vizcaíno names Santa Barbara

1786 Mission Santa Barbara established

1814 Mission rebuilt after an earthquake

1846 Mission sold under Mexican rule

1925 Another earthquake causes damage

Write a complete sentence to answer each question.

Reading Road Maps

14. Look at the map below.
`3.1.3` What kind of road is Route 5?

15. Test Preparation A _____
`3.1.3` highway begins and finishes inside a state.

16. Test Preparation A highway that
`3.1.3` connects two or more states is a(n) _____ highway.

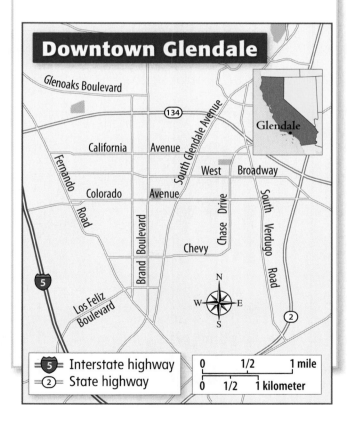

Downtown Glendale

Glenoaks Boulevard
134
California   Avenue
South Glendale Avenue
Glendale
Fernando Road
West   Broadway
Colorado   Avenue
Chase Drive
South Verdugo Road
Brand Boulevard
Chevy
Los Feliz Boulevard
2

N
W   E
S

= 5 = Interstate highway
= 2 = State highway

| 0 | 1/2 | 1 mile |
| 0 | 1/2 | 1 kilometer |

Using Primary Sources

Newspaper Articles

17. What can you learn from a
`3.3.3` newspaper article from the time of the Gold Rush?

18. What five questions do most
`3.3.3` newspaper articles answer?

Hands-on Activity

19. **Create a Skit** Choose an
`3.3.3` important event in your
ELA community's history. Write and
`LS2.2` perform a skit that explains why the event is important.

Write About History

20. **Personal Letter** Suppose you
`3.3.2` are a sales agent for the
ELA entrepreneurs who built
`W2.2` the planned community of Lakewood. Write a letter you would send to groups of people about why they should buy houses in the community.

LOG ON

For help with the process of writing, visit:

www.macmillanmh.com/ss/ca/writing

Communities Over Time

YOU ARE THERE

Communities change over time. New ways of doing things and new people can change the way a community looks, works, and celebrates. Communities also work to hold on to the past.

506—Santa Fe's "Super Chief" Traveling thru the Orange Groves, California

© CURT TEICH & CO., INC.   OB-H678

1 **Transportation Brings Change** (page 200)
Transportation affects the growth of communities. When the railroad came to San Bernardino, the city grew.

2 **Newcomers Build Communities** (page 210)
New settlers bring new ways to communities, such as San José.

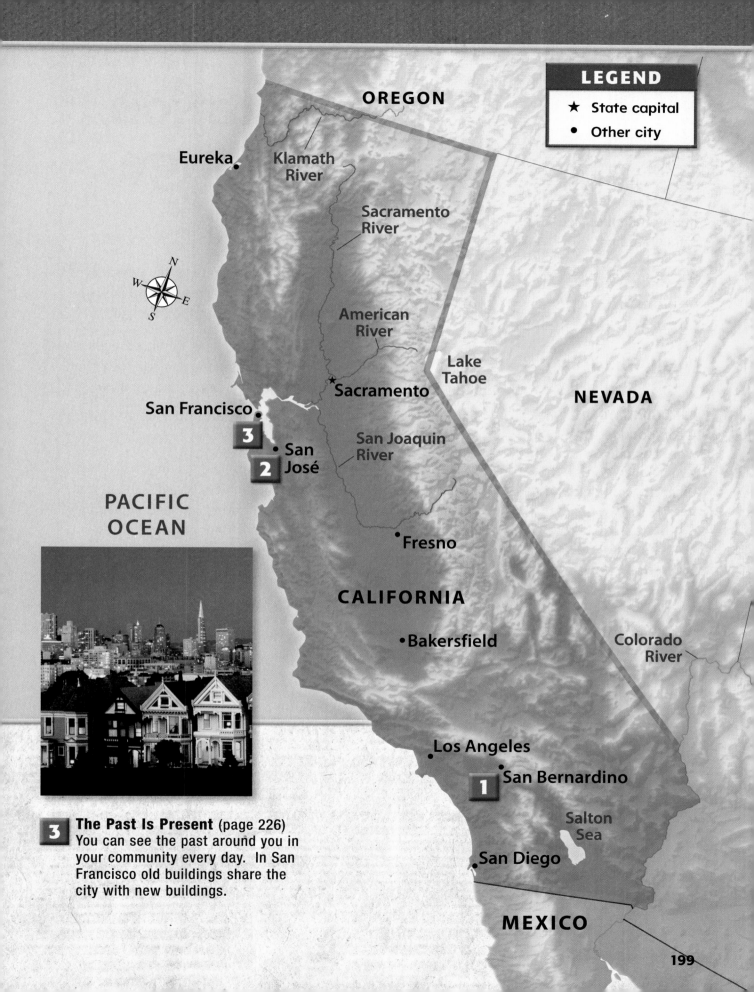

LEGEND
★ State capital
● Other city

OREGON

Eureka

Klamath River

Sacramento River

American River

Lake Tahoe

NEVADA

Sacramento

San Francisco

3

2 San José

PACIFIC OCEAN

San Joaquin River

Fresno

CALIFORNIA

Bakersfield

Colorado River

Los Angeles

1 San Bernardino

Salton Sea

San Diego

MEXICO

3 **The Past Is Present** (page 226)
You can see the past around you in
your community every day. In San
Francisco old buildings share the
city with new buildings.

FOCUS QUESTION

How did new forms of transportation change San Bernardino?

VOCABULARY

**invention
hub
freeway
mass transit**

VOCABULARY STRATEGY

COMPOUND WORDS
A compound word is made of two smaller words. What do you think a **freeway** is?

READING STRATEGY

Sequence Events
Use the chart below to sequence events in San Bernardino's past.

Transportation Brings Change

Start with Your CALIFORNIA STANDARDS

3.3 Students draw from historical and community resources to organize the sequence of local historical events and describe how each period of settlement left its mark on the land.

3.3.1 Research the explorers who visited here, the newcomers who settled here, and the people who continue to come to the region, including their cultural and religious traditions and contributions.

Explore how San Bernardino began and how new inventions helped it grow. (Begins on page 201)

3.3.3 Trace why their community was established, how individuals and families contributed to its founding and development, and how the community has changed over time, drawing on maps, photographs, oral histories, letters, newspapers, and other primary sources.

Find out how highways boosted San Bernardino's growth but also brought traffic problems. (Begins on page 204)

San Bernardino, early 1900s ▼

Each year more than half a million people who love old cars come to San Bernardino to celebrate highway history at the "Route 66 Rendezvous."

Changes in Transportation 3.3.1

It is hard to imagine a world without cars or airplanes. In the past, many people lived all their lives never traveling more than 25 miles from home. Until about 1830, the fastest way to get anywhere on land was by horseback.

Then, in the 1800s and 1900s, new **inventions** brought huge changes in transportation. An invention is something that has been made for the first time. First the railroads were built. Next came automobiles and modern roads. These improvements brought many changes to American communities.

San Bernardino

One of the communities that changed was San Bernardino, a town in Southern California. Let's see how these new technologies changed San Bernardino.

REVIEW What new kinds of transportation changed life in the 1800s and 1900s? *Sequence Events*

201

San Bernardino's Beginnings 3.3.1

The first trails through the San Bernardino Valley were made by Native Americans of the Cahuilla (kah WEE yah) and Serrano tribes. The Spanish missionaries later walked along these trails. The soldiers who came with the missionaries introduced horses as a way of travel.

As time went by, walking trails became trails for horses and horse-drawn wagons. More settlers came to the valley. In 1862, following news of a gold strike, gold seekers came pouring into the San Bernardino Valley. Then the gold ran out, and San Bernardino became a sleepy little town. It could have become a ghost town, as so many other places did, but it did not.

▼ The railroad made it easier to reach California.

Railroads Bring Change

Around 1830 a new invention, the railroad, began to change towns in the eastern United States. By 1869 the railroad reached all the way to California. That made it much easier for people from the East to move here.

The first railroad to reach San Bernardino, the Southern Pacific, arrived in 1883. In 1887 a second railroad, the Sante Fe, laid tracks through San Bernardino. Now San Bernardino was a **hub** city. A hub is a transportation center. People could arrive on one railroad and switch trains to travel on the other railroad. With the two railroads, San Bernardino's population boomed. New hotels and restaurants were built to serve visitors. Some of the visitors decided to settle in San Bernardino. Between 1900 and 1910, the town's population doubled.

REVIEW Why did the railroads come to San Bernardino? *Cause and Effect*

▲ The railroad made it possible to ship oranges from San Bernardino across the country.

▼ Southern Pacific timetable, 1892

Cars Bring More Change 3.3.3

Another new invention, the automobile, helped San Bernardino to keep growing. However, cars needed good roads. In 1926, a new road, called Route 66, came to San Bernardino. Route 66 ran from Chicago, Illinois, to Los Angeles. Route 66 brought more people to San Bernardino. You can read what a famous California author wrote about Route 66 in the Primary Source below.

Soon bigger roads called **freeways** were built. Freeways are roads that have more than two lanes and no cross streets or stoplights. Cars and freeways allowed people to make more choices about where to live and work. Now someone could live in San Bernardino and commute on a freeway to work in Los Angeles.

Roadside attractions like this dinosaur were popular with tourists. ▼

Primary Sources

A quote from **The Grapes of Wrath**
by John Steinbeck
1939

❝Highway 66 is the main migrant road. 66—the long concrete path across the country, waving gently up and down on the map, . . . and into the rich California valleys.❞

 How does John Steinbeck describe Route 66?

REVIEW How did cars and freeways change life in San Bernardino? *Summarize*

San Bernardino, Hub City 3.3.1 3.3.3

During the late 1800s and early 1900s, the railroad and an important highway brought many new people to California. Many of them passed through San Bernardino on their way west. Use the map to see the transportation routes that people could take. Read the time line to see important dates in San Bernardino transportation history.

Think About Transportation

1. What ways could someone travel from the eastern United States to San Bernardino in 1926?

2. When did Metrolink begin service?

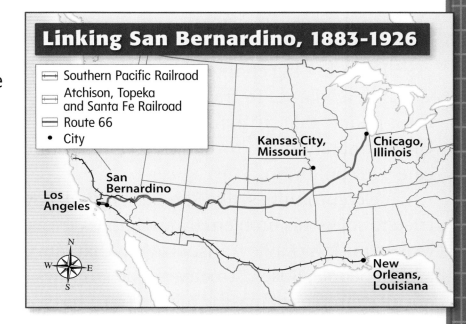

Linking San Bernardino, 1883-1926

- ▭ Southern Pacific Railroad
- ▭ Atchison, Topeka and Santa Fe Railroad
- ▭ Route 66
- • City

Kansas City, Missouri
Chicago, Illinois
San Bernardino
Los Angeles
New Orleans, Louisiana

N W E S

Transportation into San Bernardino

1875	1900	1925	1950	1975	2000
1883 Southern Pacific Railroad arrives	**1885** Santa Fe Railroad arrives	**1926** Route 66 built	**1940** First California freeway opens		**1992** Metrolink begins service

205

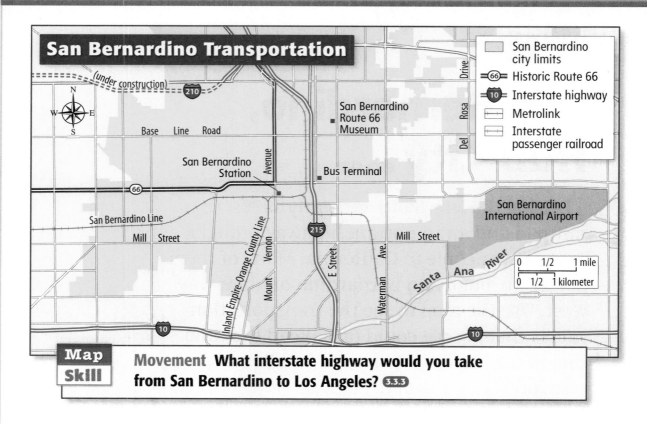

San Bernardino Transportation

(under construction) 210

Base Line Road

San Bernardino Station

Avenue

San Bernardino Route 66 Museum

Bus Terminal

Del Rosa Drive

66

San Bernardino Line

Mill Street

Inland Empire–Orange County Line

Vernon

Mount

E Street

215

Waterman

Mill Street

Ave.

San Bernardino International Airport

Santa Ana River

10

10

N W E S

Legend:
- San Bernardino city limits
- 66 Historic Route 66
- 10 Interstate highway
- Metrolink
- Interstate passenger railroad

0   1/2   1 mile
0   1/2   1 kilometer

Map Skill Movement **What interstate highway would you take from San Bernardino to Los Angeles?** 3.3.3

San Bernardino Today 3.3.3

Still another big change in transportation came with the airplane. To travel long distances today, most people take airplanes instead of trains or cars. Unfortunately, our crowded freeways and airways cause air pollution.

Some communities, like San Bernardino, have tried to solve this problem through **mass transit**. Mass transit is public transportation that moves a lot of people. Buses, streetcars, and subways are all examples of mass transit. A train service called Metrolink now gives commuters a new way to get to and from Los Angeles. Look at the map above. It shows some ways people in San Bernardino can get around.

REVIEW Compare your community's transportation to San Bernardino's. *Compare and Contrast*

Metrolink was built along old train lines. ▼

◀ San Bernardino's
restored train station

What You Learned

3.3.1 New forms of transportation have made travel easier and changed communities.

3.3.1 The coming of the railroad changed San Bernardino from a sleepy town to a hub city.

3.3.3 Cars and modern highways brought more changes to San Bernardino.

3.3.3 Mass transit is one way communities work to solve problems caused by traffic.

Lesson Review

1. **Focus Question** How did new
3.3.1 forms of transportation change San Bernardino?

2. **Vocabulary** Write one sentence for
3.3.1 each vocabulary term.
3.3.3
 freeway   invention
 hub   mass transit

3. **History** Why is 1883 an important
3.3.3 date in San Bernardino history?

4. **Critical Thinking** **Problem Solving**
3.3.1 What do you think would have happened to San Bernardino if the railroad had not chosen to go there?

5. **Reading Strategy**
3.3.3 **Sequence Events**
ELA
R.2.3 Reread the section about the railroads on page 203. Use the chart at right to sequence the events described in the section.

6. **Write about** THE **BiG** IDEA How does
3.3.3 having good transportation help a
ELA
W.2.1 community grow?

7. **Link to Science** Learn more about
3.3.3 railroads. Do some research to find out what kind of power early trains used. Find pictures of some early trains in books or online. Then report your findings to your class.

Read Bar Graphs 3.3.2

VOCABULARY

graph
bar graph

You have read about how changes in transportation helped San Bernardino grow. You can see some information about transportation by reading these **graphs**. A graph is a special kind of picture that shows information in a way that is easy to understand. A **bar graph** uses bars to show information. You can use bar graphs to compare amounts of different items.

 Learn It

Look at the graph below as you follow the steps.

- **Read the title.**
  The graph shows the monthly costs of commuting in Southern California.

- **Read the labels.**
  The labels along the bottom show different ways people commute: rail, drive alone, carpool, vanpool, or bus. The column at the far left is the monthly cost in dollars.

- **Put the information together.**
  Put your finger at the top of the orange bar. Then move your finger to the left. You can see the orange bar reaches just past the mark for $100. The cost of commuting by rail is just over $100 a month. Which way costs the least?

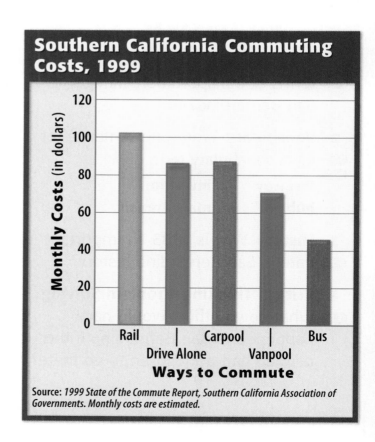

Southern California Commuting Costs, 1999

Monthly Costs (in dollars)

Ways to Commute

Source: 1999 State of the Commute Report, Southern California Association of Governments. Monthly costs are estimated.

2 Try It

Now look at the graph below to answer the questions.

- What does the graph show?

- What do the bars stand for?

- What do people in California own more of, trailers or trucks?

3 Apply It

Interview students in your class to find out different ways they get to school. Then make a bar graph to show the information. Decide which information will go along the bottom and side of the graph. Give your graph a title.

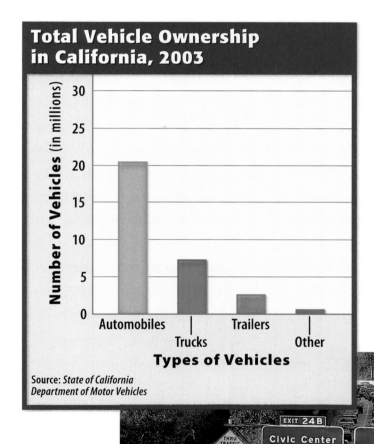

Total Vehicle Ownership in California, 2003

Number of Vehicles (in millions)

Types of Vehicles

Automobiles   Trucks   Trailers   Other

Source: *State of California Department of Motor Vehicles*

Newcomers Build Communities

FOCUS QUESTION

In what ways do newcomers contribute to California?

VOCABULARY

immigrant
opportunity
economy
real estate

VOCABULARY STRATEGY

PREFIXES The prefix **im-** means into. A migrant is someone who moves from place to place. An immigrant moves into a place.

READING STRATEGY

Identify Main Idea and Details

Use the chart to list the main idea and details of this lesson.

Start with Your
CALIFORNIA STANDARDS

3.3 Students draw from historical and community resources to organize the sequence of local historical events and describe how each period of settlement left its mark on the land.

3.3.1 Research the explorers who visited here, the newcomers who settled here, and the people who continue to come to the region, including their cultural and religious traditions and contributions.

Discover the ways recent newcomers have contributed to life in California. (page 211)

3.3.2 Describe the economies established by settlers and their influence on the present day economy, with emphasis on the importance of private property and entrepreneurship.

Explore ways in which newcomers continue to contribute to the economy of San José. (Begins on page 212)

▼ San José, California

POLLING PLACE
投票站 CASILLA ELECTORAL
投票所 LUGAR NG BOTOHAN
투표소 PHÒNG PHIẾU

California communities have always welcomed people from around the world. Today, one in four Californians is someone who was born in another country.

New People for California 3.3.1

Where is your family from? If you are like many Californians, your family moved here from somewhere else, perhaps another country. California has always attracted **immigrants**. An immigrant is a person who leaves one country to live in another country. Some immigrants come seeking freedom. Some come for greater **opportunity**. Opportunity is the chance to do something, such as go to school or get a better job.

Many immigrants have found a home in San José, a city in Santa Clara County. This was once mostly an agricultural area. Today some of the world's biggest computer companies are located here. In this lesson, you will read about why some people came to San José. You will learn about contributions these immigrants have made, too.

San José

REVIEW Why do many immigrants come to California?
Main Idea and Details

Finding Opportunity 3.3.1 3.3.2

Alfredo and Juan Barajas are brothers. They left Mexico when they were teenagers because the **economy** and the job opportunities were better in California. The economy is the way a country uses its money, goods, natural resources, and services. "I wanted to save enough money to go back to Mexico and buy a car," Alfredo says. Instead the brothers stayed in San José. Today Alfredo and Juan sell **real estate**. Real estate is land and the buildings, trees, and other things on it. The brothers have helped many Spanish-speaking people in San José to buy their own homes.

Alfredo's Mexican culture and traditions are very important to him. His children speak English at school, but Alfredo encourages them to speak Spanish at home. He wants them to speak both languages well. "By being bilingual [able to speak two languages], my children will have more opportunities," Alfredo says.

▲ Alfredo (top) and Juan (above) Barajas

San José celebrates Cinco de Mayo. ▼

Being an Entrepreneur

San José has one of the largest Vietnamese American communities in the United States. Many Vietnamese Americans came here to escape a war in Vietnam.

Linh Hoang came to California in 1990 with many dreams. Four years ago he started his own bus company. His buses take Vietnamese passengers between San José and Orange County in Southern California. Orange County also has a large Vietnamese American community. On the bus the passengers eat Vietnamese sandwiches and watch Vietnamese videos. "I just saw the opportunity," Linh says.

Every winter Linh and other San José Vietnamese celebrate Tet, the Vietnamese New Year, at the Santa Clara County fairgrounds. Linh's favorite part is watching the colorful dragon dance. Of course, he wouldn't miss eating delicious moon cakes, too!

Moon cakes ▼

REVIEW How have Alfredo and Juan Barajas and Linh Hoang found opportunities in San José? *Make Inferences*

213

A Scientist From India 3.3.1 3.3.2

Seema Handu is a scientist. Her husband, Shankar Hemmady, is an electrical engineer. Both are from India. Seema says, "When I was in India, I always wanted to come to the United States to study and do research. It was my dream since I was young."

Seema and her husband moved to Santa Clara County. They love living and working in the San José area. "We love that there are people here from many different countries. Many people have started their own businesses. There are so many opportunities here."

Immigrants have helped make places like San José into thriving communities. They have come from countries near and far. The family of Norm Mineta came from Japan. You will read about Norm Mineta on page 216.

REVIEW Why was coming to the United States a dream come true for Seema Handu? *Summarize*

▼ Immigrants like Seema and her family have helped San José grow.

◀ Dragon at San José Tet parade

What You Learned

3.3.1 Immigrants from many countries continue to come to California. Many have settled in San José.

3.3.1 **3.3.2** Immigrants have made many cultural and economic contributions to California. Some immigrants have started their own businesses.

3.3.1 **3.3.2** Some immigrants to San José are scientists.

Lesson Review

1. Focus Question In what ways do
3.3.1 newcomers contribute to California?

2. Vocabulary Write one sentence for
3.3.1 each vocabulary term.
3.3.2
   economy   opportunity
   immigrant   real estate

3. Citizenship What are some of the
3.3.1 reasons that people from other countries move to California?

4. Critical Thinking Make Decisions
3.3.1 Think about the immigrants you read about in this lesson. Give a reason each came to California.

5. Reading Strategy Identify Main
3.3.1 **Idea and Details** Reread the first
3.3.2 paragraph on page 212.
ELA Use the chart to write
R2.5 the main idea and details of the paragraph.

6. Write about THE BIG IDEA Tell how you
3.3.2 think new immigrants have changed
W2.1 San José.

7. Link to Language Arts Many
3.3.1 languages are spoken in California. Pick three of these languages. Do some research to learn how to say "Welcome to California" in each.

❝ As a kid . . . you don't realize the impact that certain people or experiences will have on your life.❞

Norman Mineta 1931–

Norman Mineta was a child who liked going to school and making friends. "Norm" was born in San José, but his parents were from Japan. Norm's life changed when he was 10 years old. That's when the United States entered World War II against Japan and other countries. Some people were afraid that Japanese Americans might help Japan in the war. Because of this fear, our government treated many Japanese Americans unfairly. Many California families were forced to leave their homes and live in guarded camps during the war.

Norm's family spent three years at a camp in Wyoming. One day, Alan Simpson, a boy from the local town, came to visit. The two boys became lifelong friends. Their friendship would have a big effect on Norm's life.

The Life of Norman Mineta

1930	1945	1960	1975
1931 Born in San José, California	**1942** Moved to Wyoming	**1967** Elected to San José City Council	**1971** Became mayor of San José	**1974** Elected to U.S. Congress

Norm finished school in San José and went on to college and a job. Alan Simpson entered politics in Wyoming. Mineta decided he would go into politics, too. In 1967 he was elected to the city council in San José. He became the first Asian American to serve in this job. Four years later, Mineta ran for mayor and became the first Asian American mayor of a large United States city. In 1974 he was elected to Congress, where he served with Alan Simpson. In 2001, he became United States Secretary of Transportation. Today he works to make sure that travel in our country is safe for all.

Write About It! How do you think Mineta's boyhood affected his decision to go into politics?

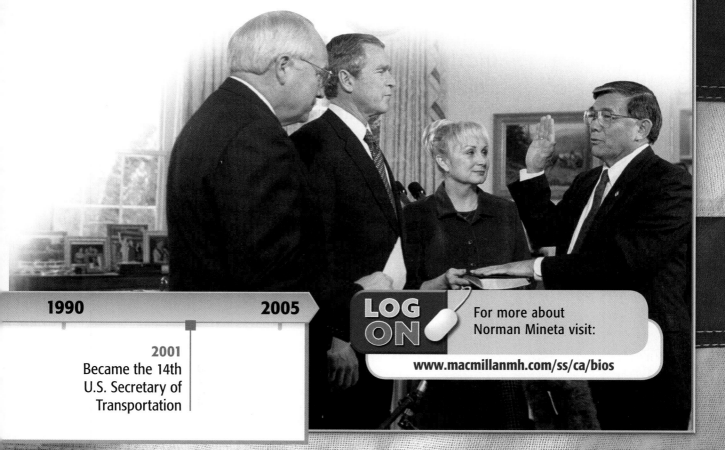

1990   2005

2001
Became the 14th
U.S. Secretary of
Transportation

LOG ON

For more about
Norman Mineta visit:
www.macmillanmh.com/ss/ca/bios

A Visit to The Past 3.3.1

—— * ——

Characters

Tour Guide

Meena *a girl from the present day*

Soo-wan *a boy from the present day*

Teacher

Sofia *a girl from 1910*

Sofia's little sisters and brothers *(non-speaking parts)*

Seppi *Sofia's brother*

Narrator: Meena and Soo-wan are in the third grade. They are on a class trip. They are visiting a museum to learn about immigration to their community long ago. To their surprise, the museum has some unexpected exhibits.

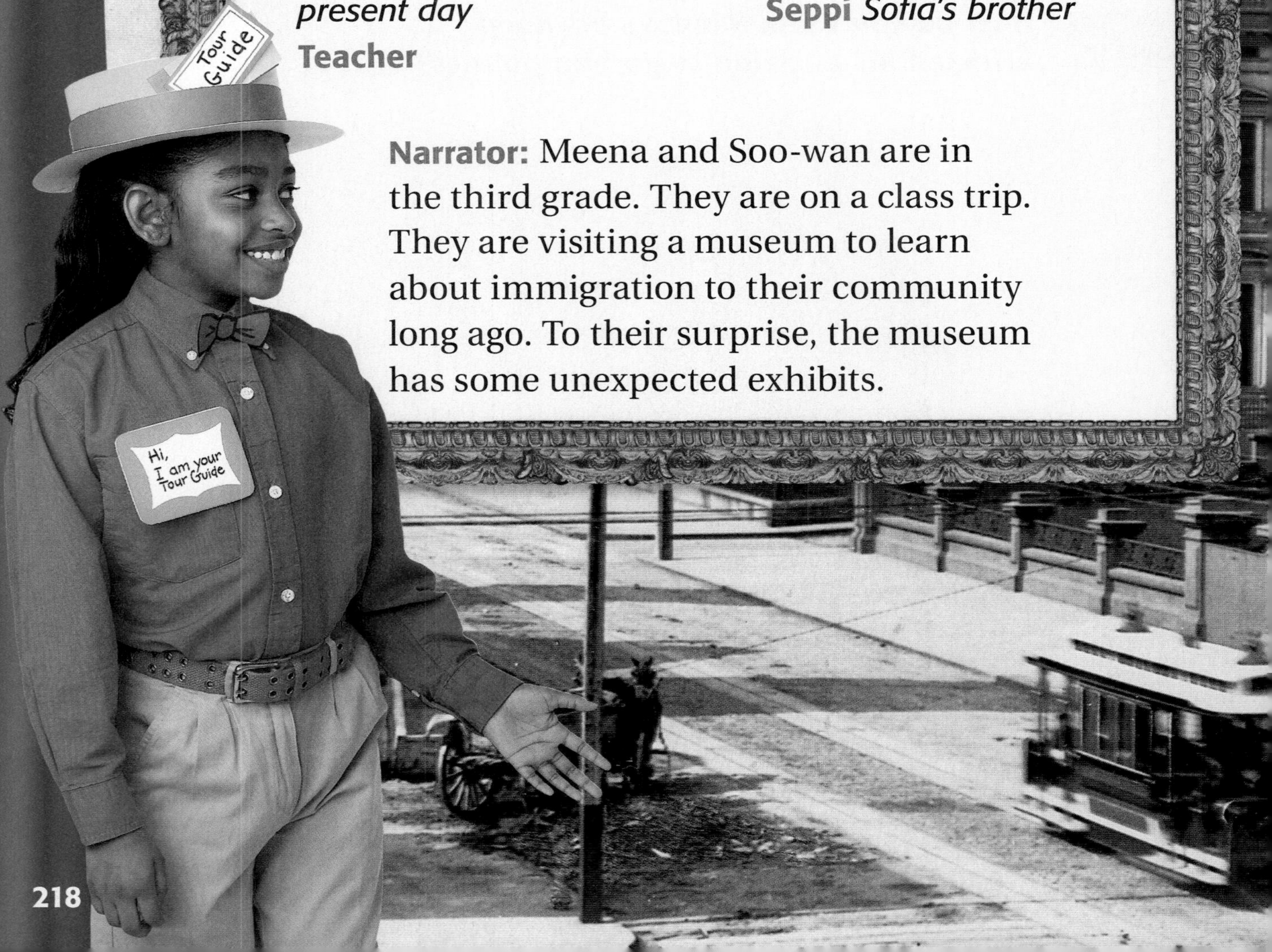

Tour Guide: Welcome to the museum. Today we are going to learn what life was like for people who came to the United States long ago.

(Meena, Soo-wan, and Teacher follow the Tour Guide.)

Tour Guide: One hundred years ago, this apartment was home to an immigrant family. Ten people might have slept in this room.

Meena: And I thought my apartment was crowded!

Tour Guide: Please follow me to the next room.

(The Tour Guide leaves. The Teacher follows. Meena turns to go, but Soo-wan stops her.)

Soo-wan: Look, Meena. A door! Let's take a look.

Narrator: This was no ordinary door. It was the door to a time machine.

(Soo-wan opens the door, and Meena follows him. Sofia, a 10-year-old girl from 1910, is cooking over a stove. She is surrounded by smaller children.)

Sofia: Hello. Are you here to rent an apartment?

Meena: I don't think so.

Sofia: Then why are you here?

Soo-wan: We're here on a school trip.

Sofia: School? Don't you have to work?

Meena: No. We're only eight.

Sofia: Well, I'm 10. I've been working since I was five.

Soo-wan: What do you do?

Sofia: I help my mother make clothes that she sells. (*Pause*) What funny clothes you are wearing. It's 1910. You have to dress in style.

Meena: *(to Soo-wan)* 1910? What is she talking about?

Soo-wan: *(to Meena)* We must have time traveled!

Sofia: Where are you from?

Soo-wan: I was born in South Korea.

Meena: I am from California.

Sofia: I was born in Italy. It's hard coming to a new country, isn't it? Do you miss your homeland?

Soo-wan: Yes, I miss my grandparents in South Korea.

Sofia: I miss my grandparents too! Back in Italy, I saw them every day.

Soo-wan: It was the same for me in South Korea.

Sofia: Now, I'll never see them again.

Meena: Can't you fly back to see them?

Sofia: Fly? What are you talking about? To go back to Italy, I'd have to take a boat. Besides, it's much too expensive.

Soo-wan: Do you like it here?

Sofia: I like a lot of things. People come to the United States from all over the world.

Meena: I like that about the United States, too.

Sofia: It was hard learning to speak English. My brother Seppi taught me. He goes to school and works at night lighting the street lamps. Oh, I hear him coming up the stairs now.

(Seppi enters. He carries books under his arm.)

Seppi: Hello, Sofia. Who are these people?

Sofia: Seppi, these are my new friends. *(to Soo-wan)* Don't worry about missing your homeland. Life will get better, I promise.

(Seppi and Sofia say "goodbye" as Meena and Soo-wan exit through the door.)

Meena: Wow! Life sure was different back then.

Soo-wan: Can you imagine going to school and working?

(The teacher walks in.)

Teacher: *(smiling)* There you are! I hope you saw something interesting.

Soo-wan/Meena: *(speaking together)* We sure did!

Write About It!

Write a journal entry about what your first day at school might be like if you moved to a different country.

Understand Hemispheres 3.3.1

VOCABULARY

sphere
hemisphere
prime
　　meridian
equator

Immigrants to San José have come from many different places around the world. You can find these places on the globe, a model of Earth. Like Earth, a globe is a **sphere**. It is round, like a ball. You can see only half of a globe at a time. The part of the globe that you see is called a **hemisphere**. The word hemisphere means half of a sphere.

1 Learn It

We can divide Earth from top to bottom or around the middle.

- The **prime meridian** is an imaginary line that runs from the North Pole to the South Pole. Any place east of the prime meridian is in the Eastern Hemisphere. Any place west of the prime meridian is in the Western hemisphere.

- The **equator** is an imaginary line around Earth, halfway between the North and South Poles. It divides Earth into two halves. Any place north of the equator is in the Northern Hemisphere. Any place south of the equator is in the Southern Hemisphere.

- A continent can be found in more than one hemisphere. It all depends on how we think of dividing Earth.

2 Try It

Look at the maps on page 225 to answer the questions.

- Name the four hemispheres.

- Which continents does the equator cross? Where would you have to be to see Earth this way?

3 Apply It

- You read that many of the immigrants to San José came from Asia. In which two hemispheres is Asia mainly found?

- Find North America on two of the maps. Which two hemispheres is it in?

- Which continents are in both the Northern Hemisphere and the Southern Hemisphere?

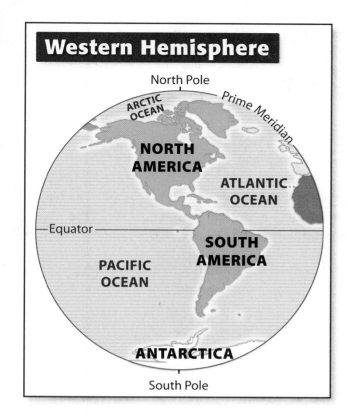

Western Hemisphere

North Pole
ARCTIC OCEAN
Prime Meridian
NORTH AMERICA
ATLANTIC OCEAN
Equator
PACIFIC OCEAN
SOUTH AMERICA
ANTARCTICA
South Pole

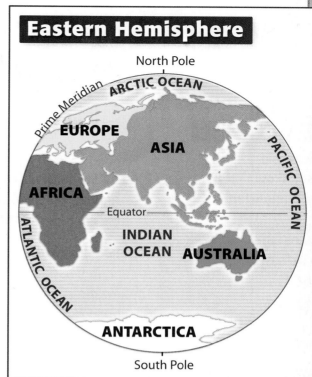

Eastern Hemisphere

North Pole
Prime Meridian
ARCTIC OCEAN
EUROPE
ASIA
PACIFIC OCEAN
AFRICA
Equator
ATLANTIC OCEAN
INDIAN OCEAN
AUSTRALIA
ANTARCTICA
South Pole

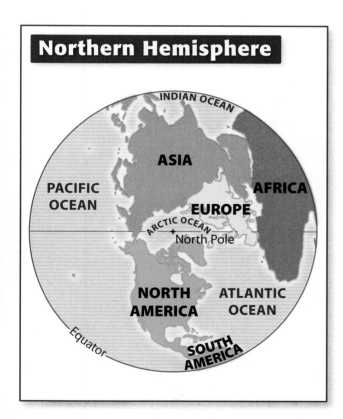

Northern Hemisphere

INDIAN OCEAN
ASIA
PACIFIC OCEAN
AFRICA
EUROPE
ARCTIC OCEAN
North Pole
NORTH AMERICA
ATLANTIC OCEAN
Equator
SOUTH AMERICA

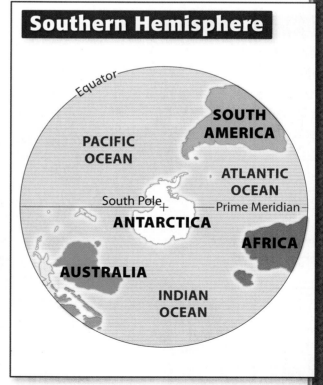

Southern Hemisphere

Equator
SOUTH AMERICA
PACIFIC OCEAN
ATLANTIC OCEAN
South Pole
Prime Meridian
ANTARCTICA
AFRICA
AUSTRALIA
INDIAN OCEAN

FOCUS QUESTION

How does San Francisco show that its history is important?

VOCABULARY

boundary
landfill
cable car
preservation
mural

VOCABULARY STRATEGY

ROOT WORDS Preserve means "save." Which term on the list is formed from **preserve**?

READING STRATEGY

Sequence Events
Copy the chart and use it to sequence events in San Francisco's history.

The Past Is Present

Start with Your
CALIFORNIA STANDARDS

3.3 Students draw from historical and community resources to organize the sequence of local historical events and describe how each period of settlement left its mark on the land.

3.3.3 Trace why their community was established, how individuals and families contributed to its founding and development, and how the community has changed over time, drawing on maps, photographs, oral histories, letters, newspapers, and other primary sources.

Explore San Francisco's past and discover how the city has changed through time. (Begins on page 227)

San Francisco, California, combines old buildings and new ones. ▼

When workers dug a tunnel for the subway in downtown San Francisco, they found many strange objects, including these buckles. How did they get under San Francisco's streets?

Linking to the Past 3.3.3

In this unit you have read how some California communities were founded. You also read about some of the reasons towns have grown and changed. Growth and change and new ways can be exciting. Yet some things about the past are valuable. Many communities today think it is important to hold on to the best of their history.

One California city that has changed greatly is San Francisco. It grew from a tiny settlement around the Presidio of San Francisco and Mission Dolores to become one of California's largest cities. The town grew quickly during the Gold Rush. Later, it survived earthquakes and fires. Let's take a look at San Francisco and see some of the ways it has kept a link to its rich and interesting past.

San Francisco

REVIEW How did San Francisco begin? *Summarize*

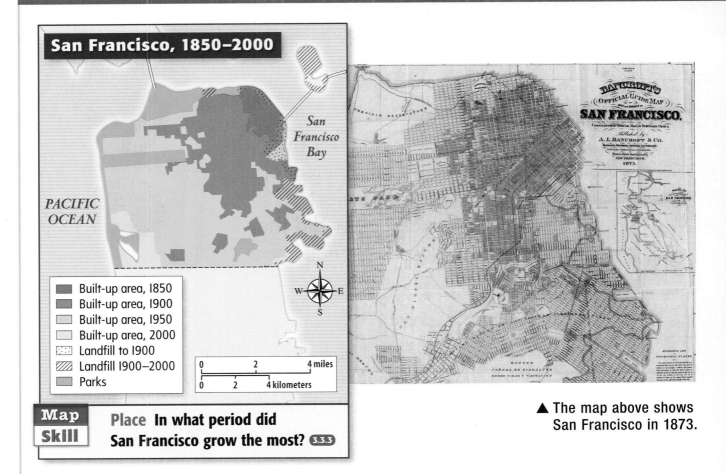

San Francisco, 1850–2000

San Francisco Bay

PACIFIC OCEAN

- Built-up area, 1850
- Built-up area, 1900
- Built-up area, 1950
- Built-up area, 2000
- Landfill to 1900
- Landfill 1900–2000
- Parks

0   2   4 miles
0   2   4 kilometers

N W E S

Map Skill   **Place** In what period did San Francisco grow the most? 3.3.3

▲ The map above shows San Francisco in 1873.

History in the Streets 3.3.3

A city's **boundaries** can change over time. A boundary is a line that marks the limit of an area. The map above shows how San Francisco's boundaries have changed. You can see that one change involved **landfill**. Landfill is dry land that people have made by filling in watery areas.

When ships carrying gold seekers arrived in San Francisco during the Gold Rush, passengers and crews rushed off to find gold. They left their ships behind in the harbor. Some of the ships were sunk to make landfill. When dirt and stones were added too, parts of the harbor filled up. In the 1960s, when tunnels were dug under this area for the subway, workers found artifacts from the ships! Today, some of San Francisco's tallest buildings stand on what was once San Francisco Bay.

Rolling History

History is on a roll in hilly San Francisco. The city is famous for its historic **cable cars**, a kind of streetcar that is pulled by a cable. The cable car was invented by Andrew Hallidie in 1873 after he watched a horse-drawn cart fall down a steep hill. Hallidie designed a car that could be pulled up and down the hills by cables. The cable car was a huge success.

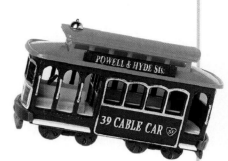

By the 1940s cable cars seemed old-fashioned. The mayor of San Francisco planned to scrap the cable cars. However, San Franciscans wanted to keep them. They fought hard for the **preservation**, or protection, of this piece of city history. Now the cars are protected by city law.

REVIEW How is history shown in San Francisco's streets? *Summarize*

How Cable Cars Work

A grip on the cable car reaches through a slot in the street to grip a cable running under the street. The cable pulls the car along at a speed of about 9 miles per hour. To stop the car, the gripman pulls on the brake and releases the grip, which lets go of the cable.

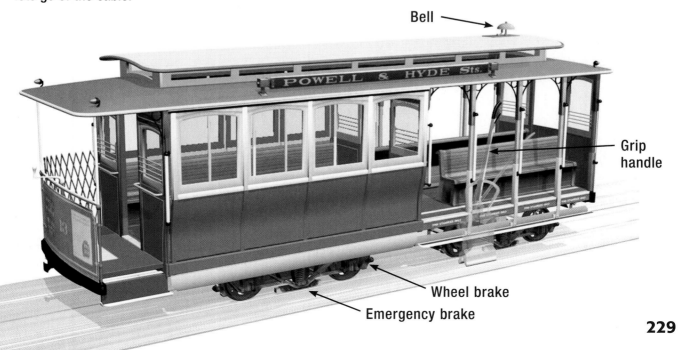

Bell

Grip handle

Wheel brake

Emergency brake

Buildings Show History 3.3.3

A city's buildings show its history, too. San Francisco still has many houses that were built in the late 1800s. You can see some of them on page 226. In 1906 a huge earthquake hit San Francisco. Leaking gas caused a fire that swept through the city. More than 28,000 buildings were completely destroyed.

One building almost destroyed by the fire was Old St. Mary's Church, a church first built in 1854 by Chinese immigrants. The church survived the earthquake, but the fire destroyed the roof and the windows, and even melted the bell. Only the outer walls and the bell tower were left standing.

▲ Buildings in Jackson Square survived the 1906 earthquake.

◀ Old St. Mary's Church after it was rebuilt

"Old St. Mary's" in the heart of Chinatown San Francisco

◀ Today Old St. Mary's Church is still important to the community.

▲ Victor Arnantoff painted "City Life" in the 1930s.

Some people wanted to tear down the church and rebuild it somewhere else. However, the people of Old St. Mary's felt that their church was an important piece of history. They worked hard to raise money and rebuild the church.

Recently the church was strengthened to make sure it can survive another earthquake. Now the church will be a part of the community for many years to come.

Painting History

Another way San Franciscans keep a link to the past is through the **murals** that decorate many buildings. A mural is a picture painted on a wall. Many murals were painted by local artists during the 1930s and show important events of that time. Others show scenes from daily life or celebrate San Francisco's different cultures.

REVIEW What are two ways San Francisco's buildings show history? *Summarize*

Families Are a Part of History 3.3.3

Families are a part of a community's history, too. Philip Choy's family came from China over 120 years ago. They settled in the Chinatown neighborhood. "It was very crowded in Chinatown then," says Philip. "Many families lived in a single house."

As a boy Philip went to a public school. He also went to a special school at night to learn about his Chinese culture. Later, after getting married, he moved out of Chinatown.

The Choys have seen a lot of changes. Philip's daughter Stephanie remembers visiting Chinatown as a girl. "Back then there were a lot of foods you could only get in Chinatown," she says. "Now there are neighborhoods with Chinese groceries and restaurants all over the city." Today, Stephanie's three children are learning Chinese language and culture, just as she did.

The Choys are a part of their city's history. They show how families, like communities, can mix old and new ways.

▲ The Choy family today

▼ Sarah and Philip Choy still live in San Francisco.

REVIEW How did Philip, his children, and his grandchildren stay connected to their culture? *Summarize*

Philip Choy (front left), age six, with his family in 1932 ▶

What You Learned

3.3.3 Many communities work to preserve their history.

3.3.3 San Francisco's changing boundaries show one way communities change over time. San Franciscans have preserved a bit of history by keeping their cable cars.

3.3.3 We can see San Francisco's past in its historic buildings and murals.

3.3.3 Families can preserve their history, too.

Lesson Review

1. Focus Question How does San
3.3.3 Francisco show that its history is important?

2. Vocabulary Write one sentence for
3.3.3 each vocabulary term.

> boundary   mural
> landfill   preservation

3. History What important event
3.3.3 changed San Francisco in 1906?

4. Critical Thinking Make
3.3.3 **Generalizations** Why do you think the Choy family continues to learn about their Chinese heritage?

5. Reading Strategy
3.3.3 **Sequence Events**
ELA
R2.3 Reread page 229. Then use the chart to sequence events about San Francisco's cable cars.

6. Write about THE **BiG** IDEA What are
3.3.3 some ways San Franciscans have
ELA
W2.2 worked to keep their history alive?

7. Link to Art Do some research to
3.3.3 learn more about San Francisco's murals. Pick one to describe. Write a paragraph to tell what the mural shows and why you like it.

Downtown Los Angeles

Los Angeles

Los Angeles is an exciting city. It has many neighborhoods, and people from all over the world, and it is a mix of the old and the new. On a visit to downtown Los Angeles, you can see the place where the city started and some of its newest sites, too.

◀ ❶ Bradbury Building

Built in 1893, this office building is a bit of a movie star. Filmmakers like to use its old-fashioned iron railings and open, cage-like elevators. They also like the dramatic shadows made by light coming in through the glass ceiling.

❷ Grand Central Market

You can buy food from all over the world at Los Angeles's oldest and largest open-air market. Here you can find everything from fresh tortillas to Chinese herbs. ▶

◀ ❸ Walt Disney Concert Hall

Walt Disney Concert Hall is one of the city's newest buildings. It was designed by Frank Gehry and opened in 2003. The outside is made of huge pieces of curved steel.

❹ El Pueblo ▲

Los Angeles started here back in 1781, when Spanish settlers founded the city. Today, at Olvera Street's busy marketplace, you can buy delicious Mexican food or dance to the music of a mariachi band.

ACTIVITY

Use the Internet to find out more about Frank Gehry. Draw a picture or make a model of another building he designed.

For more about downtown Los Angeles, visit:

www.macmillanmh.com/ss/ca/fieldtrips

What Should We Do with Old Buildings? 3.3.3

How do community leaders decide which old buildings to preserve, or protect, and which to tear down and replace? Every community has buildings from the past. Read below to find three points of view on what to do with old buildings.

"We should keep old buildings that link us to our past. You can learn about how people lived long ago. It is a lot more exciting than just reading about it in a book."

Jessica Moffett
Victorville, California
From an interview, 2004

"Sometimes old buildings just have to go. Some have unsafe chemicals or materials in them. If the building is not important, sometimes it is better to knock it down."

Kennan Raditya Choy
Pleasanton, California
From an interview, 2004

"It depends on the building. Some old buildings are worth fixing up. Another choice is to move them somewhere else. I don't like tearing them down, because it feels like killing an endangered species."

Sarah Lennon
San José, California
From an interview, 2004

Build Citizenship
Leadership

1. Why might communities need strong leaders to help preserve old buildings?

2. What can you learn about changes in your community by looking at its old and new buildings?

3. Why do you think people often disagree about whether or not to preserve old buildings?

Think About It
Points of View

1. What are the choices Sarah Lennon says people can make about old buildings?

2. Why does Jessica Moffett want to preserve some old buildings?

3. What reasons does Kennan Choy give for his opinion?

▼ Mission San Carlos Borroméo del Rio Carmelo in Carmel

Write
About It!

Choose one old building in your city or town. Write a speech telling what you think should be done with this building. Give three reasons for your opinion.

SANTA ANA

Seeing the Past in Your Community

3.3
ELA
LS2.1

José lives in Santa Ana. He wanted to learn about his town's history. Then he created a mural about historic areas in his community. He also interviewed an older resident about how his community has changed. Here are some steps you can follow to do the same things.

- Go to your local library to find books about your community's history. Look at old newspapers and photos to see what your community looked like long ago.

- On a walking tour of your community, take photographs or draw sketches of older buildings or businesses.

- Think of an older relative or neighbor who has lived in your community for a long time. Ask that person if you can interview him or her for a school report.

LOG ON

For more help in making your projects, visit:

www.macmillanmh.com/ss/ca/local

Make a Mural

Step 1 Gather your materials.

Step 2 Make a mural about your community's past. Draw pictures of older buildings or areas on your oaktag or posterboard, based on your sketches or photographs, or pictures from the library.

Step 3 Use a marker to print labels for each building or area in your mural. Include details such as the building's name, the year it was built, and what it is used for today.

Step 4 Share your mural with the class.

Materials
- notebook
- photos and drawings
- oaktag or posterboard
- markers
- crayons

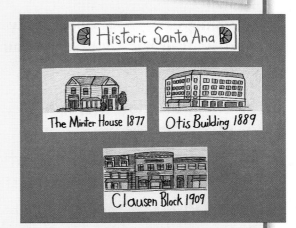

Conduct an Interview

Step 1 Before your interview, prepare a list of questions.

Step 2 During your interview, listen closely and take notes. Ask more questions about the topics the person is most interested in.

Step 3 Write a report of your interview and what you learned.

Step 4 Share your report with your classmates.

Materials
- notebook
- pencil or pen
- lined paper

Vocabulary Review

Copy the sentences below on a separate sheet of paper. Beside each number, write *C* if the underlined word is used correctly. If it is not, write the word that would correctly complete the sentence.

hub	mural
immigrant	opportunity
mass transit	preservation

1. 3.3.2 Mass transit is public transportation that moves many people.

2. 3.3.1 Opportunity is a person who comes from another country to live.

3. 3.3.1 Preservation is protecting something from damage or decay.

4. 3.3.2 A mural is a transportation center.

5. Test Preparation 3.3.3 A(n) _____ is the line that marks the limits of an area.

A. mural   C. freeway
B. boundary   D. hub

Comprehension Check

6. 3.3.1 What are some reasons immigrants have come to California?

7. 3.1.2 How was new land created in San Francisco's harbor?

8. 3.3.3 How do San Francisco's murals tell people about the past?

9. 3.3.2 Why is it good for places to have mass transit?

10. Critical Thinking 3.3.2 How do you think new inventions, such as railroads, cars, and airplanes, have changed people's lives?

11. Critical Thinking 3.3.1 What are some ways that immigrants add to a community?

Read Bar Graphs

12. What does this graph show?
3.3.2

13. Which airport was busier in 2003, San Diego or San José?
3.3.2

14. About how many passengers came through San José airport in 2003?
3.3.2

Understand Hemispheres

15. Test Preparation The _____ is the imaginary line that divides Earth into Northern and Southern Hemispheres.
3.3

16. Test Preparation All of North America is in the _____ Hemisphere and the _____ Hemisphere.
3.1

California Airport Passengers, 2003

Number of People (in millions)

Los Angeles | San Francisco | San Diego | Oakland | San José

Airports

Sources: *Los Angeles, San Francisco, San Diego, Oakland, Mineta San José airports.*

Using Primary Sources

17. What is something Seema Handu likes about San José?

18. What do the two photographs of the church on page 230 tell you about how the neighborhood of Old St. Mary's Church has changed?

Hands-on Activity

19. Make a Mural Work in groups to create a mural on paper that answers the question:
3.3.1

Why do immigrants come to California?

Write About History

20. Personal Letter Suppose you lived in San Francisco during the 1940s when the mayor wanted to get rid of the cable cars. Write a letter to the mayor giving your opinion. Give reasons to support your opinion. Be sure to include a date, proper salutation or greeting, closing, and signature.
3.3.3
ELA W2.3

LOG ON

For help with the process of writing, visit:

www.macmillanmh.com/ss/ca/writing

Comprehension and Critical Thinking Check

Write a sentence or more to answer each question.

1. How were the **ranchos** different from the missions? **3.3.2**

2. How did **landfill** change San Francisco? **3.3.3**

3. How can **tourists** contribute to a community's economy? **3.3.2**

4. How did railroads make it easier to **migrate** to California? **3.3.1**

5. How did the railroad change the **economy** of San Bernardino? **3.3.1**

6. How did **freeways** make suburbs grow? **3.3.3**

7. What are some signs of Santa Barbara's Spanish **heritage**? **3.3.1**

8. What is one way people work for **preservation** in their communities? **3.3.3**

9. **Critical Thinking** What **opportunity** caused people to go to Placerville? **3.3.2**

10. **Critical Thinking** Give an example of an **entrepreneur** who helped California grow. **3.3.2**

Reading Social Studies Check

Sequence Events

Reread "Cars Bring More Change" on page 204. Use the chart to place the events from that section in order. Then answer the questions. **3.1.2** **ELA R2.3**

11. How did you know how to order events? **ELA R2.3**

12. When did Route 66 come to San Bernardino? **ELA R2.3**

13. What new kind of highway was built after Route 66? **ELA R2.3**

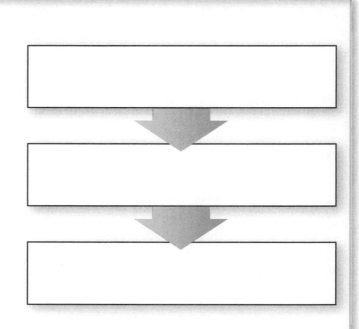

Read the paragraphs. Then answer the questions.

In the early 1800s, English engineers built the first railroad that used a steam engine. Before that, horses pulled cars on iron rails. Steam power was much faster. It could also pull more weight. The first steam locomotive could pull six loaded cars nine miles in one hour.

Beginning in the 1830s, railroad lines were built in the eastern part of the United States. The railroads brought big changes. The railroads made it much easier for people to travel long distances. They also made it easier to ship goods.

14. How did the first railroads change life in **3.3.3** the United States?

A Railroads replaced automobiles.

B Steam power was faster.

C Railroads made it easier to travel and ship goods.

D Railroads were built in the East.

15. What is the main idea of the passage?
3.3.3

A Before steam engines people used horses to pull heavy loads.

B The railroad created jobs for people.

C Railroads made money for the government.

D Railroads were an important invention.

Write About History

16. Personal Letter Pretend you are a gold **3.3** miner who came to California for the **ELA** **W2.3** Gold Rush. Write a letter to a friend back home describing what your life is like.

17. Descriptive Suppose you are a **3.3** tour guide in San Francisco. Write a **ELA** **W2.3** paragraph describing two places you might take people on a tour. Tell why each place is important.

18. Narrative Think about what it would **3.3** be like to move to a new country. Write **ELA** **W2.1** a short story about your first day in the new place.

For help with the process of writing, visit:

www.macmillanmh.com/ss/ca/writing

REVIEW
THE BIG IDEA

Why do communities change over time?

Write About the Big Idea 3.3.3 ELA W2.1

Descriptive Composition

Think about the communities you read about in Unit 3. All of them changed over time. What were some events that caused the changes? Complete the graphic organizer below. Add events that influenced California's growth.

Then choose one event from your graphic organizer. Explain what changes it caused, and why.

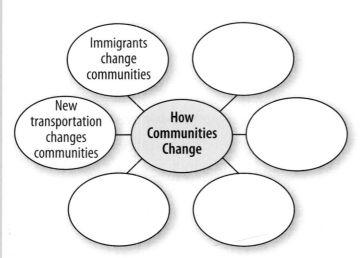

Write a Descriptive Composition

1. Plan
• Decide on a topic. Keep in mind your purpose for writing. You will explain an event and the changes that it caused.

2. Write a First Draft
• Begin with a sentence that tells the topic of your composition.
• Add sentences to explain how the event you chose caused California communities to change.
• Write a concluding sentence. It should summarize your main idea.

3. Revise and Proofread
• Check your composition. Does it have a topic and supporting sentences? Does your last sentence summarize your composition?
• Be sure all the words are spelled and capitalized correctly.
• Rewrite your composition neatly before you give it to your teacher.

Speak About the Big Idea 3.3.3 ELA LS2.1

Community Time Line Story

Make and narrate a time line story of events in your community.

1998
The
John Steinbeck
Center opens

2004
Mayor
Anna Caballero
Re-elected

Prepare As a class, list important events in your community's history. Then work in small groups. Each group should choose one event and research it. Make a time line piece with the date and name of the event.

Present One member of each group should stand in a line with that group's time line piece. The time line pieces should be in order from first to last. Then the members of each group should present the story of each event.

LAUNCH PAD For help with the Big Idea activity, visit:

www.macmillanmh.com/ss/ca/launchpad

Read More About the Big Idea

Boom Town

Sonia Levitin Read how a young girl during the Gold Rush turns a mining settlement into a boom town by selling pies to miners.

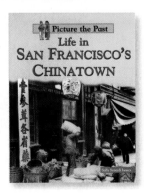

Life in San Francisco's Chinatown

Sally Senzell Isaacs Learn about what life was like for Chinese immigrants in San Francisco in the 1800s.

A Mission for the People

Mary Ann Fraser Find out about the effects of the Spanish mission of La Purisma on the Chumash people of Southern California.

Communities at Work

"Never turn down a job because you think it's too small; you don't know where it can lead."

— Julia Morgan, California's first female architect

◄ San Francisco Farmers' Market

EXPLORE THE BIG IDEA

How do people in a community meet their needs?

As you read Unit 4, you will learn about how people make and spend money to meet their needs. You will also see how trade and farming affect communities.

Copy the graphic organizer below. As you read the chapters in this unit, note the ways that people in a community meet their needs.

Complete the graphic organizer as you read Unit 4. For each way that people meet their needs, list two steps they need to take. The first one has been done for you.

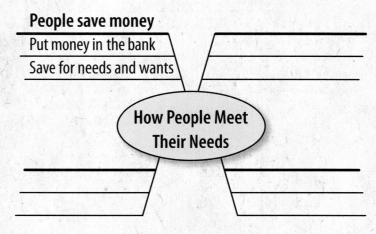

People save money

Put money in the bank

Save for needs and wants

How People Meet Their Needs

Backyard Carnival

**from *Max Malone Makes a Million*
by Charlotte Herman**

When Max Malone read about a boy his age who got rich selling cookies, Max and his friend Gordy decided to make their fortune, too. Their first tries went all wrong. Then Max had another idea . . .

"I don't know why I didn't think of it before. A backyard **carnival** is a great way to make money. We'll have food and prizes, and we'll make the games ourselves."

"You need money to start a carnival," said Rosalie. "And you don't have any."

"I'll take out a loan," said Max.

On Friday morning Max and Gordy were on their way to buy food and prizes. Max had **convinced** his mother to lend him ten dollars. He would pay her back as soon as he made money from the carnival. Gordy took out a ten-dollar loan from his mother too. First they went looking for food.

"Taffy apples," Max suggested. "That's a good carnival food." He thought that cotton candy was a good carnival food too. But he didn't know how he could make it in his backyard.

"Good idea," said Gordy. "We can buy them cheap at the outlet store. No one will mind the broken sticks.

At the store they bought twenty taffy apples for twenty-five cents apiece. "We'll sell them for fifty cents each," said Max. "Double our money. And now for the fun stuff. Let's go get the prizes. We've got fifteen dollars to spend."

"My father said we should try to find quality prizes," said Gordy. "People will be more likely to play the games if they know they can win quality prizes."

---

carnival (KAHR nuh vuhl) fair
convinced (kuhn VINSD) caused to do

"Yeah. None of that junky stuff," said Max as they were walking. "No liquid bubbles, or slime, or things like that. We'll look for prizes kids will want to win."

Max and Gordy brought their prizes and taffy apples to Max's house. Then they went into the backyard to plan their carnival.

"We can have them knock over tin cans with a ball," said Max.

"And pitch balls into pails," said Gordy.

"And guess the number of jelly beans in a fishbowl," said Max. He thought of the two packages of jelly beans Mrs. Malone had bought for Rosalie the other day. Max didn't care much for jelly beans. They got stuck in his teeth. But Rosalie loved them.

All day long, Max and Gordy cut, drew, pasted, and hammered. They gathered empty cans that Mrs. Malone had been saving for recycling to use for their game. And they filled Max's old fishbowl with Rosalie's jelly beans.

On Saturday, Max and Gordy put up signs all around the neighborhood, announcing their main event on Sunday. And when Sunday arrived, everything was ready.

Kids came from all around. Some even came with their parents. Rosalie was in charge of ticket sales: five for a dollar. The kids knocked over the cans. They pitched balls into pails. Mrs. Malone served iced tea at twenty-five cents a glass. And she sold all the taffy apples. There was only one problem. Max and Gordy were running out of prizes.

"Everyone's winning," said Max.

"We made the games too easy," said Gordy.

Rosalie volunteered to run out and buy more prizes and taffy apples with the money they were making from the carnival.

A half hour later, she was back, eating a taffy apple.

"I'm back," she called to Max. "Just look at all the **sensible** prizes I bought for you."

Max poked his head into a bag full of liquid bubbles, slime, plastic jewelry, and school supplies.

"You bought school supplies for a carnival?" cried Max. "Who wants to win erasers and pencil sharpeners?"

"They were on sale," said Rosalie. "And besides, school will be starting soon. They're very practical."

Max didn't have time to argue. Too many people were waiting for their prizes.

When all the prizes were gone, Max and Gordy decided that the carnival was over. Everyone went away happy. Especially Austin Healy, who'd won the jelly beans by guessing that there were two hundred and ten of them in the fishbowl. He'd won the fishbowl, too.

"Just look at all this money," said Max after everyone left. "I can't wait to see how much we made." They counted up all the nickels, dimes, quarters, and dollar bills.

"Wow!" said Max. "Twenty-five dollars. We almost made a fortune."

"Not quite," said Gordy, reaching into the pile. "I owe my mother ten dollars."

Max slapped his forehead. "Oh, no. I forgot all about that." He let out a deep sigh and took ten dollars from the pile too. That left them with just five dollars. "Two dollars and fifty cents each," he said. "Bummer. Not much of a fortune, is it?"

"You can say that again," said Gordy

---

sensible (SEN suh buhl) having good sense; wise.

Write About It!

Write a paragraph explaining why you think Max and Gordy didn't make very much money.

Identify Cause and Effect:

Making Money Choices _{ELA} R2.3 3.5.3

Think about the last time you spent money. You had a reason. A cause, or reason, is why something happens. An effect is what happens. Thinking about causes and effects will help you understand events you read about.

1 Learn It

- To find a cause, ask, "Why did it happen?"

- To find an effect, ask, "What happened?"

- Look for words such as *because, as a result,* and *so.* These words often link causes and effects.

- Now look for causes and effects in the paragraph.

Cause
This sentence tells why Ana had money.

Effect
The words "as a result" and "so" are clue words that show effects.

Ana's grandparents and aunts gave her money for her birthday this year. As a result, Ana had $70. She decided to save $50 of her birthday money, so she opened a savings account. Now she has $20 to spend on things she wants.

 **Try It**

Copy the cause and effect chart below. Then, complete the chart with causes and effects from the paragraph on page 254.

Cause and Effect Chart

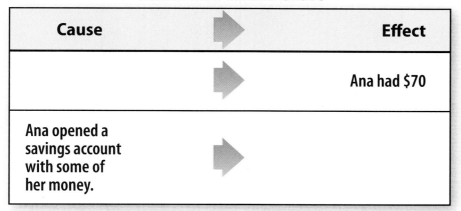

Cause		Effect
		Ana had $70
Ana opened a savings account with some of her money.		

 **Apply It**

- Review the steps for understanding cause and effect in Learn It.

- Read the paragraph below. Then make a chart to show two causes and two effects.

José has saved all the money he made delivering newspapers. Therefore, he has enough money to buy something special. He wants a new computer game. He also wants new skateboard wheels. He only has enough money for one or the other. So he needs to make a decision.

People Use Money

YOU ARE THERE

In this chapter you will read about how people work to earn money for the things they need and want. You will also read why it is important for people and businesses to make smart choices about how to spend their money.

1 **Earning and Spending** (page 258)
Most people earn money by working at businesses.

2 **Making Money Choices** (page 266)
People need to make smart choices about how to spend their money.

OREGON

Eureka

Klamath
River

Sacramento
River

American
River

Lake
Tahoe

NEVADA

Sacramento

San Francisco
Oakland

San
José

San Joaquin
River

PACIFIC
OCEAN

Fresno

CALIFORNIA

Bakersfield

Colorado
River

3 Los Angeles

Anaheim

1

Salton
Sea

3 **A Community Business** (page 274)
Businesses like El Dorado Foods in Los
Angeles provide goods, services, and jobs
to people in a community.

San Diego

2

MEXICO

Earning and Spending

VOCABULARY

consumer
income
budget
expenses
savings account
interest

VOCABULARY STRATEGY

PREFIXES Knowing prefixes can help you with new words. **Ex-** means "out of." Which term in the list begins with **ex-**?

READING STRATEGY

Identify Cause and Effect

Use the chart below to show how people's needs affect what they do with their money.

Start with Your
CALIFORNIA STANDARDS

3.5 Students demonstrate basic economic reasoning skills and an understanding of the economy of the local region.

3.5.3 Understand that individual economic choices involve trade-offs and the evaluation of benefits and costs.

Learn how people decide to spend and save their money. (Begins on page 260)

3.5.4 Discuss the relationship of students' "work" in school and their human capital.

Think about how your work in school prepares you for your work in the future. (Begins on page 260)

California's communities provide a lot of jobs for the people who live in them. How many jobs? In 2004 there were almost 17 million jobs in California.

People Need Money 3.5 3.5.3

What has your family spent money on lately? Maybe you bought new sneakers or went to an amusement park. Maybe your parents or guardian paid someone to fix the family car. Each time that you and your family buy something or pay someone to do a job, you are **consumers**. A consumer is any person who buys things he or she needs or wants.

Anaheim

Consumers need money to buy the things they need and want. *Needs* are things you cannot live without, like food and clothing. *Wants* are things you don't really need but are nice to have. In this lesson you will read about Theo and his family. They live in Anaheim. They made a plan to help them decide how to spend the money they earn so they could get the things they need and want.

REVIEW Name something you bought recently that was a *want*. *Cause and Effect*

◄ At a fair like this one, families would have many choices to make about spending.

Earning Money 3.5.3 3.5.4

People get the money they need by working to earn it. People in a community might work at many different kinds of jobs. They might be construction workers, bankers, teachers, or truck drivers. Theo's dad works as a bus driver. His mother works at a doctor's office.

Wherever they work or whatever they do, people have jobs in order to earn an **income**. Income is money received for working. The amount of income someone earns depends on the job he or she does.

Perhaps you already know what you would like to do someday. Right now, your "job" is going to school. By going to school, by exploring different subjects, and by learning many skills, you are preparing to earn an income of your own one day.

Theo's parents work to earn an income, so they can buy things the family needs.

Theo wants a telescope. He dreams of being an astronomer one day. ▼

Making a Money Plan

Theo's family uses a **budget** to help them make smart spending choices. A budget is a plan for using money. A budget shows how much money is available and the ways it will be spent.

Theo likes astronomy. He wants a telescope so he can study the stars. His parents looked at their budget to see if they could afford it. In the budget, Theo's mom and dad wrote their total income for the month. They also wrote how much they will need for **expenses**. An expense is money spent to buy or do something. Theo's mom and dad set some money aside for savings. Then, they checked to see if there was money left to buy the telescope.

REVIEW How does a budget help a family plan their spending? *Summarize*

Family Budget

Income	Expenses	
	Needs	
Mom $1,756.00	Groceries	$375.00
	Clothing	$225.00
Dad $2,170.00	Rent	$1,400.00
	College fund	$150.00
	Wants	
	Fun things	$100.00

Choosing to Save 3.5 3.5.3

Theo's family saves some money for the future, too. They know they want money for Theo to go to college someday. They also want money for unexpected things, such as when the car needs to be fixed. So their budget includes a plan for saving money.

Theo's mom and dad have opened a **savings account**. A savings account is money that a person keeps in a bank. Theo's family puts some money into the savings account each month. The bank pays Theo's family a small amount of money each month, called **interest**. This gets added to the money the family saves. Little by little the money in the account grows.

Primary Sources

A section from **Poor Richard's Almanack** (1732–1757)
sayings by Benjamin Franklin,
politician, author, and inventor

- **Beware** of little expenses. A small leak will sink a great ship.
- Our **necessities** never equal our wants.
- He that goes borrowing goes a sorrowing.

---

beware be careful   **necessities** needs

Write About It! What did Benjamin Franklin think people should do with their money?

Benjamin Franklin

REVIEW How is a savings account helpful? *Summarize*

◀ **Theo hopes he'll make an important discovery about astronomy someday.**

What You Learned

3.5 **3.5.3** Consumers use money to buy the things they need or want.

3.5.3 **3.5.4** People work to earn an income so that they have money to buy things. Many people make a budget to keep track of their income and expenses.

3.5 **3.5.3** People often save money by putting it in a savings account in a bank.

Lesson Review

1. **Focus Question** What are some
3.5 ways people manage their money?

2. **Vocabulary** Write one sentence for
3.5 each vocabulary term.
   budget   income
   expenses   savings account

3. **Economics** What is an example of
3.5.3 an expense a family might have?

4. **Critical Thinking** **Make Decisions**
3.5.3 What might you say to a friend who says, "I really need that new CD!"

5. **Reading Strategy**
3.5.3 **Identify Cause and**
ELA **R2.3** **Effect** Reread page 262. Use the chart to show why Theo's family saves part of their money.

6. **Write about** **THE BIG IDEA** Write about
3.5.3 a time when you saved up for
ELA **W2.1** something you wanted.

7. **Link to Language Arts** Write a
3.5 paragraph about a job that you
ELA **W2.1** would like to have someday. What would be exciting about this job? Why do you want this job?

Make Decisions 3.5.3

A **decision** is a choice about what to do. You make many decisions every day. Some decisions, such as choosing what to eat for a snack, are easy. Choosing which camera to buy with money you saved is harder. Sometimes, when both choices are good things, it is not easy to know which to choose. Then it is wise to think about your **goals**. A goal is something you want to accomplish. You should also think about the result of each choice.

VOCABULARY

decision
goal

1 Learn It

Follow these steps to help you make good decisions.

- Decide what goals are important to you.

- Identify the different choices, or options, you have. You will not know what the best choice is until you know what your choices are. When you are making a decision about what to buy, you can choose one product or service over another, or you can choose not to buy anything.

- Think about the possible results of each choice. If you choose one option, will the results be different than if you chose another option?

- Select the best choices to meet your goal.

2 Try It

Read the paragraph and then answer the questions below.

Jim has been saving up for four months to get a new skateboard. He also wants to get his sister a birthday present. Jim knows his sister really wants a radio. If Jim buys his skateboard, he won't have enough money left for the radio. He could buy his sister something less expensive than the radio, but she may not want it. He could buy her the radio and save up another month and then get the skateboard. Jim has a decision to make.

■ What goals are important to Jim?

■ What are the choices Jim has?

■ Tell what might happen with each choice.

■ How can knowing your goals help you make decisions?

3 Apply It

Suppose you are in charge of planning a family vacation. You may travel to any place in the United States, but you can only go to one place.

■ What is your goal for this vacation?

■ What choices do you have?

■ Where will you decide to go? Why?

Making Money Choices

FOCUS QUESTION

What are some things to think about when you decide to buy something?

VOCABULARY

cost
benefit
trade-off
opportunity cost

VOCABULARY STRATEGY

WORD FAMILIES
The word **benefit** comes from the Latin word meaning "good." What do you think benefit means?

READING STRATEGY

Compare and Contrast

Use the diagram below to compare the choices Grace has in the lesson.

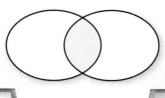

Start with Your
CALIFORNIA STANDARDS

3.5 Students demonstrate basic economic reasoning skills and an understanding of the economy of the local region.

3.5.3 Understand that individual economic choices involve trade-offs and the evaluation of benefits and costs.

Learn how people make choices about what to buy. (Begins on page 268)

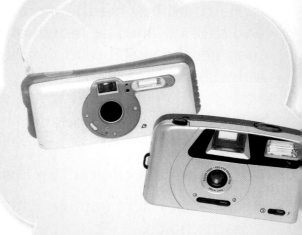

How can I decide which one to buy?

The Brownie camera was introduced in 1900. It cost just $1, and the film cost 15 cents. Soon, nearly everyone was taking pictures!

Choosing What to Buy 3.5 3.5.3

Back in 1900, the Brownie was the camera everyone wanted. Today, we have many choices. When was the last time you bought something? What made you decide to buy it? Every day we are faced with choices about how we spend money. In this lesson you will read about some ways to make wise money choices.

Grace lives in San Diego. She saved her allowance, and she received some money for her birthday. Now Grace has $30 and wants to buy a camera. She's having a hard time deciding which camera to buy.

At the store Grace sees two cameras that she likes. She has enough money to buy either one. Both cameras take good pictures and both have automatic focus. Both use the same kind of film. How can Grace decide which camera to buy?

San Diego

REVIEW How are the two cameras that Grace sees alike?
Compare and Contrast

Comparing Costs and Benefits ⬤3.5.3

Before choosing what to buy, it is a good idea to compare. That is what Grace did. She thought the first camera was really cool! It comes in blue, purple, and pink, her favorite color. It has a wrist cord, too. The second camera comes only in silver and it doesn't have a cord.

Next, Grace looked at the **cost**, the amount she would have to pay for the camera. The first camera costs $30. The second camera costs $20.

Then Grace looked at the **benefits** of each camera. A benefit is something that helps a person. Both cameras have automatic focus and take good pictures. The $30 camera has other benefits, too. Its cord makes it easier to carry. And pink is Grace's favorite color! However, the silver camera costs only $20. If she buys that one, Grace will have money left over.

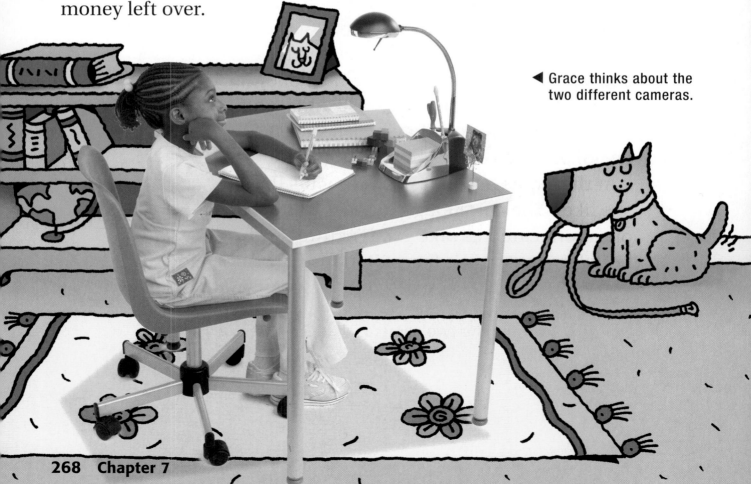

◀ Grace thinks about the two different cameras.

Grace makes a list to compare her choices. ▶

Pink Camera	Silver Camera
My favorite color	Silver not as cool
Takes good pictures	Takes good pictures
Automatic focus	Automatic focus
Takes 35mm film	Takes 35mm film
Wrist cord	No cord
Costs $30	Costs only $20

Making a Choice

Grace liked the pink camera. She liked the cord, but she knew she could carry the camera in her backpack. In addition, she knew the silver camera takes pictures as well as the pink one.

Grace bought the silver camera for $20. She will not have the color she first wanted, and she will not have a cord, but she does have money left over. With the extra money, she can buy some film.

Choices about spending money always involve **trade-offs**. A trade-off means that you give up one thing you want when you choose another. Grace gave up the pink camera in order to have money left for film. In a way, not getting the pink camera or the cord is part of the cost of being able to buy film. It is the **opportunity cost**, which means what she gave up by picking one thing over another.

REVIEW Compare what Grace would get with each camera. *Compare and Contrast*

269

Communities and Money Choices 3.5.3

In the last lesson, you saw how a family made a budget to help them decide how to spend their income. In this lesson you saw how a person might weigh the costs and benefits of different choices.

Communities also have budgets and have to decide how to spend money. A community may not have enough money in the budget to do everything it would like to do. It might have to choose between buying more books for the library and constructing a new playground in the park. Learning how to make wise money choices is an important part of everyone's life.

REVIEW What choices might a community make about spending money? *Summarize*

◀ Grace took these pictures in her community.

What You Learned

3.5
3.5.3 Spending money means making choices.

3.5.3 When you make a choice, you need to look at both the costs and the benefits of your choices.

3.5.3 When you buy something, you often make a trade-off, giving up one thing when you choose another.

Lesson Review

1. **Focus Question** What are some
3.5.3 things to think about when you decide to buy something?

2. **Vocabulary** Write one sentence for
3.5.3 each vocabulary term.

   benefit   opportunity cost
   cost   trade-off

3. **Citizenship** Who do you think
3.5.3 makes decisions about how your community spends money? How could you find out?

4. **Critical Thinking Problem Solving**
3.5.3 How does Grace solve the problem of making her decision about the camera?

5. **Reading Strategy Compare and**
3.5.2 **Contrast** If the pink camera was
ELA
R.2.0 $5 cheaper, do you think Grace would have bought it? Use the diagram to compare the choices Grace would have then.

6. **Write about** THE BIG IDEA Write about
3.5.3 a time you chose between two
ELA
W.2.1 things to buy. Tell whether you were happy with your decision.

7. **Link to Drama** Work with a partner
3.5.3 to plan a skit about shopping for something. In the skit use the terms *cost, benefit,* and *trade-off* as you decide between two things.

CITIZENSHIP
POINTS OF VIEW

Why Is It Important to Save? 3.5.3

There are good reasons to save money, but saving is not easy. It is hard to decide when to spend money on present needs and when to save for future needs. What makes people decide to save money? Read below to find three different points of view on why saving money is important.

"If you don't save money, you won't be able to pay for important things you might need. I save money to buy lunch at school and school supplies like a backpack."

Riane Garcia
Whittier, California
From an interview, 2004

"Some day you might want to buy your own car. If you save money, you'll have plenty. I just put money in my piggy bank and leave it alone so I won't be anxious to spend it."

Robert Bryant
Altadena, California
From an interview, 2004

"Saving money can affect your future. You can get educated and go to a good college. Someday I will start saving so my children will be able to have opportunities."

Philip Yu
Los Angeles, California
From an interview, 2004

Build Citizenship
Responsibility

1. What are some reasons for saving money?

2. How does saving money help in planning for the future?

3. The speakers talk about both their needs and their wants. Which do you think it is easier to save money for—needs or wants?

Think About It
Points of View

1. Why does Riane Garcia think it is important to save money?

2. Why does Philip Yu think it is important to save for the future?

3. What other points of view might people have about this question?

Write About It!

Ask three people if they have any suggestions for how to save money. Explain their answers in a paragraph or make a list of their ideas for saving money.

A Community Business

FOCUS QUESTION

What things does a business owner have to think about to make a profit?

VOCABULARY

producer
free enterprise
profit
employee
human
 resources
competition

VOCABULARY STRATEGY

SUFFIXES The suffix -**er** means "one who does something." Which term from the list means "one who produces"?

READING STRATEGY

Summarize
Use the chart below to summarize the important ideas in the lesson.

Start with Your
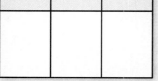
CALIFORNIA STANDARDS

3.5 Students demonstrate basic economic reasoning skills and an understanding of the economy of the local region.

3.5.1 Describe the ways in which local producers have used and are using natural resources, human resources, and capital resources to produce goods and services in the past and in the present.

Meet the owners of a community business.
(Begins on page 276)

3.5.2 Understand that some goods are made locally, some elsewhere in the United States, and some abroad.

Learn about a product that is made locally.
(Begins on page 276)

Lincoln Heights,
Los Angeles ▼

When she was seven, Taylor Crabtree started making and selling hair clips. With the profits, she bought teddy bears for people who have cancer. Today she has raised more than $100,000 and given away more than 20,000 teddy bears.

Minding a Business 3.5.1

Many people earn money by operating their own business. Some businesses are **producers**. A producer makes and sells a product. The business might sell its product to another business or it might sell the product directly to consumers like you. The product could also be a service, such as cleaning houses or delivering packages.

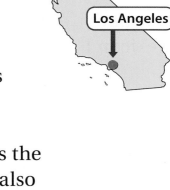

Los Angeles

In the United States, people can operate any kind of business they want to, as long as the business is allowed by law. Consumers can also buy whatever they choose and can afford. They can buy these things from whomever they want. The freedom to make these choices is called **free enterprise**.

Let's look at a small business in Los Angeles. It is called El Dorado Mexican Foods.

REVIEW Give examples of some things a producer makes.
Summarize

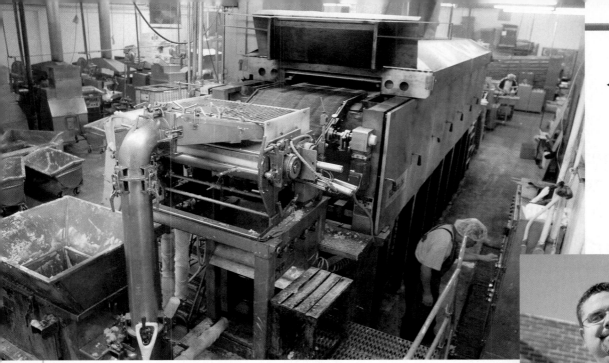

◀ Machines and the electricity to run them are business expenses.

▲ Philip Manly

A Family Business ⓧⓧ

Do you ever make tacos at home? If so, you may have used a product made by El Dorado Mexican Foods. El Dorado is a family business that makes and sells tortillas, tamales, and other food products. It was started in 1946 by Bernardo Gutirerrez and Helen Lugo. Today the business is run by their grandchildren, Philip and Chris Manly.

All businesses have expenses. For example, before El Dorado can make tortillas, they must buy the flour and other ingredients. They also had to buy machines to help make the tortillas. They have to pay for the electricity to run the machines. They also must pay rent on the building that their business is in.

The amount of money left after all the costs of operating the business have been paid is called the **profit**. In order to make money, the Manlys have to make sure that the money El Dorado takes in from sales adds up to more than its expenses.

Hiring Helpers

Of course, Phil and Chris can't do all the work themselves. So they employ, or hire people to help them. These people are called **employees**. The employees earn income by working for El Dorado. Paying the employees is another expense of the business.

Carlos Torres is a production supervisor. He keeps track of which markets and restaurants have ordered products like tortillas and tamales, and he keeps track of how much they've ordered. He figures out how long it will take to make the food, and then makes sure it's finished on time. Salvador Gonzalez runs the machine that cooks the tortillas. Arturo Sanchez is a grinder. He runs the machine that grinds the corn into masa.

El Dorado could not operate its business without Carlos, Salvador, and all of its other employees. The people, their ideas, and their labor are the **human resources** that El Dorado Foods uses.

REVIEW What are some jobs the employees at El Dorado Foods do? *Summarize*

◀ The tortillas are ready for sale.

277

Making Tortillas

1 Corn is harvested.

2 Corn is washed and then ground to form masa.

3 The masa is pressed into a thin sheet. Then it is cut into the round shape of tortillas.

Producers and Products 3.5.2

Where does El Dorado Foods get ingredients like corn and flour—the things they need to make their tortillas, tamales, and other products? They need to buy so much corn and flour that they can't just get them at the market, the way your family might when cooking a meal at home.

Instead El Dorado Foods gets things they need from different producers. El Dorado buys flour from flour mills. Some of the flour mills are in other states. They buy corn from a producer in Texas. The products are all shipped to El Dorado. Without these producers, El Dorado would not be able to make the products they sell.

4 The tortillas are baked. After they leave the oven, they are cooled.

5 The tortillas are put into packages to be sold.

Serving the Customers

El Dorado sells some of its products directly to families. It also sells its products to stores and restaurants. Phil and Chris know that their customers do not have to buy from them. There are other businesses making the same products. These other businesses are in **competition** with them. That means they are trying to attract the same customers. Phil and Chris try to give their customers what they want. If they don't, people may buy from someone else!

To be sure the tortillas get to the stores and restaurants where they will be sold, El Dorado has a delivery service. "People want to be able to buy a good, fresh tortilla," Phil says. "That's why we get ours out to stores on the day they're made."

REVIEW What does El Dorado Foods do with its products after they are made? *Sequence Events*

The Business and the Community 3.5.1

El Dorado Mexican Foods is in Lincoln Heights, a neighborhood in Los Angeles. Even a small business like El Dorado is an important part of the economy of the neighborhood. Many of El Dorado's employees live in the neighborhood. People from the neighborhood come to El Dorado to buy their products. The products are sold to restaurants and stores in other parts of Los Angeles, and in other California cities, too.

Phil remembers visiting his grandfather's factory when he was a boy. "I always remember the smell of the cooking corn, and taking hot tortillas off the conveyors. I thought that was the neatest thing." Little did he dream that someday the business would be his.

REVIEW Why is El Dorado Foods an important part of its neighborhood? *Summarize*

El Dorado makes sure its products are delivered fresh. ▼

◄ Tortillas are part of
many delicious foods.

What You Learned

3.5.1 Some businesses earn money by selling products to make a profit.

3.5.1
3.5.2 Businesses have expenses, such as rent, electricity, and paying employees.

3.5.2 Businesses use natural resources, and human resources to make products. Businesses depend on other producers to make things they need.

3.5.1 A business is an important part of its community.

Lesson Review

1. Focus Question What things does a **3.5.1** business owner have to think about to make a profit?

2. Vocabulary Write one sentence for **3.5** each vocabulary word.
3.5.1

competition   producer
employee   profit

3. Economics Why do you think it **3.5.1** would be important for a business like El Dorado to use a budget?

4. Critical Thinking Make Decisions **3.5.1** What things could you do to prepare now for owning a business someday?

5. Reading Strategy
3.5.2 **Summarize** Reread
ELA
R2.3 page 280. Use the chart to summarize the information in the section.

6. Write about THE BIG IDEA How does **3.5.2** a business like El Dorado help the **ELA** **W1.1** community meet its needs?

7. Link to Language Arts Work in a **3.5.2** small group to write a TV commercial **ELA** **W2.1** for El Dorado Foods. In your ad, give information about the products and why people would want to buy them. Then act out your commercial for your class.

BAKERSFIELD

Businesses in Your Community 3.5.1

Peter lives in Bakersfield. He learned about businesses in his community by interviewing people and making an accordion book about what he found out. Here's what you can do to learn about businesses in your community:

- Make a list of businesses or jobs in your community that interest you.

- Think of questions you would want to ask people about working in those businesses.

- Have an adult come with you to interview people at three different businesses in your community. Write down what each worker tells you. If you have a camera, ask if you can take pictures of them at work.

LOG ON For more help in making your accordion book, visit:

www.macmillanmh.com/ss/ca/local

Make an Accordion Book

Step 1 Gather the notes and photographs you took during the interviews.

Step 2 To make your book, start with a large piece of stiff paper. Paper about 36" long by 8" wide is a good size. Fold the paper into even parts.

Step 3 On each page, write the name of a worker you interviewed and paste a photo of the person. Summarize the things the worker told you, and write them below the photo or on the back. Make a cover for your book. Give your book a title.

Step 4 Share your book with your classmates.

Materials
- notebook
- pencil or pen
- camera
- stiff paper
- markers
- scissors
- glue
- oaktag or posterboard

1. Construction Worker
2. Librarian
3. Banker
4. Shop Owner
5. Police person

Vocabulary Review

Copy the sentences below on a separate sheet of paper. Use the list of vocabulary words to fill in the blanks.

benefit	producer
cost	profit

1. The _____ is the amount of
3.5.3 money left after the costs of running a business are paid.

2. A _____ is something that
3.5.3 helps a person.

3. A person or business that
3.5.1 makes and sells a product is a _____ .

4. The _____ is the amount you
3.5.3 pay for things.

5. Test Preparation Money received
3.5.1 for working is _____ .

   A. interest   **C.** opportunity cost
   B. employee   **D.** income

Comprehension Check

6. How are needs and wants
3.5.2 different?

7. Why do people need an
3.5.2 income?

8. Why are savings accounts
3.5.2 important?

9. Explain what free enterprise is
3.5.3 and how it works.

10. How do businesses help
3.5.2 communities?

11. Critical Thinking How is
3.5.2 competition good for customers?

12. Critical Thinking Why is it good
3.5.3 to compare costs and benefits?

Read the passage. Then write a complete sentence to answer each question.

Make Decisions

Anna's mother says that Anna can have a pet, but it must be clean, quiet, and easy to care for. Anna is trying to choose between a dog, a parrot, and a guinea pig. Anna knows that dogs can bark and they need a lot of care. She thinks parrots are beautiful and it would be fun to teach one to talk. She did some research and found that parrots can be noisy. They also can make a mess with their seeds. Anna knows guinea pigs are usually quiet. They are friendly, too. Anna's friend has an extra guinea pig cage she can have, so Anna wouldn't need to buy a cage.

13. What goal is important to **3.5.3** Anna? What are her choices, or options?

14. Make a list of the good points **3.5.3** and bad points for each option.

15. Test Preparation A choice about **3.5.3** what to do is a _____ .

16. Test Preparation A _____ **3.5.3** is something you want to accomplish.

Book Excerpts

17. What do you think Franklin **3.5.3** meant by saying "Beware of little expenses"?

18. What did Franklin think of **3.5.3** borrowing money?

19. Plan a Product or Service
3.5.2 Work in a group and think
ELA about a product or service your
W1.0 school or community needs. Research what you would need to do to make the product or provide the service. Create a plan that tells what is needed and why.

20. Descriptive Think about **3.5.3** something you might want **ELA** to buy. Write a paragraph **W2.2** describing how you would go about making a choice.

LOG ON For help with the process of writing, visit:

www.macmillanmh.com/ss/ca/writing

Communities Produce Goods

YOU ARE THERE

In this chapter you will read about how people and businesses in communities work to produce things that people need and want. You will also read how communities trade to get other products.

PACIFIC OCEAN

OREGON

Eureka

Klamath River

Sacramento River

American River

Lake Tahoe

San Francisco

Oakland

3

Santa Cruz

2

NEVADA

Sacramento

San Joaquin River

Fresno

1

CALIFORNIA

Bakersfield

Colorado River

Los Angeles

Long Beach

Salton Sea

San Diego

MEXICO

3 Communities Trade with Each Other (page 312)
Oakland is one of the largest trading communities in California.

287

FOCUS QUESTION

How do California farmers help provide what people need?

VOCABULARY

human resources
demand
supply
capital resources
food processing
union

VOCABULARY STRATEGY

ROOT WORDS The word **union** comes from the Latin word for one. In a union, many workers speak with one voice.

READING STRATEGY

Identify Cause and Effect

Use the chart below to show how the supply of crops and the demand for foods affects what you pay.

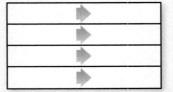

A Farming Community

Start with Your
CALIFORNIA STANDARDS

3.5 Students demonstrate basic economic reasoning skills and an understanding of the economy of the local region.

3.5.1 Describe the ways in which local producers have used and are using natural resources, human resources, and capital resources to produce goods and services in the past and the present.

Learn how California farmers produce goods for their communities, and how other workers provide services for farmers. (Begins on page 289)

3.5.2 Understand that some goods are made locally, some elsewhere in the United States, and some abroad.

Discover how farmers in different parts of the world are able to grow similar crops. (page 294)

Harvesting grapes
in Fresno ▼

★ ☆ ★

Each harvest season about 50,000 California workers cut bunches of grapes. Most workers harvest 8,000 to 10,000 pounds of grapes each day.

Farming in Fresno 3.5.1

In the last chapter, you read that people work to earn money. In California, many people earn money in agriculture. Agriculture is the business of growing crops or raising animals for food. Agriculture is a huge business in California. More food is grown in California than in any other state.

The community of Fresno is in the heart of California's farming region. The area around Fresno has rich soil, nearby water, and hot dry summers, important natural resources for farming. It's the perfect place to grow grapes, cotton, tomatoes, and many other crops. Let's take a look at how people live and work in this farming community.

Fresno

REVIEW What makes the Fresno area a perfect place for growing certain crops? *Cause and Effect*

STATE CENTER BRAND
CALIFORNIA
MAIN OFFICE FRESNO CAL.
PAUL A. MOSESIAN & SONS, INC.
GROWERS · PACKERS · SHIPPERS
REG. U.S. PAT. OFF.
NT. WGHT.

Working on a Farm 3.5.1

Natural resources, such as rich soil, are not enough to make a farm or any business successful. Farms need **human resources**, too. Human resources are people, including owners and workers, who work for a business.

Cher Sue and Bor Yang Lor own a small farm near Fresno. In 1989 they came to California from Laos, a country in Asia. In Laos, Bor Yang and Cher Sue grew Asian vegetables such as bok choy and long beans. In Fresno, they grow many of the same crops. Their 13 children all help out on the farm. That is a lot of human resources!

Because many people from Asia live in the Fresno area, there is a high **demand** for the family's vegetables. Demand is the number of people who want certain goods or services. Because not many farms near Fresno grow Asian vegetables, the **supply**, or the amount of goods available, is low.

Bor Yang (left) and her daughter (right) sell their vegetables at the Farmers Market in Aptos, California.

▲ Tractors are a kind of capital resource.

When demand is high and the supply is low, a farmer or business person can charge more for his or her goods or service. The Lors have no trouble finding customers for what they grow. They are able to sell their crops for a profit.

Machines for Farming

Capital resources are an important part of farming and other businesses, too. Capital resources are the tools and machines people use to produce goods. Most farms in California, even small farms like the Lors', use some capital resources. The Lors use a tractor. Other farms use computers to track weather and water usage.

REVIEW When demand for a farmer's vegetables is low, should he or she raise or lower prices? *Cause and Effect*

Farm-related Jobs 3.5.1

Not everyone in the Fresno area is a farmer. Some people work in businesses that provide services for farmers. Richard Molinar and Michael Yang work for a Fresno County government office. They help farmers who come to Fresno from other countries learn what works best on farms in the dry climate of Fresno county. Molinar and Yang also help solve other problems. "Farmers bring sick plants in. We try to identify the problem, whether it's insects or disease. We find ways to solve the problem," says Yang.

▲ Richard Molinar (left) and Michael Yang (center) help a farmer.

Turning Grapes into Raisins

Other people in the Fresno area work in the **food processing** business. In food processing, people take a crop and change it by cooking, drying, or preserving it. Putting tomatoes in cans or turning wheat into flour and then into bread are examples of food processing.

Grapes are cut by hand. ▶

Raisins are a big processed food in Fresno. Raisins begin as grapes. Grapes thrive in Fresno's rich soil and sunny climate. When the plump grapes are ready to pick, farm owners hire workers to pick them. The workers lay bunches of grapes on paper to dry in the sun. It is hard work. Many of the workers are members of a **union**. A union is a group of workers who join together to improve their working conditions. The farm workers union was started by César Chávez.

After a few weeks, the grapes dry out and become raisins. The raisins are packed into big boxes, loaded onto trucks, and taken to a food processing factory. At the factory, the raisins are inspected. Next, a large machine removes all of the stems. Another machine washes the raisins. Finally, another machine puts the raisins into small boxes for sale in stores. Raisins from the Fresno area are shipped all over the world.

REVIEW What are some of the natural, human, and capital resources involved in making raisins? *Summarize*

The grapes are put on paper to dry in the sun. ▼

New Crops for California Farmers 3.5.1 3.5.2

Growing the right crop in the right place is important. However, to make a profit, a farmer should grow a crop in high demand. Richard Molinar helped some Fresno farmers learn that capers were a promising crop. Capers are flower buds from the caper plant. There is a big demand for capers in restaurants. Cooks use them in sauces and seasonings. At one time, few California farmers grew capers. Today, small farmers in Fresno County who followed Molinar's advice, are making money by selling capers.

◄ Caper branch

REVIEW What might happen if every farmer in the Fresno area started growing capers? *Draw Conclusions*

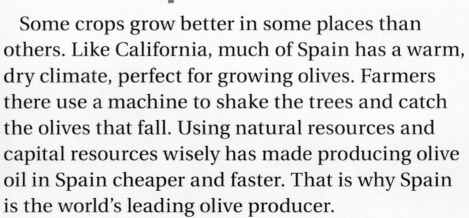
◄ Capers

Global Connections

Spain

Olives in Spain

Some crops grow better in some places than others. Like California, much of Spain has a warm, dry climate, perfect for growing olives. Farmers there use a machine to shake the trees and catch the olives that fall. Using natural resources and capital resources wisely has made producing olive oil in Spain cheaper and faster. That is why Spain is the world's leading olive producer.

How do Spanish farmers harvest olives cheaper and faster?

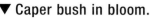
▼ Caper bush in bloom.

3.5.1 The climate around Fresno, California, makes it a perfect place for a farming community.

3.5.1 Farms in the Fresno area use natural resources, human resources, and capital resources, to produce crops.

3.5.1 Some workers in Fresno provide support for farmers and farm workers, while others work in food processing.

3.5.1
3.5.2 California farmers try new crops to meet market demand.

Lesson Review

1. Focus Question How do California
3.5.1 farmers help provide what people need?

2. Vocabulary Write one sentence for
3.5.1 each vocabulary term.

demand	supply
food processing	union

3. Economics What might Bor Yang
3.5.1 do if the demand for her vegetables dropped?

4. Critical Thinking Problem
3.5.1 **Solving** Why did Richard Molinar
3.5.2 want small farmers in Fresno to try growing capers?

5. Reading Strategy Identify Cause
3.5.1 **and Effect** Reread "New
3.5.2 Crops for California
ELA Farmers," on page 294.
R2.3 Use the chart to show the effect of Richard Molinar's advice to farmers.

6. Write about THE BIG IDEA Which
3.5.1 other people in a farm community,
ELA besides farmers, have jobs that
W2.0 depend on farms? How are their jobs connected?

7. Link to Science Rainfall is important
3.5.1 to farmers. Use the Internet or your library to find out how much rain usually falls in Fresno each month. Which months are the wettest? Which are the driest?

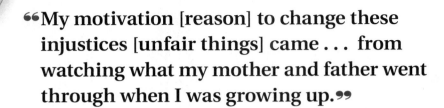
"My motivation [reason] to change these injustices [unfair things] came . . . from watching what my mother and father went through when I was growing up."

César Chávez 1927–1993

As a boy, César Chávez spent many happy days on his grandfather's farm in Arizona. It was the Great Depression, a hard time for our country. When César's family could not pay their bills, they had to give up their farm. They left for California to find work.

They found work traveling from farm to farm picking crops. The pay was low, and workers lived in crowded camps with no running water or electricity. If workers complained, they would lose their jobs.

César read about leaders like Martin Luther King, Jr., and Mahatma Gandhi of India. They brought people together to work for justice and never used violence to get their way. César thought he could help farm workers in the same way.

The Life of César Chávez

1925		1945		1965	
	1927 César Chávez born near Yuma, Arizona	**1938** Chávez family lost their farm during Great Depression		**1962** Formed union for farm workers	**1966** Led 340 mile march to support union

In 1962, César Chávez and Dolores Huerta formed a union, the National Farm Workers Association. Now farm workers could work together for better treatment. Many farm owners did not want the union. Some used violence against the union, but Chávez refused to answer violence with violence. Instead, he asked consumers to boycott, or refuse to buy, grapes. People all over the country boycotted grapes. The growers lost money.

Finally, in 1970, grape growers agreed to give workers more pay and better working and living conditions. The union later won many other victories for the rights of farm workers.

César Chávez died in 1993. His birthday is now a California state holiday, so everyone can honor a man who worked for justice.

▲ Presidential Medal of Freedom

Chávez in Salinas, 1972 ▼

Write About It! How did César Chávez win better treatment for California farm workers?

1985		2005
1993 Died in San Luiz, Arizona	1994 Awarded the Presidential Medal of Freedom	

LOG ON

For more information about César Chávez, visit:

www.macmillanmh.com/ss/ca/bios

A Farm Child in 1910 3.5.1

There was always something to do on a farm! Children had regular chores. Animals had to be given food and water. Children helped with chores in the house, too. In the past, many farm children only went to school when they didn't have to help with planting or picking the crops.

Children helped process food, such as peaches. ▼

▲ Hand-cranked freezers like this made homemade ice cream.

▲ Even after gas-powered tractors were invented, many farmers still used horse-drawn machines.

▲ Children of different ages studied together in one-room schools.

Write About It!

Suppose you were a visitor on a farm in 1910. Write a postcard home telling about your visit.

LOG ON

For more about farm life in 1910, visit:

www.macmillanmh.com/ss/ca/dayinthelife

Use Flow Charts 3.5.1

Do you like strawberry jam? Have you ever made jam at home? There are several steps to follow to turn fruit into jam. These steps have to be done in a certain order. A **flow chart** shows the different steps necessary to complete an activity. It can help you understand and remember the steps in the right order.

VOCABULARY

flow chart

1 Learn It

Look at the chart below as you read about using a flow chart.

- Read the title of the chart. This flow chart shows the steps to turn fruit into jam.

- Look at the pictures and read the labels. Both the pictures and the labels give information.

- The arrows and numbers show the order of the steps. Read the steps in number order and follow the arrows. You can see that the strawberries must be washed before they are cooked.

Make Jam

1. Pick strawberries
2. Wash strawberries
3. Cook strawberries
4. Add sugar and pectin
5. Jar and seal jam

2 Try It

Answer the questions by reading the flow chart on this page.

- What does the chart show?

- How many steps are there in the activity? What is the first step? What is the last step?

- What does the picture tell you about how farmers harvest corn?

- What happens after the corn is harvested?

3 Apply It

Make your own flow chart to show the steps in a process that you know well. Draw a picture for each step. Then write a label to go with each picture. Use arrows and numbers to show the order of the steps. Do you know how to bake a cake, plant a garden, or make papier-mâché? Show how you do it with a flow chart.

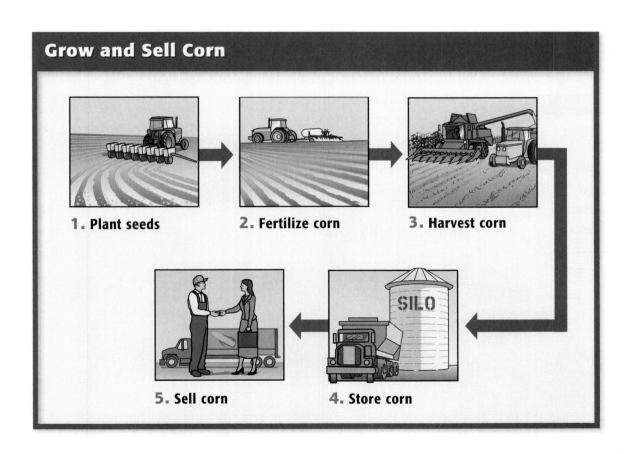

Grow and Sell Corn

1. Plant seeds
2. Fertilize corn
3. Harvest corn
5. Sell corn
4. Store corn

VOCABULARY

**factory
manufacturing
assembly line**

VOCABULARY STRATEGY

COMPOUND WORDS To **assemble** something means to put it together. An **assembly line** is people working to put a product together.

READING STRATEGY

Identify Main Idea and Details

As you read, use the chart below to list the main ideas and details in this lesson.

How Goods Are Made

Start with Your
CALIFORNIA STANDARDS

3.5 Students demonstrate basic economic reasoning skills and an understanding of the economy of the local region.

3.5.1 Describe the ways in which local producers have used and are using natural resources, human resources, and capital resources to produce goods and services in the past and the present.

Find out how California companies make skateboards. (Begins on page 303)

3.5.2 Understand that some goods are made locally, some elsewhere in the United States, and some abroad.

Explore how manufacturers buy goods locally and from producers in other states or countries. (page 306)

Building
a spacecraft ▼

Did you know that more products are made in California than in any other state in the country? From computer chips to chocolate chip cookies, California makes all sorts of things!

Made in California 3.5.2

In Lesson 1 you read that California is a great place for agriculture. California is also known for making many things. Machines, clothes, toys, sports equipment, and many other things are made in California's **factories**. A factory is a place where products are made.

The business of making or processing something is called **manufacturing**. In the past, most manufacturing was done by hand in small workshops. Today, most manufacturing uses machines. In many factories, people work alongside robots and other machines.

REVIEW How has manufacturing changed over time? *Main Idea and Details*

A worker watches a robot build airplane parts. ▶

1 The wood is inspected.

2 Seven layers of maple wood are glued together in a press.

Making Skateboards 3.5.1

If you have a skateboard, it was probably manufactured in California. Factories here make thousands of skateboards each day. Many of them are made in Santa Cruz.

Santa Cruz

A skateboard has three parts: the deck, the trucks, and the wheels. The deck is the board you stand on. The trucks are the parts that connect the wheels to the deck.

Working Together

Skateboard decks are made on an **assembly line**. An assembly line is a line of people and machines that work together to make a product. Each worker and machine in an assembly line does one step in the process.

◄ A skateboard has three main parts: deck, trucks, and wheels.

3 The wood is cut into a skateboard shape. Holes are drilled for trucks and wheels.

4 The skateboard is painted and decorated.

In the past, just a few people might work together to manufacture something as big as a car. It took a long time to make something this way.

Workers on an assembly line, however, can make more products in less time than if everyone works alone. The less time it takes to make something, the less it costs to make the product. So products made in assembly lines are less expensive to buy.

Each part of the skateboard is made separately. Decks are made from pieces of maple wood and take about a day to manufacture. Other companies in California manufacture trucks, and still others manufacture wheels. In a store, a skateboarder can purchase the deck, wheels, and trucks separately.

5 The finished decks are inspected and packaged. Boxes of decks are sent to companies and stores to sell.

REVIEW Why are skateboard decks made in assembly lines?
Make Inferences

Using Resources to Make Things 3.5.1 3.5.2

To make its products, a skateboard company uses natural resources, capital resources, and human resources. The company needs maple wood, a natural resource, to make the deck. The company also needs machines to cut and shape the wood. These machines, and the factory building they are in, are capital resources. Without human resources, however, the skateboards could not be made. People design, cut, shape, and paint the skateboards.

Businesses try to buy the natural resources they need for as low a price as possible. Sometimes that means buying natural resources from local businesses. Other times it means buying from businesses far away. A skateboard company in Santa Cruz, for example, might get its maple wood from Canada.

REVIEW What might happen to the price of skateboards if there was not enough maple wood? *Draw Conclusions*

◀ Many skateboard decks are made from Canadian maple trees.

What You Learned

3.5.2 Many products are manufactured in California factories.

3.5.1 People and machines work together in assembly lines to make products quickly.

3.5.1
3.5.2 Producers in California use local materials and materials from outside the state to make their products.

Lesson Review

1. **Focus Question** How do producers
3.5.1 manufacture goods?

2. **Vocabulary** Write one sentence for
3.5 each vocabulary term.

   **assembly line   manufacturing
   factory**

3. **Geography** How might the kinds
3.5.1 of natural resources that a place has affect what a local producer can make?

4. **Critical Thinking** **Problem**
3.5 **Solving** Suppose you owned a skateboard factory. What would you do if another skateboard company was selling its skateboards at a lower price than you were?

5. **Reading Strategy** **Identify Main**
3.5.1 **Idea and Details**
3.5.2
ELA Reread page 306.
R2.3 Use the chart to show the main idea and details for the page.

6. **Write about THE BIG IDEA** Think of
3.5.1 other goods or service jobs that
ELA
W2.1 are connected to manufacturing skateboards, and tell how these jobs are connected.

7. **Link to Science** Maple trees
3.5.1 are hardwood trees. Find out which other trees are considered hardwoods, and which are considered softwoods. What is an important difference in the way the two kinds of trees grow?

The **LIBRARY**
of **CONGRESS**

Understanding Historic Photographs 3.5.1

Photographs are an important primary source. Photographs give us a record of daily life and let us see people, places, and events exactly as they were at a certain moment in history.

Photograph of an Airplane Factory Assembly Line, 1942

During World War II, airplane factories in Southern California built thousands of planes to help the United States win the war. The photograph on page 309 can help you understand what life— and manufacturing—were like at that time.

 1 Learn It

■ Read the caption for information.

■ Note where the photograph was taken. Was it indoors or outdoors?

■ Note any people in the photograph. What are they doing? Do you think they knew the photograph was being taken?

■ Look for other clues in the photograph, such as buildings, signs, tools, or animals.

■ Think about why the photograph was taken.

Study the photograph below.

flag

P-51s on
assembly
line

factory
workers

▲ P-51 Mustang fighters being
manufactured at a plant in
Inglewood, California, about 1942

■ Write a paragraph telling
what sounds you would
hear if you were there
when the photograph
was taken.

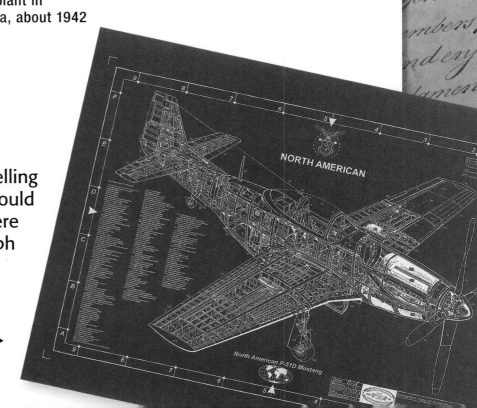

P-51 Mustang
blueprint ▶

Use Line Graphs 3.5.1

Many things are manufactured in California, from airplanes to computer chips. Suppose you wanted to find out how many people worked in manufacturing jobs in California for the last 50 years. A **line graph** could help you. A line graph shows information that changes over time.

VOCABULARY

line graph

1 Learn It

Look at the graph on this page as you follow the steps below.

- Look at the graph title and the labels to tell what the graph shows. The labels on the left show the number of manufacturing jobs. The dates along the bottom of the graph show the years being measured. This graph shows the number of people in California who worked in manufacturing jobs from 1950 to 2000.

- Look at the dots to see information for the years shown. In 1980, for example, there were 2 million manufacturing jobs in California.

- Trace the line connecting the dots to see changes over time. The graph shows that California had more people working in manufacturing in 2000 than in 1970.

California Manufacturing Jobs, 1950-2000

Jobs (in thousands)

2,500
2,000
1,500
1,000
500
0

1950 1960 1970 1980 1990 2000

Year

Source: *California Statistical Abstract, 2002*

2 Try It

Now look at the graph below.

- What type of graph is this?

- What does this graph show?

- About how many people worked in transportation in California in 1970?

- Did the number of people working in transportation go up or down between 1950 and 2000?

California Transportation Jobs*, 1950-2000

Jobs (in thousands) — vertical axis: 0, 500, 1,000, 1,500, 2,000, 2,500

Year — horizontal axis: 1950, 1960, 1970, 1980, 1990, 2000

Source: *California Statistical Abstract, 2002*
*Includes Jobs in Transportation and Utilities

3 Apply It

Make a line graph to show information about a third-grade class that printed and sold T-shirts.

- In the first week, the class sold 10 T-shirts; in the second week, 12 T-shirts; in the third week, 50 T-shirts; in the fourth week, 25 T-shirts; and in the fifth week, 20 T-shirts.

- What title will you give your graph?

- What information will you put along the bottom of the graph? What will you put along the side?

- In which week did the class sell the most T-shirts?

- What does the graph show about the class's sales?

◀ Workers building cars in Stockton, California

international trade
export
import
container

VOCABULARY STRATEGY

ROOT WORDS Import and **export** both come from the Latin word for carry. The prefix **im-** makes the word **import**, or carry **in**. What do you think **export** means?

READING STRATEGY

Identify Cause and Effect
Use the chart to show the effects of international trade on the city of Oakland.

▶	
▶	
▶	

Communities Trade with Each Other

Start with Your
CALIFORNIA STANDARDS

3.5 Students demonstrate basic economic reasoning skills and an understanding of the economy of the local region.

3.5.2 Understand that some goods are made locally, some elsewhere in the United States, and some abroad.

Discover how trade between nations helps the city of Oakland. (Begins on page 313)

Oakland's City Center ▼

These 200-foot high cranes were delivered to the Port of Oakland from China in 2002. They made it under the San Francisco-Oakland Bay Bridge—with just five feet to spare!

Trading Goods 3.5.2

Long ago, communities often made or grew most of the things they needed. Today most communities cannot do this. They rely on **international trade** to get the goods and services they need. International trade is trade between countries.

The United States is a major trading country. It **exports** many of the things it makes and grows. To export means to send goods to other countries to be sold. For example, the California raisins you read about in Lesson 1 are sold all over the world. The United States also **imports** things that are made or grown in other countries. To import means to bring goods in from other countries to be sold here. Let's take a closer look at Oakland, California. It is a port city that plays an important role in international trade.

Oakland

REVIEW What is one effect of being able to trade with other countries? *Cause and Effect*

▲ Ships from many countries dock at the Port of Oakland.

Oakland, a Port City 3.5.2

The Port of Oakland is a busy place. It has more than four miles of shoreline where ships can dock. Each day hundreds of **containers** pass through the port. A container is a steel box the size of a railroad car. It is used to carry goods.

Some containers arrive by sea on ships. These containers carry goods imported from other countries. The port's huge cranes lift the containers from the ships and place them onto trains or trucks. The trains and trucks then leave the port and bring the containers to communities all over the country.

Other containers arrive at Oakland by land, also on trains or trucks. These containers carry products from the United States that will be loaded onto ships and exported to other countries.

Trade and the Economy

Most of the goods imported through Oakland come from countries in Asia. The Pacific Ocean serves as a link between California ports, such as Oakland, Long Beach, and Los Angeles, and Japan, China, and Taiwan. Look at the Datagraphic on page 316 to read how goods from Asia come to Oakland and the United States.

The port is important to Oakland. Many workers in the city have jobs there. The port is also important to the United States economy. Read the Primary Source below. It tells about the role of the port in the United States economy.

▲ Containers get loaded right onto trucks.

Primary Sources

Jerry Bridges

Jerry Bridges, Executive Director of the Port of Oakland, 2004

❝We move about $26 billion worth of goods in and out of the United States each year. . . . Without seaports like the Port of Oakland, you might find some things missing from your home – sneakers, DVD players, cell phones, and some of the clothes in your closet, for example.❞

Write About It! What are some things that are imported through the Port of Oakland?

REVIEW How do goods enter and leave the Port of Oakland?

Sequence Events

Imports and Exports at the Port of Oakland 3.5.2

Ports bring communities together through trade. Imports from other countries arrive at the Port of Oakland. The United States also sends exports to other countries through the Port of Oakland. Read the graphs below and use the flow chart to follow how one import, automobile engines, travels from Japan to Ohio.

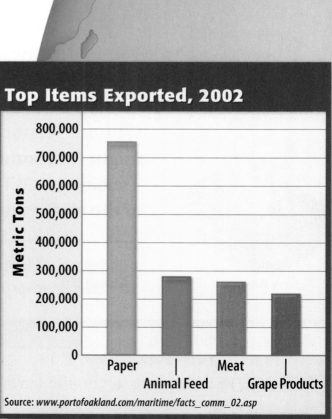

Japanese workers make car engines for export.

Japan

Top Countries Imports Came From, 2003

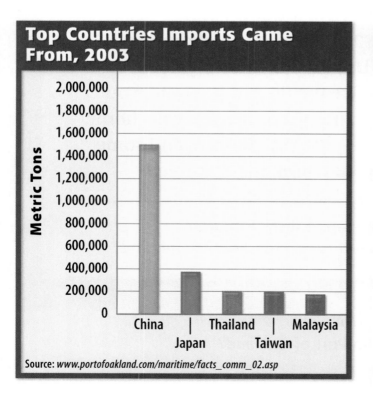

Metric Tons

2,000,000
1,800,000
1,600,000
1,400,000
1,200,000
1,000,000
800,000
600,000
400,000
200,000
0

China | Thailand | Malaysia
Japan | Taiwan

Source: www.portofoakland.com/maritime/facts_comm_02.asp

Top Items Exported, 2002

Metric Tons

800,000
700,000
600,000
500,000
400,000
300,000
200,000
100,000
0

Paper | Meat
Animal Feed | Grape Products

Source: www.portofoakland.com/maritime/facts_comm_02.asp

2 Engines arrive at the Port of Oakland.

3 Engines travel by train.

4 A car manufacturer places them in new cars.

5 The new car is sold to a customer in the United States.

PACIFIC OCEAN

California

Ohio

2 **3** **4** **5**

Tennessee

Think About Imports and Exports

1. In 2003, how many countries shipped more goods to Oakland than Japan did?

2. What happens after a car engine arrives at the Port of Oakland?

3. What ocean does the car engine cross when it travels from Japan to the United States?

317

Sister Communities 3.5.2

Communities trade more than goods and services. They also trade ideas and friendship. Oakland has six "sister cities" around the world. They are in Japan, China, Cuba, Jamaica, Ghana, and Russia. People in Oakland share ideas and friendship with people in these faraway communities.

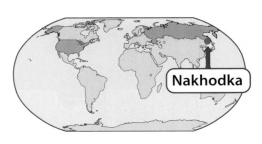

Oakland and Nakhodka, Russia, became sister cities in 1975. Teachers, high school students, librarians, and musical groups from the two cities have visited each other over the years.

Sister cities also introduce businesses to other businesses. For example, an entrepreneur from Oakland could meet a factory owner from Nakhodka. When people meet in a friendly way, there are many ways to trade.

REVIEW How does having a sister city help the people of Oakland? *Cause and Effect*

▼ Nakhodka, Russia is a port city, too.

◀ A girl from Nakhodka, wearing a special costume.

What You Learned

3.5.2 Communities rely on trade to meet their needs.

3.5.2 Ships, trains, and trucks carry goods in and out of ports such as Oakland.

3.5.2 Communities around the world also exchange ideas and friendship.

Lesson Review

1. Focus Question How do
3.5.2 communities around the world get the goods they need?

2. Vocabulary Write one sentence for
3.5.2 each vocabulary word.

container   import

export

3. Economics Why are human resources
3.5.2 important to the Port of Oakland?

4. Critical Thinking Make Inferences
3.5.2 Other than delivering goods and services, what are some other benefits of trade between countries?

5. Reading Strategy
3.5.2
ELA
R2.2 **Identify Cause and Effect** Use the chart to show how Oakland's location as a transportation center helps the port.

6. Write about THE **BIG** IDEA Choose any
3.5.2 product you use in your home. Write
ELA
W2.1 a description of how that product may have gotten to your home through the Port of Oakland.

7. Link to Mathematics Look at the
3.5.2 graphs on page 316. Is there more paper, or more animal feed and meat (together), exported from the Port of Oakland?

Producers in Your Region 3.5.1

LOS ANGELES

Jenny lives in Los Angeles. She was curious about businesses in her city. She made a chart showing how one local business uses resources to produce goods and services. Here's what you can do to learn about resources that businesses in your community use:

- Think about a business in your community that interests you.

- Think about the three kinds of resources the business uses—human resources, natural resources, and capital resources.

- Go to your local library to find out more about the kind of business that interests you. You could also visit the business with an adult and ask questions about the resources it uses.

LOG ON

For more help in making your chart, visit:

www.macmillanmh.com/ss/ca/local

ACTIVITY

Make a Chart

Materials
- poster board or stiff paper
- markers
- photographs
- paste

Step 1 Choose a business you learned about.

Step 2 Organize your notes. Draw pictures to show the resources the business uses, or get pictures from the Internet.

Step 3 Make a chart on poster board or stiff paper. Your chart should show human resources, natural resources, and capital resources. Write the name of the business on the top and paste on your photographs or drawings.

Step 4 Share your chart with your classmates.

321

Chapter Review

Vocabulary Review

Copy the sentences below on a separate sheet of paper. Use the list of vocabulary terms to fill in the blanks.

factory	import
human resources	supply

1. The amount of goods available
(3.5.1) is called the _____ .

2. _____ are the people who
(3.5.1) work for a business.

3. To _____ is to bring goods
(3.5.2) made or grown in one country to be sold in another.

4. A place where products are
(3.5.1) manufactured is a _____ .

5. Test Preparation The business of making things is called _____ .

    A. **manufacturing**   C. **migrant**
    B. **processed**   D. **container**

Comprehension Check

6. Give two examples of capital
(3.5.1) resources used by farms.

7. What makes Oakland a good
(3.5.2) port?

8. How have assembly lines
(3.5.1) changed manufacturing?

9. What are the three kinds of
(3.5.1) resources a company uses?

10. What happens to the cost of
(3.5.1) goods when supply is low?

11. Critical Thinking How does trade
(3.5.2) connect countries with one another?

12. Critical Thinking How do
(3.5.1) machines help both farmers and factories?

Write a complete sentence to answer each question.

Use Line Graphs

13. What does the graph below
3.5.2 show?

14. How many years does the
3.5.2 graph cover?

15. Has world trade increased or
3.5.2 decreased in the past 40 years?

16. Test Preparation A graph that
3.5.2 shows how things change over
time is a _____ graph.

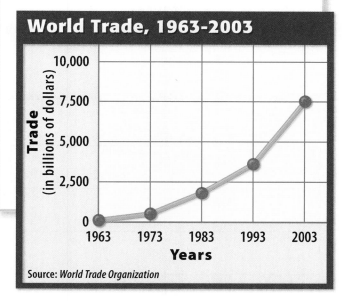

World Trade, 1963-2003

Source: *World Trade Organization*

Historic Photographs

17. Why are photographs an
3.5.1 important source of information
about the past?

18. What is an example of
3.5.1 something a photograph could
tell you?

19. Make a Flow Chart Work in
3.5.1 groups to make a flow chart
showing how a product is
made.

**Show at least four steps in making
the product.**

20. Descriptive Suppose you are
3.5.1 the owner of a small farm. You
ELA realize there is less demand
W2.1 for the crops you grow. Write
a paragraph telling what steps
you could take to solve your
problem.

For help with the
process of writing, visit:

www.macmillanmh.com/ss/ca/writing

UNIT 4 Unit Review and Test Prep

Comprehension and Critical Thinking Check

Write a sentence or more to answer each question.

1. Give an example of a **trade-off** made when you bought something. *3.5.3*

2. What are some **expenses** a company has to pay? *3.5.1*

3. Why is making a **profit** important to a business? *3.5.1*

4. How do people earn an **income**? *3.5.4*

5. Why do **producers** depend on other producers? *3.5.2*

6. How does **interest** help people save money? *3.5.3*

7. What happens if there is a low **supply** of something and a high **demand** for it? *3.5.1*

8. Why are **human resources** important to a business? *3.5.1*

9. **Critical Thinking** Why do countries **import** and **export** goods? *3.5.2*

10. **Critical Thinking** What kinds of things would you include in a family **budget**? *3.5.3*

Reading Social Studies Check

Identify Cause and Effect

Reread "Oakland, a Port City" beginning on page 314. Use the chart to help explain why communities trade with each other. *3.5.2* *ELA R2.3*

11. Why do communities trade with other countries? *ELA R2.3*

12. Why is the port important to the city of Oakland? *ELA R2.3*

13. Why do many goods from Asia come into Oakland's port? *ELA R2.3*

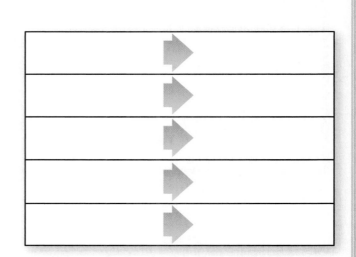

Read the paragraphs. Then answer the questions.

California makes more products than any other state. Many of these products are things people use every day, such as paper and clothing. California companies also make computer parts which go into computers and are also used in cars and machinery.

California is also the leading state for a special product—movies! Many movies today also use special effects created on computers from California. From actors and writers to camera operators and computer artists, California's movie industry gives work to thousands of people in California.

14. *3.5.2* Based on what you have read, what can you say about California?

    A California doesn't make many kinds of products.

    B California needs to make more computers.

    C Computers and computer parts are important to California.

    D Making products is not important in California.

15. *3.5.2* Why is the movie industry important to California?

    A We need movies to live.

    B The movie business gives work to many people.

    C If California didn't make movies, there wouldn't be any.

    D California is the only place movies are made.

Write About Economics

16. **Descriptive** *3.5.1* *ELA W2.2* Capers are a new crop for California. Explain why some California farmers began planting capers.

17. **Descriptive** *3.5.2* *ELA W2.2* Suppose you work at a port. Write a paragraph that describes what your day might be like.

18. **Narrative** *3.5.1* *ELA W2.1* Write a story about what it might be like if your family had a business. Tell how the business got started and what it's like for your family to work together.

LOG ON For help with the process of writing, visit:

www.macmillanmh.com/ss/ca/writing

How do people in a community meet their needs?

Write About the Big Idea 3.5.2 ELA W2.3

A Letter of Request

Complete the graphic organizer that you started on page 247. Add more ways that communities meet their needs.

Then use the graphic organizer to help you write a letter to a local business. Ask for information about what they produce and how they spend money. Ask what services the business provides to your community.

People save money
Put money in the bank
Save for needs and wants

How People Meet Their Needs

Write a Letter

1. Plan

- Identify a business to write to.
- Make a brief list of questions you will ask. Plan to use formal language.

2. Write a First Draft

- Include the parts of a letter. You need a heading, greeting, body, and closing.
- Tell the business why you are writing the letter in your first sentence.
- State your questions clearly. Be as brief as possible.

3. Revise and Proofread

- Be sure the information you are requesting is clear.
- Check to see that you used complete sentences.
- Be sure you have used correct capitalization, punctuation, and spelling.
- Ask your teacher to review your letter. Rewrite it neatly before you mail it.

ACTIVITY

Speak About the Big Idea 3.5.2 ELA LS2.3

Job Fair

Create a class job fair. List jobs that people in your community do.

Prepare Work in small groups. Have groups decide on a job category—for example, small business, agriculture, or manufacturing. Group members will research jobs in that category.

Present Each group should set up a desk or table to be their job station. Each group will report in turn on the jobs in their category. Use props or costumes to help you describe the jobs in your category.

LAUNCH PAD For help with the Big Idea activity, visit:

www.macmillanmh.com/ss/ca/launchpad

Read More About the Big Idea

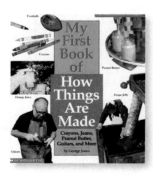

My First Book of How Things Are Made

George Jones Read about how crayons, jeans, and other products are made.

Great-Grandma Tells of Threshing Day

Verda Cross A child learns about what life was like on a Missouri farm in the early 1900s.

If You Made a Million

David Schwartz A magician explains what can be done with a million dollars.

UNIT 5

Many Communities, One Nation

"One flag, one land,
one heart, one hand,
One Nation evermore!"
— Oliver Wendell Holmes, Sr.

◀ Celebration in
Washington, D.C.

Why do communities need governments?

In Unit 5 you will read about national, state, and local governments. You will read about some Americans we honor, too.

Copy the **KWL** chart. Before you read, fill in the first two columns, writing what you already **K**now and what you **W**ant to know about government. As you read the unit, note the different reasons that people in a community need governments. After you read Unit 5, fill in what you **L**earned.

What I Know	What I Want to Know	What I Learned
1. Police and fire departments protect our community	1. Who is responsible for police and fire departments?	1. My local government is . . .
2.	2.	2.
3.	3.	3.
4.	4.	4.

America

Words by Samuel F. Smith
Music by Henry Carey

We Americans are proud of our country. One way we show that pride is through song. You may know this song by the name "My Country 'Tis of Thee."

Samuel Francis Smith wrote the words and set them to a tune he found in a music book. He probably did not know that the same tune was used for "God Save the King!" — the British national anthem.

America

Music by Henry Carey
Words by Samuel F. Smith

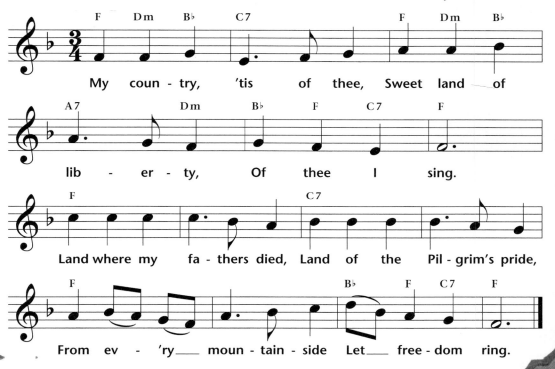

My coun - try, 'tis of thee, Sweet land of

lib - er - ty, Of thee I sing.

Land where my fa - thers died, Land of the Pil - grim's pride,

From ev - 'ry moun - tain - side Let free - dom ring.

Write About It!

Choose a song you know and like. Write your own words to it telling how you feel to be an American.

Compare and Contrast:

National Landmarks 3.4.3 ^{ELA} R2.6

Compare means to see how things are alike. Contrast means to see how they are different. Comparing and contrasting will help you understand what you read in social studies.

1 Learn It

- To compare two things, look for how they are alike.
- To contrast two things, look for ways in which they are different.
- Now, read the passage below. Think about how the Washington Monument and the Lincoln Memorial are alike and different.

Alike
Both are located on the mall.

Different
There is no statue of Washington.

Different
Another difference is visitors can look out on the city from the Washington Monument.

The Washington Monument and the Lincoln Memorial honor two of our country's greatest Presidents. Both structures are located along the Mall in Washington, D.C. They are symbols of the United States. The Lincoln Memorial has a statue of President Lincoln inside. Visitors can also go inside the Washington Monument. There is no statue of Washington, but there is an elevator. It speeds visitors 500 feet to a lookout from where they can see the city.

2 Try It

Copy the Venn diagram. Then, fill in the left-hand side with details about the Washington Monument. Fill in the right side with details about the Lincoln Memorial. Fill in the center with details that tell about both landmarks.

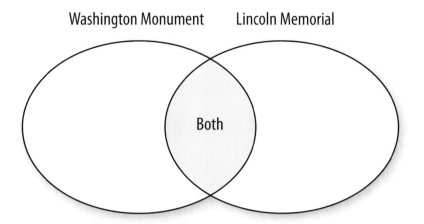

Washington Monument   Lincoln Memorial

Both

3 Apply It

- Review the steps for comparing and contrasting in Learn It.

- Read the passage below. Then make a Venn diagram to compare and contrast the two leaders.

The President of the United States and the governor of California are powerful leaders. Both are elected for four-year terms. The President makes sure our country's laws are followed. The governor makes sure state laws are followed. Presidents are more powerful than governors. Only the President, for example, makes decisions about war and peace.

Governing the United States

YOU ARE THERE

In this chapter you will read about how the United States is a community. You will learn how rules and laws are made to protect everyone. You will also read about the levels of government in the United States: national, state, and local.

Sacramento
River

Sacramento ★ **3**
Stockton • **4**

1

PACIFIC
OCEAN

1 **Our American Community** (page 336)
People all over our country share common beliefs.

2 **Rules and Laws Protect Everyone** (page 342)
Our country has laws, like the United States Constitution, that all people must follow.

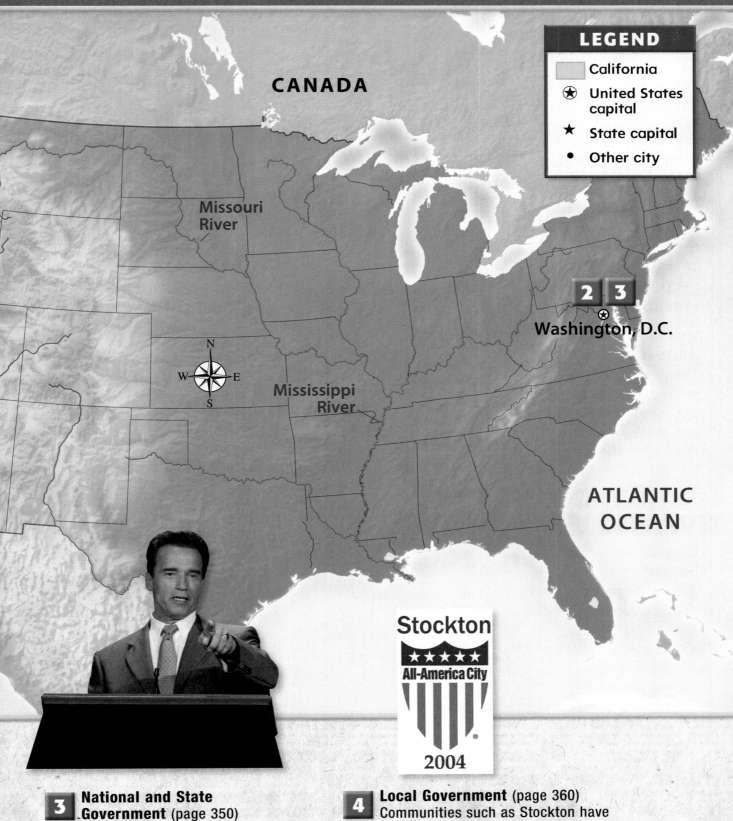

CANADA

Missouri River

Mississippi River

N
W E
S

LEGEND

☐ California
⊛ United States capital
★ State capital
• Other city

2 **3**
⊛
Washington, D.C.

ATLANTIC OCEAN

Stockton
★★★★★
All-America City
2004

3 **National and State Government** (page 350)
Our country's government is centered in Washington, D.C. Our state's government is centered in Sacramento.

4 **Local Government** (page 360)
Communities such as Stockton have their own governments to keep the streets clean and the people safe.

What are some things Americans have in common?

motto
right
responsibility

VOCABULARY STRATEGY

MULTIPLE MEANINGS
The word **right** has many meanings. It can mean "correct." It can mean a direction. What other meanings for **right** can you think of?

READING STRATEGY

Compare and Contrast
Use the diagram below to compare and contrast the way your classroom works and the way our country works.

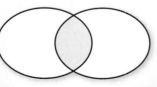

Our American Community

Start with Your
CALIFORNIA STANDARDS

3.4 Students understand the role of the rules and laws in our daily lives and the basic structure of the U.S. government.

3.4.2 Discuss the importance of public virtue and the role of citizens, including how to participate in a classroom, in the community, and in civic life.

Learn how all Americans have certain rights and important responsibilities. (Begins on page 337)

The Latin words *e pluribus unum* have appeared on official United States papers since leaders such as Benjamin Franklin and Thomas Jefferson made them our national saying in 1776. The words also appear on all of our coins. But what do these words mean?

Many Make One 3.4.2

Where do you live? To answer, you might name your local community. Or you might say, "California," or, "the United States." All three answers are right, because you live in your community, our state, and our country.

Many different people make up the 50 United States. Our country has a **motto** about its people: *e pluribus unum*. A motto is a short sentence or phrase that says what someone believes. Our motto is Latin, and it means "out of many, one." Our motto tells everyone that while we are different people, living in 50 different states, we are all one country.

REVIEW What is one way all people in California communities are alike? *Compare and Contrast*

Our Common Beliefs 3.4.2

People in the United States share common beliefs. For example, we believe that everyone has the **right** to be treated fairly. A right is something that everyone deserves. In the United States, we have the right to say or write what we want, to live where we want, and to practice any religion we want.

We also believe that people have **responsibilities**. A responsibility is a duty or job. For example, everyone in your classroom has a responsibility to treat others with respect.

Caring about our country is another belief we share. We show we care when we say the Pledge of Allegiance. Read the Pledge below.

Primary Sources

Pledge of Allegiance

First written by Francis Bellamy, 1892

"I pledge **allegiance** to the flag of the United States of America, and to the **Republic** for which it stands, one Nation, under God, **indivisible**, with liberty and justice for all."

allegiance loyalty	**Republic** our country's government
indivisible not to be divided	

Write About It! Which words of the Pledge of Allegiance describe rights people have?

REVIEW What are some rights citizens of our country have? *Summarize*

◀ We show loyalty to our country when we say the Pledge of Allegiance.

What You Learned

3.4.2 You are a citizen of your community and of your country. The motto of the United States, "Out of many, one," means that many states and people make up one country.

3.4.2 We believe that everyone has rights, such as freedom of speech and writing, and freedom of religion. People also have responsibilities.

Lesson Review

1. **Focus Question** What are some
3.4.2 things Americans have in common?

2. **Vocabulary** Write one sentence for
3.4.2 each vocabulary word.

   motto   **right**
   responsibility

3. **Citizenship** What are some of your
3.4.2 responsibilities in the classroom?

4. **Critical Thinking** **Draw Conclusions**
3.4.2 Why is *E pluribus unum* a good motto for our country?

5. **Reading Strategy**
3.4.2 **Compare and Contrast**
ELA
R2.3 Use the diagram to compare and contrast our rights and responsibilities.

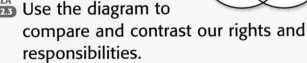

6. **Write about** THE **BiG** IDEA Write about
3.4.2 a time when you were loyal to
ELA
W2.1 someone or something. Why was it important to be loyal?

7. **Link to Mathematics** Find out how
3.4.2 many different languages are spoken by your classmates' families. Show your results in a bar graph.

Understanding Letters 3.4.3

Letters are an important primary source. Letters tell us how people felt and what they thought at the time events took place.

The Letters of Thomas Jefferson

Thomas Jefferson was a leader who helped our country win its independence. After the War of Independence, Jefferson lived in Paris, France, where he worked for our country's government. Later, Jefferson was President of the United States. He strongly believed in our right to say and write what we want. This right is called freedom of the press.

▲ Thomas Jefferson

1 Learn It

Read the steps below to help you find information in historical letters.

- Look for the time and place the letter was written.

- Review what you already know about the letter writer.

- Read to find out what the writer said. What new information does the letter give you?

Jefferson invented a machine to copy letters. ▶

2 Try It

Read the letter below to understand important parts of historical letters.

Time and Place → Paris, Jan. 18, 1786

Dear Sir,

. . . . [I]n truth, it is [troubling] that a man who has [passed] his life in serving the public, . . . who tho' poor, has never permitted himself to make a **shilling** in the public employ, should yet . . . have his peace of mind so much disturbed by any [person] who shall think proper to **arraign** him in a newspaper.

What does Jefferson say about this important right? → It is however an evil for which there is no **remedy**, our liberty depends on the freedom of the press, and that cannot be limited without being lost. To the sacrifice of time, labor, fortune, a public servant must count upon adding that of peace of mind and even **reputation**.

I am with sincere esteem . . .,
Your friend & servt.

Letter writer → Thomas Jefferson

---

shilling: a coin of small value
arraign: accuse of wrongdoing
remedy: cure; fix
reputation: what people think of a person

This is the actual letter Thomas Jefferson wrote ▼

3 Apply It

- What troubles Jefferson in this letter?

- Tell what you think Jefferson would say about this statement: "Newspapers should not print letters that disagree with what our country's leaders say."

FOCUS QUESTION

What are some rules that all Americans must follow?

VOCABULARY

law
common good
volunteer
Bill of Rights

VOCABULARY STRATEGY

MULTIPLE MEANINGS
A bill can be a list of items or a summary of ideas. The **Bill of Rights** is a list of citizens' rights in the United States. What other kinds of bills can you think of?

READING STRATEGY

Summarize
Use the chart below to summarize the most important ideas in the lesson.

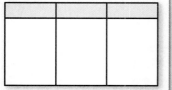

Rules and Laws Protect Everyone

Start with Your
CALIFORNIA STANDARDS

3.4 Students understand the role of the rules and laws in our daily lives and the basic structure of the U.S. government.

3.4.1 Determine the reasons for rules, laws, and the U.S. Constitution; the role of citizenship in the promotion of rules and laws; and the consequences for people who violate rules and laws.

Discover why our country has laws to protect its citizens and why our government must follow laws, as well. Understand why people who break the law are punished.
(Begins on page 343)

3.4.2 Discuss the importance of public virtue and the role of citizens, including how to participate in a classroom, in the community, and in civic life.

Learn why it is important for all citizens to follow laws and get involved in the community by voting and helping others.
(Begins on page 344)

Rules and laws protect citizens, even at the beach. ▼

When Benjamin Franklin, George Washington, and other leaders met in Philadelphia in 1787 to write the United States Constitution, they wanted their talks to be secret. Although it was a hot summer, they kept the doors closed and the windows shut.

Rules and Laws Protect People 3.4.1

Raise your hand to speak. Take turns. Share with others. Does your class have rules like these? Rules help people get along and work together.

Communities and countries also need rules. When a rule is made by a government for people in a community it is called a **law**. Some laws help keep people safe, such as laws that tell drivers what speed is allowed. Other laws protect property. Laws say that no one may come into your home or take something of yours without your permission. People who break laws are punished. They may have to pay money or go to jail.

REVIEW What is a law?
Summarize

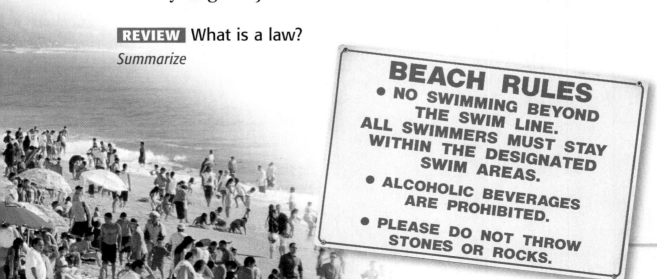

BEACH RULES
• NO SWIMMING BEYOND THE SWIM LINE. ALL SWIMMERS MUST STAY WITHIN THE DESIGNATED SWIM AREAS.
• ALCOHOLIC BEVERAGES ARE PROHIBITED.
• PLEASE DO NOT THROW STONES OR ROCKS.

Being a Good Citizen 3.4.1 3.4.2

Following rules and laws is part of being a good citizen. Good citizens believe in the **common good**—doing what is best for everyone.

Good citizens also know that rules and laws protect everyone. For example, many places have laws against locking a bicycle to a fire hydrant. If firefighters had to get water from the hydrant, it would take them extra time to move the bicycle. People could get hurt. Disobeying laws can put others in danger.

▲ Good citizens help people in need.

Getting Involved

Have you ever helped out at school or in your community? A person who offers help without being paid is a **volunteer**. Volunteering is another way to be a good citizen. You are being a good citizen if you read to younger children at school, pick up trash, or collect cans for a food drive.

◀ Planting trees is one way to help your community.

▲ State Senator Liz Figueroa, seated, meets with Senators Bowen (right) and Karnette (far right).

Being involved in school government is another way to help your school community. You can continue to stay involved with government when you grow up. Liz Figueroa, a state senator from Fremont, California, says, "It is important to get involved and help your community." As a state senator, she works to improve schools. She also works to make sure that sick people can see doctors even if they cannot pay for them.

Voting is one way for citizens to be involved. It is one of the responsibilities that goes with being a good citizen. When we vote we make decisions about laws and about which people we want to serve in government.

REVIEW What are some of the things you can do to be a good citizen? *Main Idea and Details*

Governments Follow Rules 3.4.1

Just as people have to follow rules, our government has to follow rules, too. Some of the most important rules the government must follow are in the United States Constitution. A constitution is a plan for government. Our country's Constitution was written more than 200 years ago. It says what our government can and cannot do. The people we elect promise to obey the Constitution. That means they cannot pass a law that goes against any laws already in the Constitution.

The **Bill of Rights** is part of the United States Constitution. It tells the most important rights that people in our country share. For example, in some countries, people can be put in jail just for saying that they disagree with the government. In the United States, you cannot be arrested for disagreeing. The Bill of Rights makes sure that we have the freedom to say what we want.

REVIEW What does the Bill of Rights tell us? *Summarize*

This historic photograph shows people speaking out for their beliefs. This right is protected by law in the Bill of Rights. ▼

What You Learned

3.4.1 A law is a rule made by a government for all of the people in a town, state, or country.

3.4.1 **3.4.2** An important reason to follow laws is for the common good. Following laws protects everyone.

3.4.1 The United States Constitution says what the government can and cannot do. The Bill of Rights is part of the Constitution. It lists important rights we all share.

Lesson Review

1. **Focus Question** What are some **3.4.1** **3.4.2** rules that all Americans must follow?

2. **Vocabulary** Write one sentence for **3.4.1** **3.4.2** each vocabulary term.

   Bill of Rights   **law**
   common good   **volunteer**

3. **Citizenship** Ask some adults about a **3.4.2** time when they voted. How did they decide what or whom to vote for?

4. **Critical Thinking Draw** **3.4.1** **Conclusions** Why is it a good idea to have a Constitution that tells the government what it cannot do?

5. **Reading Strategy** **3.4.1** **3.4.2** **ELA R2.3** **Summarize** Reread the "Getting Involved" section that begins on page 344. Use the chart to summarize the section.

6. **Write about** THE BIG IDEA Why do **3.4.1** **ELA W2.2** communities need laws?

7. **Link to History** When the Constitution **3.4.1** **3.4.2** was written, only white men who owned land could vote. Find out about how another group—women, African Americans, or young people—got the right to vote. Who led the fight to win the group's right to vote?

Use Reference Sources 3.4.3 ELA W1.3

Suppose you wanted to find out more about the Pledge of Allegiance and its author, Francis Bellamy. Where could you find this information? You would use a **reference source**. A reference source is a book, CD-ROM, or Web site that has facts about different subjects.

VOCABULARY

reference
source
dictionary
encyclopedia
guide words

1 Learn It

There are several kinds of reference sources.

- A **dictionary** gives you the meanings of words and their pronunciation. Sometimes dictionaries have sample sentences that show you how the word is used.

- An **encyclopedia** is a set of books or a CD-ROM with articles about many subjects.

- Dictionaries and encyclopedias have **guide words** to help you find the word or subject you are looking for. Guide words tell you the first and last words on a page. By looking at the guide words, you can tell quickly whether the word you want is on the page.

2 Try It

Look at the dictionary page and the encyclopedia page as you read the following.

- Find the word "pledge" on the dictionary page. What is a pledge?

- Entries in an encyclopedia are listed in alphabetical order. The article gives you information about the subject. Where was Francis Bellamy born?

3 Apply It

Use an encyclopedia to find out more information about the motto of the United States.

Dictionary

Guide words

pleasure ➤ pluck **P**

pleasure **1.** A feeling of enjoyment or happiness: *The clowns gave* ***pleasure*** *to the children.* **2.** Something that gives a feeling of enjoyment or happiness: *It was a* ***pleasure*** *to see you again.* **pleas•ure** (plezh'er) *noun, plural* **pleasures**

pled A past tense and a past participle of plead: *The prisoner* ***pled*** *not guilty.* **pled** (pled) *verb.*

definition

pledge **1.** A serious promise: *The children made a* ***pledge*** *to keep the secret.* **2.** Something given to another person for a time, as part of an agreement: *I gave the storekeeper my watch as a* ***pledge*** *that I would come back and pay what I owed.* **pledge** (plej) *noun.* **1.** To promise: *The children* ***pledge*** *allegiance to the flag each morning.*

Sample sentence

Encyclopedia

Bellamy • Bellini

entry

Bellamy, (BEHL uh mee), **Francis Edward** • (1855-1931), an American religious figure and writer. Born in Mount Morris, New York, Bellamy was the son of a Baptist minister. Following an education at the Rome Free School in Rome, New York, Bellamy attended the University of Rochester, where he studied to be a Baptist minister. He left the ministry in 1891 and took a job with a Boston magazine, *Youth's Companion*, published by one of his nephews. It was as a writer for the magazine that Bellamy wrote the Pledge of Allegiance, on which his fame today rests. The Pledge was published in the magazine on September 8, 1892. Bellamy lobbied Congress to make reciting of the pledge a central part of Columbus Day celebrations scheduled for that year. The Pledge soon caught on. Over the years, Bellamy changed the wording of the Pledge. The current wording dates from 1954, when Congress added the words "under God". Bellamy later worked in advertising. He died on August 28, 1931. He is buried in Rome, New York. The words of the Pledge are

Body of article

What are the branches of government in our country and state?

legislative
executive
judicial
federal
governor
tax

VOCABULARY STRATEGY

ROOT WORDS Many words have Latin roots. **Legislator** comes from the Latin word for law.

Compare and Contrast

Use the diagram below to compare and contrast California's government and the national government.

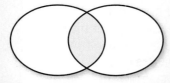

National and State Government

Start with Your
CALIFORNIA STANDARDS

3.4 **Students understand the role of the rules and laws in our daily lives and the basic structure of the U.S. government.**

3.4.4 Understand the three branches of government, with an emphasis on local government.

Find out about the three branches, or parts, of the United States government, and how government works at the national, state, and local levels. (Begins on page 351)

3.4.5 Describe the ways in which California, the other states, and sovereign American Indian tribes contribute to the making of our nation and participate in the federal system of government.

Discover how California contributes to the nation, and how Native American groups have their own governments and leaders. (Begins on page 352)

Judicial Branch: The Supreme Court makes sure the laws of our country are fair. ▼

Legislative Branch: Congress makes laws for our country. ▼

Did you know that more than 10 million people work for you? Employees of our government work in jobs that range from defending our country to delivering the mail.

Parts of Our Government 3.4.4

The Constitution divides the United States government into three parts, or branches. You can see the branches in the photographs below.

The **legislative** branch is called the Congress. It writes our laws. The job of the **executive** branch is to make sure the laws are followed. The President of the United States leads the executive branch. The third branch is the **judicial** branch, or our courts. The courts decide what the laws mean and whether the laws follow the Constitution. All three branches work in Washington, D.C., our nation's capital.

REVIEW How is the legislative branch of government different from the executive branch? *Compare and Contrast*

◀ **Executive Branch:** The President makes sure the laws of our country are followed.

351

Sharing Government 3.4.4 3.4.5

In the United States, we have a **federal** system of government. That means that power is shared among different levels of government. The three levels of government are national, state, and local. Each level of government has different responsibilities.

National Government

Our national government is the highest level of government. It makes sure we have an army and navy to protect us. It runs the post office and prints money. It cares for our national forests and parks, and does many more things. Its decisions affect the whole country.

Congress makes laws that apply in all 50 states. Each state elects people to serve in Congress and make laws. Because California has the largest population, it sends more people to Congress than any other state.

Park rangers are part of our national government. ▼

▲ These sailors are helping people in Asia affected by the 2004 tsunami [syew NAH mee].

State Governments

Each state has a government, too. The state government looks after state roads and state parks. It decides what you learn in school, how old you must be to drive a car, and many other things. Like the national government, state governments have three branches.

The legislative branch of California's state government is made up of the State Assembly and the State Senate. Both groups meet in the state capital, Sacramento, to make laws. The head of a state's executive branch is called the **governor**. The judicial branch reviews state laws to see if they are fair.

You also have a local government. You will learn more about local government in the next lesson.

Where does the money come from to pay for the different levels of government? It comes from **taxes**. A tax is money that people must pay to support the government. The Datagraphic on the next page shows where some of California's tax money goes.

REVIEW What might happen if a town needed money to build a new library? *Draw Conclusions*

▲ The California State Seal is a symbol of its government.

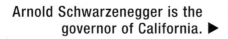

Arnold Schwarzenegger is the governor of California. ▶

California and the United States 3.4.4 3.4.5

Like every state, California sends lawmakers to Congress and pays taxes to the federal, or national, government. The map and two graphs compare California's share of lawmakers and taxes to that of two other states.

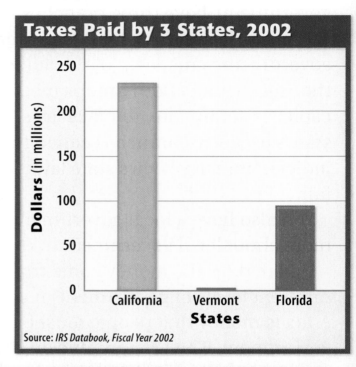

Taxes Paid by 3 States, 2002

Dollars (in millions)

States: California, Vermont, Florida

Source: *IRS Databook, Fiscal Year 2002*

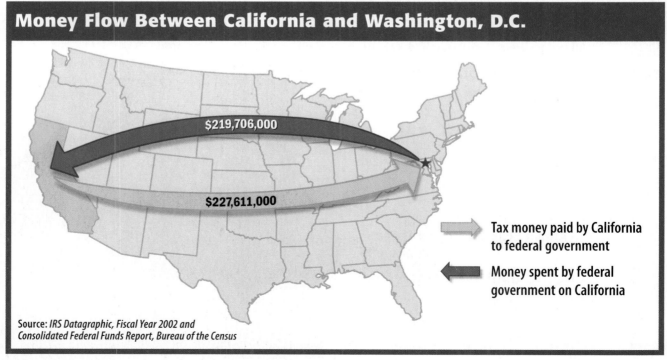

Money Flow Between California and Washington, D.C.

$219,706,000

$227,611,000

Tax money paid by California to federal government

Money spent by federal government on California

Source: *IRS Datagraphic, Fiscal Year 2002 and Consolidated Federal Funds Report, Bureau of the Census*

Members of Congress (Selected States)

Congress has two parts, or "houses." The Senate has 100 members, two for each state. The House of Representatives has 435 members. States with more people get more representatives. The pictograph below shows the number of people in Congress from California, Florida, and Vermont.

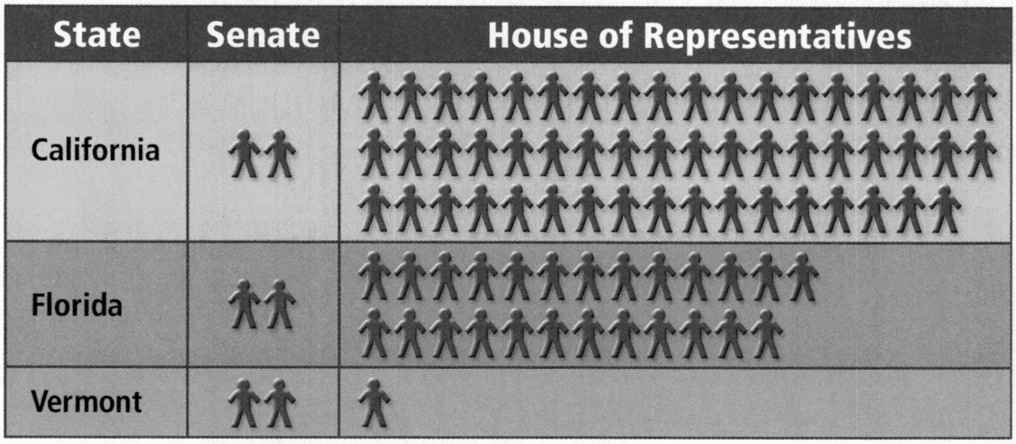

State	Senate	House of Representatives
California	🚶🚶	🚶🚶🚶🚶🚶🚶🚶🚶🚶🚶🚶🚶🚶🚶🚶🚶🚶🚶 🚶🚶🚶🚶🚶🚶🚶🚶🚶🚶🚶🚶🚶🚶🚶🚶🚶🚶 🚶🚶🚶🚶🚶🚶🚶🚶🚶🚶🚶🚶🚶🚶🚶🚶🚶
Florida	🚶🚶	🚶🚶🚶🚶🚶🚶🚶🚶🚶🚶🚶🚶🚶 🚶🚶🚶🚶🚶🚶🚶🚶🚶🚶🚶🚶
Vermont	🚶🚶	🚶

Think About Government

1. Which state shown on the graph on page 354 contributes the most tax dollars to the federal government?

2. Why do you think that is? (Hint: Look at the "Members of Congress" graph.)

3. In what way is Vermont equal to California and Florida?

Native American Government 3.4.5

Native Americans are citizens of the United States. They vote in local, state, and national elections, and follow United States law. However, Native Americans are also citizens of their tribes. Many Native American reservations are sovereign, or independent. Many tribes have their own governments. They elect their own leaders and make their own laws, and at the same time they follow local, state, and national laws.

For example, the Agua Caliente Indian Reservation in Palm Springs in Southern California has a five-member tribal government. The Agua Caliente have sovereignty over their land. Their government is free to make laws for the tribe and to protect the tribal property. It also works with the California and national governments on issues that are important to the tribe.

REVIEW What does sovereignty mean?
Summarize

▼ The Agua Caliente tribal government makes decisions for the tribe.

▲ Tribal leaders such as Cheryl Seidner of the Wiyot and local leaders, such as Eureka Mayor Peter La Vallee, work together to solve problems.

What You Learned

3.4.4 The United States government has three branches: legislative, executive, and judicial.

3.4.4
3.4.5 Our federal system of government has three levels: national, state, and local. Each uses tax money to pay for its public services.

3.4.5 Native Americans are citizens of the United States, but many groups also have their own sovereign governments.

Lesson Review

1. Focus Question What are the
3.4.4 branches of government in our
3.4.5 country and state?

2. Vocabulary Write one sentence for
3.4.4 each vocabulary word.
3.4.5

executive	judicial
governor	legislative
federal	tax

3. Government What are some of the
3.4.4 public services that each level of
3.4.5 government provides?

4. Critical Thinking Make Inferences
3.4.4 Why do you think the government of our country is divided into branches?

5. Reading Strategy Compare
3.4.4 **and Contrast** Use the
ELA
R2.3 diagram to compare and contrast the two parts of Congress.

6. Write about THE **BiG** IDEA How do the
3.4.5 members of our state's legislature
ELA
W2.2 help the state?

7. Link to Music Our national anthem
3.4.5 is a song that represents our country.
ELA
W2.2 Each state also has an anthem. The California state song is "I Love You, California." Find the music and lyrics to the song. Try singing it, then write a new verse telling how you feel about the state.

MAP and GLOBE Skills

Use Grid Maps ⌜3.4.4⌝ ⌜3.4.5⌝

Suppose you and your family went on a trip to visit Sacramento. One way to find your way around is to use a **grid map**. A grid map has a grid, or set of lines that cross to form boxes. The grid helps you to find places on the map quickly and easily.

1 Learn It

Look at the map below. Then follow the steps to use a grid map.

- Read the map title to see what the map shows.

- Grid maps have two sets of lines that make boxes. Rows are lettered from top to bottom. Columns are numbered from left to right.

- Look at the index for the name of the place you want to locate. An **index** is an alphabetical list that tells you where information can be found. For a grid map, the letters and numbers in the index tell you in which grid boxes you will find places.

- Find a place on the map by using the letter and number of its grid box. To find the state capitol, slide your finger down the left side of the map to the row marked C. Then move your finger across the map to the column numbered 6.

Sacramento: State Capitol

2 Try It

Look at the map below to answer the questions.

- In which grid box is the California State Railroad Museum?

- What place of interest is found in both B3 and B4?

- If you walked from the California State History Museum to the Crocker Art Museum, in what direction would you be going?

- Use the map scale to find the distance from the Old Governor's Mansion to the U.S. District Court.

3 Apply It

Draw a grid map of an imaginary town.

- Include important landmarks such as a school, grocery store, local library, fire and police stations, and any other landmarks you think should be included.

- Give your town a name.

- Make an index that lists each location.

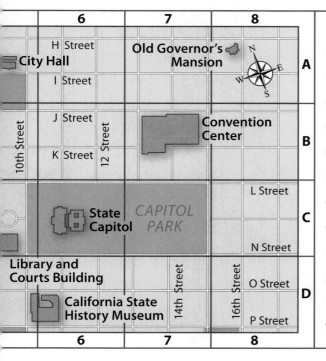

INDEX

Local Government

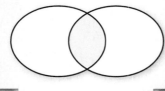

Start with Your
CALIFORNIA STANDARDS

3.4 Students understand the role of the rules and laws in our daily lives and the basic structure of the U.S. government.

3.4.4 Understand the three branches of government, with an emphasis on local government.

Find out how a local government meets the needs of one California city. (Begins on page 361)

The city of Stockton has 18,000 streetlights. That's a lot of light bulbs to change. Who is in charge of changing all those bulbs?

Local Government 3.4.4

Who decides if a busy corner needs a traffic light? Who takes care of the parks in your town? Who hires the police and firefighters? Who paves the streets and picks up the garbage? The answer to all of these questions is, your local government. It is the level of government that most closely touches our everyday lives.

Most Californians live in cities. The state has nearly 500 cities, and each has its own government. Let's look at Stockton, a city in the San Joaquin Valley, to see how one local government works.

Stockton

REVIEW What are some of the things local government takes care of? *Main Idea and Details*

◀ Stockton was named an All-American City in 2004.

How a City Works 3.4.4

Stockton is home to almost 300,000 people. It takes a lot of teamwork to run such a large city. Stockton's team begins with its seven-member **city council**. The council is the legislative branch of the city. It makes the city's laws. The **mayor** is the head of the city council. Citizens of Stockton vote for the mayor and city council members.

The head of Stockton's executive branch is the **city manager**. He or she is chosen by the city council to put the council's decisions into action.

Most California cities follow this plan, but larger cities such as Los Angeles have no city manager. Instead, the mayor is head of the executive branch.

The chart below shows the different parts of Stockton's government. Each part has specific jobs. Public Works, for example, cleans the streets and changes the bulbs in the streetlights.

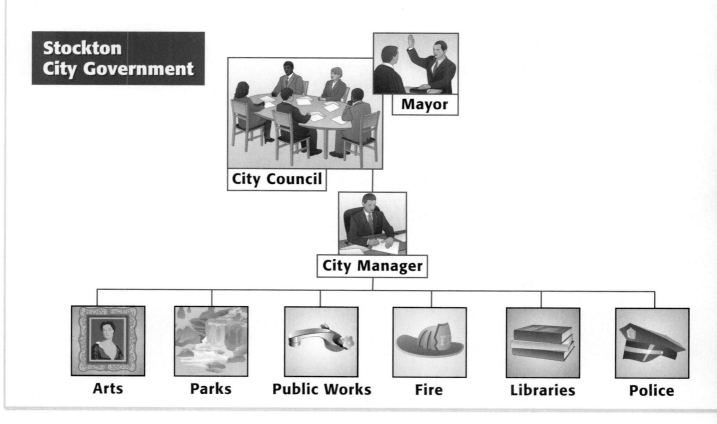

Stockton City Government

City Council

Mayor

City Manager

Arts Parks Public Works Fire Libraries Police

◄ Stockton's city manager (far left), members of the city council, and other Stockton leaders

Making a City Better

Stockton's city council meets weekly at city hall. Citizens can watch these meetings on television or in person. At each meeting the council listens to the concerns of citizens and decides what to do.

A few years ago, the council decided that downtown Stockton needed a better place for people to sit and have a picnic by the water. Where could they build such a project? There was a piece of land near downtown that was full of litter and harmful chemicals. The city council decided to clean it up. They made it into a park! They added sculptures and fountains. Now Stockton's downtown and waterfront look better than ever.

Stockton
★★★★★
All-America City

2004

REVIEW What is the job of the city council? *Summarize*

Local Courts 3.4.4

Local governments are also in charge of courtrooms. Some cities in California have their own courts. Most cities, however, use the county court system, which is part of the county government. A county is larger than a city and has many cities within its boundaries.

Stockton is the county seat of San Joaquin County. The county seat is the town where the county government is located. The county seat is like the capital of the county. San Joaquin County's central courthouse is in Stockton.

Many minor crimes are judged in local courts, such as traffic tickets and arguments between people. A judge or team of judges listen to the problems brought before them and try to make fair decisions under the law.

▲ The city of Stockton has a seal, just like the county and state do.

REVIEW Does Stockton run its own courts? *Make Decisions*

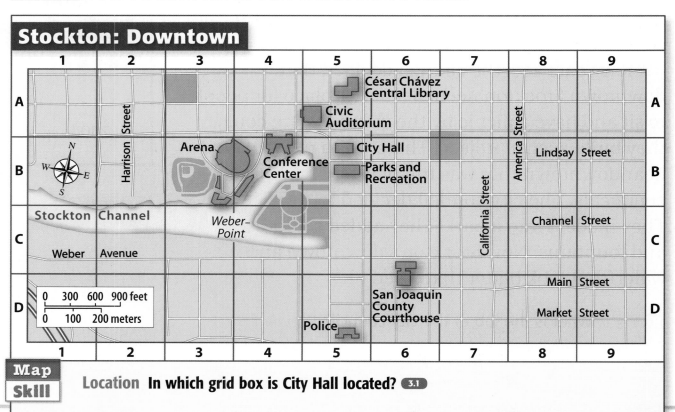

Stockton: Downtown

Map Skill **Location In which grid box is City Hall located?** 3.1

◄ The San Joaquin County courthouse is in Stockton.

What You Learned

3.4.4 Local governments provide many services for citizens, such as providing police protection, cleaning streets, and keeping parks neat.

3.4.4 The local government is made up of a city council and mayor who make decisions for the city. Often, a city manager is hired to put these decisions into action.

3.4.4 Courts are part of local government too, but they are often run by counties, not cities.

Lesson Review

1. **Focus Question** How does local
3.4.4 government work?

2. **Vocabulary** Write one sentence for
3.4.4 each vocabulary term.

city council   mayor
city manager

3. **Government** How is a county seat
3.4.4 like a state capital?

4. **Critical Thinking** **Problem Solving**
3.4.4 Why do you think Stockton puts its city council meetings on television? How do you think this helps Stockton citizens to take part in their government?

5. **Reading Strategy** **Compare**
3.4.4 **and Contrast** Reread
ELA
R2.3 page 362. Use the diagram to compare and contrast the jobs of city manager and mayor.

6. **Write about** **THE BIG IDEA** Tell how
3.4.4 local government affects your life.
ELA
W2.2

7. **Link to Arts** Many cities invite
3.4.4 performers to visit their communities.
ELA
W2.3 Write a letter to your mayor or city manager describing the kind of performer you would like to see come to your town. Include tips on how to act on your idea.

CITIZENSHIP
DEMOCRACY IN ACTION

Being Informed 3.4.2

Several third graders at the school across from Green Valley Park heard this report on local television news:

"At its next meeting, the city council will vote on a plan to close Green Valley Park and sell the city-owned land. City officials say the land can be better used to locate new businesses in town."

The next day, the students told their classmates the news. Some students were unhappy to learn that they might lose the park. Others wondered what might replace it. No one knew what to think. They needed to become informed, or learn more about the issue.

To be informed means to find out all you can about an issue. That will help you make up your mind about it. Read these steps to learn how to become informed.

Build Citizenship

1. **Identify the issue.** Make a list of what you already know and what you need to know about a subject to understand it better.

2. **Get information.** Read local newspapers, watch television, search the Internet, talk with people who know about the issue.

3. **Examine the information.** Try to decide which information is fact and which is opinion. Are the opinions supported by facts?

4. **Find out who is in charge.** Many public issues are the responsibility of government officials. Find out who is responsible for the issue you're interested in.

Think About It

1. What are some ways Green Valley students could learn more about this issue?

2. What opinions might people have about the land sale?

3. Why is it sometimes hard to tell facts from opinions?

4. Which government officials might the students contact about selling the park? How do you know?

Write About It!

Choose an issue in your school or community that people might disagree about. Gather all the information you can. Then, write a letter to a local newspaper, your principal, or a city official, telling what you learned about the issue and what you think should be done.

Local Connections

Your Local Government 3.4.4

OXNARD

Zachary lives in Oxnard. He was interested in his local government. He made a chart showing the leaders in his community and their responsibilities. Here's what you can do to learn about the leaders in your community:

- Go to your library to find out who your mayor is, who is on your city council, and who your city manager is (if your city has one). This information is also on the Internet.

- Make notes about things the city government might be responsible for, such as trash removal.

- Ask people in your community which city leaders are responsible for those services, or find the information on the Internet or in newspapers.

LOG ON For more help in making your chart, visit:

socialstudies.macmillanmh.com/ss/ca/local

Make a Local Government Organizational Chart

Materials
- poster board
- pencil
- markers
- scissors
- photographs
- paste

Step 1 Gather your notes and the information you found. Get photos of the leaders from the Internet or newspapers.

Step 2 Write the names of your mayor, city councilors, city manager, and other leaders on labels. Arrange the labels on poster board to show the parts of your city's government.

Step 3 Under each name, list the responsibilities for that person's part of government. Add drawings of responsibilities such as trash pickup or streetlights. Give your chart a title.

Step 4 Share your chart with your classmates.

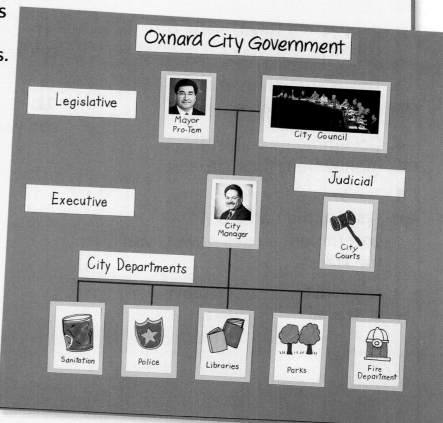

Oxnard City Government

Legislative

Mayor Pro-Tem

City Council

Judicial

Executive

City Manager

City Courts

City Departments

Sanitation   Police   Libraries   Parks   Fire Department

Chapter Review

Vocabulary Review

Copy the sentences below on a separate sheet of paper. Beside each number, write the word from the list below that best matches the description.

law	right
legislative	tax

1. This branch of the government **3.4.4** writes our laws.

2. This is a rule made by a **3.4.1** government for all of the people in a town, state, or country.

3. This is something that **3.4.1** everyone deserves.

4. Governments collect this **3.4.1** money from their citizens.

5. **Test Preparation** In a _____ **3.4.1** system, the national government shares power with the states.

    A. **judicial**   C. **executive**
    B. **federal**   D. **local**

Comprehension Check

6. Why are laws important?
3.4.1

7. Why is voting a responsibility of **3.4.2** citizens?

8. What is the Bill of Rights?
3.4.1

9. What are some jobs done by **3.4.2** our national government?

10. How are the positions of **3.4.4** President, governor, and mayor the same and different?

11. **Critical Thinking** How are the **3.4.4** responsibilities of each branch of government different?

12. **Critical Thinking** Name three **3.4.1** ways a person can show he or she is a good citizen.

Write a complete sentence to answer each question.

Using Grid Maps

13. What can grid maps tell us?
`3.4.3`

14. Name something found in box B2.
`3.4`

15. In which grid box is Saint James Park located?
`3.4.3`

16. **Test Preparation** A map that has a set of lines that cross to form boxes is a _____ .
`3.4`

San José: Downtown

	1	2	3	4	
A			Santa Clara County Courthouse		**A**
B	HP Pavillion at San José	San Pedro Square	St. James Park / City Hall		**B**
C		Center for the Performing Arts	Plaza de César Chávez	San José State University	**C**
D	Children's Discovery Museum	Convention Center			**D**
	1	2	3	4	

0   1/8   1/4 mile
0   1/8   1/4 kilometer

Using Primary Sources

Letters

17. Why are letters an important source of information about history?
`3.4.3`

18. What important right did Jefferson speak about in the letter on page 341?
`3.4.3`

Hands–on Activity

19. **Create a Skit** Work in groups to think about one right that people in this country have. Write and perform a skit that shows why it is an important right.
`3.5.1` ELA `LS2.2`

Write About Government

20. **Personal Letter** Think about the rules in your class. What rule would you add? Write a letter to the students in your class about the new rule and why you think it is needed.
`3.5.1` ELA `W2.2`

For help with the process of writing, visit:

www.macmillanmh.com/ss/ca/writing

Celebrating America

In this chapter you will read about America's heroes and symbols. Our country's heroes have made the United States a better place by standing up for freedom and fairness. Our national symbols stand for beliefs we all share.

Sacramento River

Sacramento

Colorado River

PACIFIC OCEAN

1 **American Heroes** (page 374)
People we look up to, such as Frederick Douglass, help us understand important ideas.

Our Country's Symbols (page 386)
Symbols, such as the American bald eagle, stand for important beliefs that Americans share.

LEGEND

California

⊛ United States capital

★ State capital

CANADA

Missouri River

Mississippi River

Rio Grande

MEXICO

•New York

⊛ Washington, D.C.

ATLANTIC OCEAN

N W E S

How have American heroes fought for freedom?

hero
slavery
Underground Railroad
segregation

VOCABULARY STRATEGY

SUFFIXES The suffix **-ion** changes a verb into a noun. The verb **segregate** means to separate people by race. What do you think **segregation** means?

Compare and Contrast

Copy the diagram below. Compare and contrast two of the heroes from this lesson.

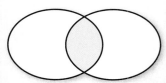

American Heroes

Start with Your
CALIFORNIA STANDARDS

3.4 Students understand the role of rules and laws in our daily lives and the basic structure of the U.S. government.

3.4.6 Students describe the lives of American heroes who took risks to secure our freedoms.

Read about real people who risked their lives for our freedoms. (Begins on page 375)

Firefighters of the United States Forest Service battle a fire in San Diego County. ▼

Rudy Garcia-Tolson is a hero. He needs artificial legs to walk. But walking wasn't enough for Rudy—he learned to run, bike, and swim, too. At age 10 he took part in his first triathlon, or three-event race. In 2004 he won a gold medal with the United States Paralympic swim team.

Heroes Make a Difference 3.4.6

Who is your **hero**? You have probably seen superheroes in movies or on television. Real people can be heroes, too. A hero is someone people look up to or admire because of great achievement or fine qualities. Your hero might be a firefighter in your community or a teacher who has helped you.

In our nation's past there have been many heroes who fought bravely for freedom. Some fought for the freedom to believe what they wanted. Some fought to make sure all Americans were treated fairly. Some fought so that all Americans would have equal rights.

In this lesson you will read about some American heroes. All of them were real people who risked their lives for freedom. The stories of their lives will help you understand why freedom is so important.

REVIEW What is a hero? *Summarize*

Fighting for Freedom 3.4.6

Anne Hutchinson is an American hero. We remember her as someone who stood up for freedom of religion. Freedom of religion is the right to practice any religion you choose, or no religion at all.

Anne was born in England and came to North America with her family in 1634. When she was a child her father taught her to think for herself and to speak her mind.

Anne was deeply religious. She began to meet with other people in her home to talk about religion. She said, "He who has God's grace in his heart cannot go astray." Her ideas were different from what the ministers of her community taught.

The ministers had Anne arrested and put on trial. During her trial Anne Hutchinson stood by what she believed. She said that only God could be her judge.

Heroes do not always win. The court ordered Anne to leave the community. She left, but she never gave up her ideas, or her right to think for herself.

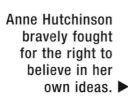

Anne Hutchinson bravely fought for the right to believe in her own ideas. ▶

Winning Independence

We remember Thomas Jefferson and Benjamin Franklin as heroes who helped our country gain its independence from Great Britain. Jefferson and Franklin were two of the men chosen in 1776 to write the Declaration of Independence. This document told Great Britain why Americans wanted to be free. Jefferson wrote most of this important document. Publishing the Declaration was the beginning of a long war with Britain.

Jefferson wrote that "all men are created equal." At that time, however, **slavery** was legal in the United States. Slavery is the practice of keeping people against their will and forcing them to work. Jefferson owned slaves, but Franklin did not. In 1789, after our country won its freedom, Franklin asked Congress to end slavery. Congress refused. In the next section you will read about other Americans who worked to end slavery.

REVIEW What did Hutchinson, Jefferson, and Franklin have in common in their struggles for freedom? *Summarize*

▲ Thomas Jefferson (top) and Benjamin Franklin fought for democracy.

Freedom for All 3.4.6

Harriet Tubman and Frederick Douglass are heroes. They both fought to free enslaved Africans.

Harriet Tubman was born into slavery in the South. She escaped to the North, where she became free. For many years after her escape, Tubman risked her life leading other enslaved people to freedom. The routes she followed, and the system of stopping places where people could hide, were known as the **Underground Railroad**. In all she helped lead more than 300 people to freedom.

Frederick Douglass was also born into slavery and escaped to the North. There he started a newspaper and used it to speak out against slavery. He also traveled and gave speeches. Later, he served as an adviser to President Abraham Lincoln, who helped end slavery in the United States.

◀ Frederick Douglass (left) and Harriet Tubman (above) fought to free enslaved people.

Votes for Women

Elizabeth Cady Stanton and Susan B. Anthony were great friends who worked for more than 50 years to gain rights for women. When they first met in 1851, women in our country had few rights. In most places women could not vote or even own land.

Stanton and Anthony worked to change that. They wrote books, held meetings, made speeches, and talked to Congress. They even led **protests**. A protest is an action that is meant to show that you believe something is wrong. Both women died before women gained the right to vote, but they are remembered for their fight for women's rights.

Read the section from a letter that Anthony wrote Stanton. It tells of one protest they led.

▲ Elizabeth Cady Stanton

Primary Sources

Susan B. Anthony

A section from a letter
by Susan B. Anthony
November 5, 1872

❝Well I have gone and done it!!—positively voted. . . . I hope the morning's telegrams will tell of many women all over the country trying to . . . [uphold] the existing Constitution.❞

Write About It! What effect do you think Anthony hoped her action would have on other women?

REVIEW How were Tubman, Douglass, Stanton, and Anthony heroes? *Summarize*

Freedom and Fairness 3.4.6

When Martin Luther King, Jr., was born in 1929, the United States did not treat African Americans fairly. King spoke out against **segregation**. Segregation is the separation of people by race or the color of their skin. In many states African Americans could not eat in the same restaurants or go to the same schools as whites. In some cities African Americans had to sit in the back of buses or in special sections in movie theaters.

Dr. King asked government leaders to change segregation laws. He led protest marches, and refused to use violence to meet his goals. King was killed in 1968. Today we remember him as a hero who fought for freedom and fairness.

▲ Martin Luther King, Jr., won the Nobel Peace Prize in 1964.

REVIEW How did Dr. King lead the fight against segregation? *Summarize*

Global Connections

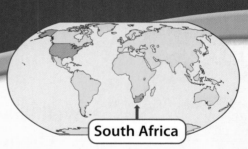

South Africa

Nelson Mandela

For most of his life, Nelson Mandela (man DEL uh) worked to change unfair laws. These laws said that non-white people could only work in certain jobs and live in certain places. They could not vote.

Nelson Mandela protested these unfair laws. He was arrested and went to prison for 27 years! While he was in prison, he wrote many books and became famous as a leader. Finally, in 1990, he was set free. In 1994 Nelson Mandela was elected president of South Africa.

How did Nelson Mandela change South Africa?

▲ Dr. King leads a march in Montgomery, Alabama, in 1965.

What You Learned

3.4.6 American heroes have fought bravely for freedom.

3.4.6 Anne Hutchinson fought for religious freedom. Benjamin Franklin and Thomas Jefferson fought for independence.

3.4.6 Harriet Tubman and Frederick Douglass fought for freedom for enslaved Africans. Susan B. Anthony and Elizabeth Cady Stanton fought for women's rights.

3.4.6 Martin Luther King, Jr., fought for equal rights for all Americans.

Lesson Review

1. Focus Question How have American **3.4.6** heroes fought for freedom?

2. Vocabulary Write one sentence for **3.4.6** each vocabulary term.

| hero | slavery |
| segregation | Underground Railroad |

3. Citizenship What are three ways **3.4.6** the United States treated African Americans unfairly during Martin Luther King, Jr.'s, time?

4. Critical Thinking Make 3.4.6 Inferences Why did the Declaration of Independence lead to a war with Great Britain?

5. Reading Strategy Compare and 3.4.6 Contrast Copy the **ELA R2.3** diagram. Use it to compare and contrast the ways Harriet Tubman and Susan B. Anthony helped people win their freedom.

6. Write about THE BIG IDEA Write about **3.4.6** how one American hero helped to **ELA W2.2** change the way our government works.

7. Link to the Arts Find out more **3.4.6** about an event in the life of an American hero. Work with a group to write a short play about the event. Present the play to your class.

Use Cutaway Diagrams 3.4.3

You already know that Thomas Jefferson helped write the Declaration of Independence. He was also our country's third President. Did you know that he designed buildings, too? One of the buildings he designed was his own home. It is called Monticello. You can learn about Monticello from this **cutaway diagram**. A cutaway diagram shows the inside and outside of an object in the same picture.

1 Learn It

Follow the steps for reading a cutaway diagram. Look at the diagram on page 383 as you read.

- A cutaway diagram is like a window that lets you look inside something. Look closely at the diagram to tell which parts show the inside of Monticello and which parts show the outside.

- Read the labels to see which parts of Monticello are shown in the diagram. The labels are written next to **leader lines**. Leader lines lead your eye to the part of the diagram that is labeled.

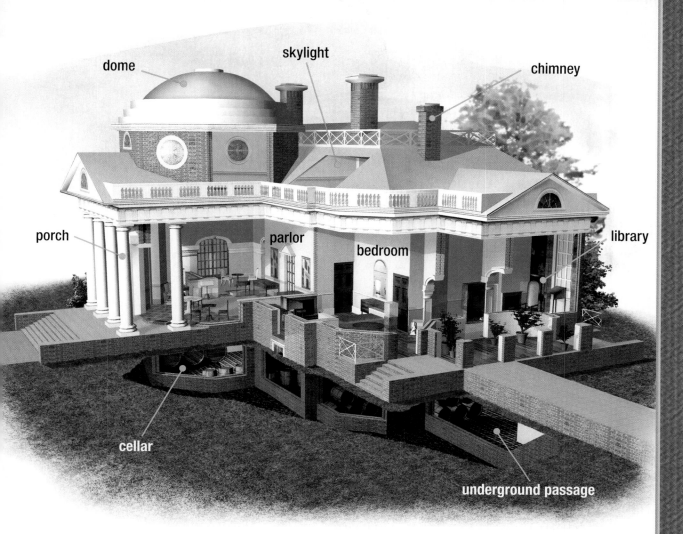

dome · skylight · chimney · porch · parlor · bedroom · library · cellar · underground passage

2 Try It

Answer the questions by reading the cutaway diagram above.

- What does the diagram show that the photograph does not?

- Which labels tell you about the outside of Monticello?

- Which labels tell you about the inside of Monticello?

- What does this diagram tell you about how Jefferson lived?

3 Apply It

Make your own cutaway diagram of a place you know inside and out, such as your home or room. Use colored markers to draw your cutaway diagram. Use labels and leader lines to show information.

Biography
Focus on Justice

"It was we, the people; not we, . . . the male citizens; but we, the whole people, who formed the Union."

Susan B. Anthony 1820–1906

Not so long ago—only about 100 years—women in our country did not have the right to vote. Susan B. Anthony worked to change that. She died in 1906, but thanks to her work, the 19th Amendment to the Constitution gave women the right to vote in 1920.

When Susan was born, many families did not believe that girls needed an education. One day Susan came home from school and said that her teacher would not let girls learn long division. Her father took Susan out of the school. He started a school in his home where girls were treated equally.

The Life of Susan B. Anthony

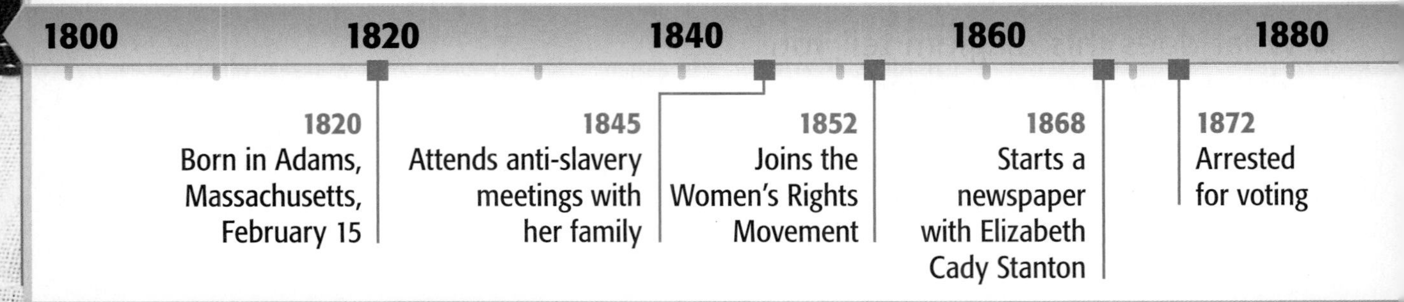

1800	1820	1840	1860	1880

1820 Born in Adams, Massachusetts, February 15

1845 Attends anti-slavery meetings with her family

1852 Joins the Women's Rights Movement

1868 Starts a newspaper with Elizabeth Cady Stanton

1872 Arrested for voting

When she grew up, Anthony taught for 10 years. Then she began work to change the law that said women could not vote.

Anthony organized meetings of people who supported more rights for women. She spoke before the United States Congress many times. She also put out a newspaper about women's rights.

During the 1872 election for President, Anthony led a protest. She and other women decided they would try to vote, even if they were arrested for doing so. When Anthony first tried to sign up to vote, she was told "No." Still, she kept trying, and on November 5, she voted. About two weeks later, the police arrested her, and she was ordered to pay a fine. At her trial, Anthony made a powerful speech and refused to pay the fine.

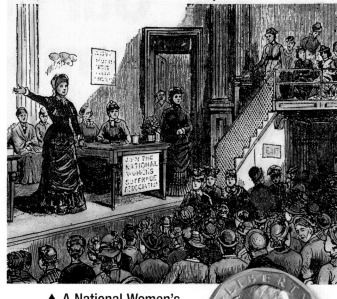

▲ A National Women's Suffrage Association meeting in the 1870s

Write About It! **Why did Susan B. Anthony try to vote in 1872?**

1900   1920

1906
Dies in Rochester, New York

1920
Women win the right to vote in the United States

LOG ON

For more about Susan B. Anthony, visit:

www.macmillanmh.com/ss/ca/bios

FOCUS QUESTION

What are some symbols of our country?

VOCABULARY

symbol
liberty
democracy
landmark

VOCABULARY STRATEGY

COMPOUND WORDS A compound word, such as **landmark**, is made up of two smaller words. Knowing the meanings of the smaller words—**land** and **mark**—helps you define the compound word.

READING STRATEGY

Summarize
Copy the chart below. Summarize the three types of symbols and landmarks you read about in this lesson.

Our Country's Symbols

Start with Your
CALIFORNIA STANDARDS

3.4 Students understand the role of rules and laws in our daily lives and the basic structure of the U.S. government.

3.4.3 Know the histories of important local and national landmarks, symbols, and essential documents that create a sense of community among citizens and exemplify cherished ideals.

Read about some of the ideas that bring us together as a country. (Begins on page 389)

The Statue of Liberty ▶

Did you know that the eagle is our national bird? The beauty, strength, and proud independence of the eagle stand for the strength and freedom of the United States.

Symbols of Our Country 3.4.3

What do you think of when you see an American flag? You probably know that the flag is a **symbol** for our country. A symbol is something that stands for something else. The stars of our flag stand for the 50 states. The stripes stand for the original 13 colonies. In the Pledge of Allegiance, we honor the flag as a symbol of our country and its promise of "liberty and justice for all."

▲ Symbols remind us of important ideas.

The Statue of Liberty is another symbol. **Liberty** is an important idea for people in the United States. It means freedom from control by someone else. The Statue of Liberty stands on an island in New York Harbor. It was the first thing millions of people saw when they came to this country by boat. For many it symbolizes our country's freedoms.

REVIEW What is a symbol? *Summarize*

Symbols of Government 3.4 3.4.3

You have read about the Declaration of Independence. This is the document that explained to the world why the United States wanted to be a free and independent country. It is a symbol of how our country began. The Declaration said that "all men are created equal." We remember the ideas of freedom and equality when we see it.

The Constitution of the United States is another symbol of our country. After winning independence from Great Britain, the United States needed a plan to govern itself. People wanted a government that would protect their freedoms and rights. So the Constitution was written to make sure the government was strong but fair. The Constitution became a symbol reminding us that our freedoms are protected by law.

▲ The Declaration of Independence is a symbol of freedom.

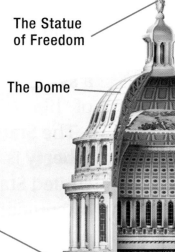

The Statue of Freedom

The Dome

The United States Capitol Building

The House of Representatives Chambers

The Rotunda

A Government Landmark

Our government is a **democracy** (duh MOK rah see). That means it is a government run by the people. In the United States, citizens vote to elect leaders who make the laws for our country. These lawmakers are called senators and representatives. They work in the United States Capitol building in Washington, D.C. Look at the diagram to see some rooms inside the Capitol.

The Capitol is a special kind of symbol known as a **landmark**. A landmark is an important building, structure, or place. The Statue of Liberty is a landmark, too. It stands for the promise of freedom that the United States offers people. The Capitol stands for democracy—the idea that people can govern themselves.

REVIEW What are some symbols of the United States government? *Main Idea and Details*

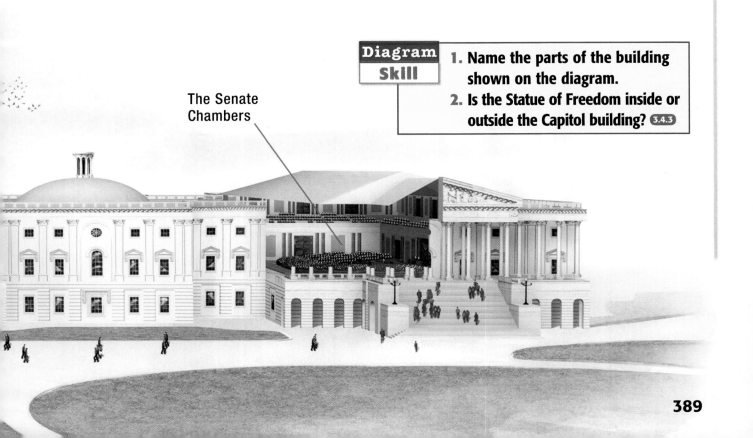

The Senate Chambers

Diagram Skill

1. **Name the parts of the building shown on the diagram.**
2. **Is the Statue of Freedom inside or outside the Capitol building?** 3.4.3

Local Landmarks and Symbols 3.4.3

Communities have important symbols and landmarks, too. Just look around and you will find them. These symbols and landmarks tell us about the history of our communities. They also tell us what our communities think is important.

The city flag of Glendale shows a city landmark. The landmark is the first house built by Spanish settlers over 200 years ago. By having the house on the city flag, people in Glendale honor the city's Spanish heritage.

The city flag of Oakland honors one of its landmarks, the large oak tree in front of City Hall. The oak tree is a symbol of strength. It also reminds people of Oakland's natural beauty and resources.

Are there symbols and landmarks in your community? Look around. You may be surprised by what you find.

REVIEW Why is it imporant for communities to have symbols and landmarks? *Summarize*

▲ The flag of the City of Glendale

▼ The oak tree is a symbol of Oakland.

◀ The word *Eureka* on the California seal reminds us of the discovery of gold.

What You Learned

3.4.3 Our country has many symbols. The flag, the Statue of Liberty, and the bald eagle are symbols of the United States.

3.4
3.4.3 The Declaration of Independence, the United States Constitution, and the Capitol building are symbols of our government.

3.4.3 Communities have landmarks and symbols.

Lesson Review

1. **Focus Question** What are some **3.4.3** symbols of our country?

2. **Vocabulary** Write one sentence for **3.4** each vocabulary term.
3.4.3

democracy   liberty
landmark   symbol

3. **Government** Which important ideas **3.4** do the United States Constitution and Capitol building remind us of?

4. **Critical Thinking Draw Conclusions** **3.4.3** Was New York Harbor the right place to put the Statue of Liberty? Why or why not?

5. **Reading Strategy** **3.4.3** **Summarize** Copy the **3.4.3** chart. Use it to **ELA** **R2.3** summarize what the flag, the Statue of Liberty, and the United States Capitol represent.

6. **Write about** THE BIG IDEA Choose one **3.4** symbol of our government to write **ELA** **W2.2** about. Explain the meaning of the symbol and why it is important.

7. **Link to Art** Design a building or **3.4.3** landmark for your community. Choose items that stand for what is important to you. Present your drawing to your class, and explain what the landmark means.

Fact and Opinion 3.4.3

When you are reading, it is important to be able to tell the difference between two kinds of statements. A **fact** is a statement that can be proven to be true. You could prove a fact by checking it in a reference source. An **opinion** tells what someone believes or feels. It may or may not be true. Knowing the difference between facts and opinions can help you become a better reader.

1 Learn It

■ To find facts, look for things like dates or amounts that you can check. "The Statue of Liberty was given to the United States by the people of France in 1885. It stands 151 feet high." The information in these statements can be checked in a reference source.

■ To identify opinions, look for clue words like *better*, *probably*, *should*, and *believe*. They often show that a statement is an opinion. Other words like *most*, *best*, and *worst* can also be clue words. "I believe the Statue of Liberty is the most beautiful statue in the world." This statement is an opinion. It is someone's belief and cannot be proved.

2 Try It

Read the paragraph about Mount Rushmore. Look for facts and opinions.

Mount Rushmore is probably the best-known monument in the United States. It is located in South Dakota. It honors four presidents—George Washington, Abraham Lincoln, Thomas Jefferson, and Theodore Roosevelt. Sculptor Gutzon Borglum carved the heads of the famous presidents into the mountainside. The work took 14 years to complete.

- Is the first sentence a fact or an opinion? How do you know?

- How could you prove that the second sentence is a true statement?

- Why is it important to be able to tell the difference between facts and opinions?

3 Apply It

Read the paragraph below and try to identify which statements are facts and which are opinions.

The bald eagle is a symbol of our country. Many people believe it is the most beautiful bird in the United States. It first appeared on the Great Seal of the United States in 1784. At the time, however, Benjamin Franklin did not like the choice of an eagle. He wanted the turkey to be chosen instead. If Franklin had gotten his way, we would have a turkey instead of an eagle on the dollar bill.

Washington, D. C.

Washington, D.C.

Washington, D.C., is our nation's capital. It was named for George Washington, and is the home of all three branches of our government. The city is not part of any state, but is part of a special district, called the District of Columbia. More than 18 million people visit the city each year to see its monuments, museums, and landmarks.

❶ The Lincoln Memorial ▶

This landmark honors Abraham Lincoln, our country's 16th President. It is also a symbol of how our country remains united. You can read words from Lincoln's speeches carved into the walls.

◀ ❷ National Air and Space Museum

You can see the world's first airplane here. It was invented by Wilbur and Orville Wright. You can also see a spaceship that went to the moon, and touch a moon rock that the astronauts brought back.

❸ National Museum of the American Indian ▶

This museum celebrates the art and culture of Native American groups from North, Central, and South America. Each tribe got to choose objects they wanted the museum to show.

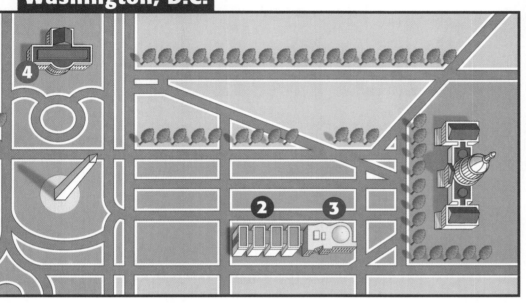

Washington, D.C.

❹ The White House

The President of the United States lives and works in the White House. On most days you can take a tour of the White House and see where history is made. ▼

ACTIVITY

Write a travel brochure describing one of the sites on the tour. You can also research and write about a different site in Washington, D.C.

LOG ON

For more about our nation's capital visit:

www.macmillanmh.com/ss/ca/fieldtrips

The Story of
Paul Bunyan 3.4.3

Characters

———— * ————

Father   Elmer

Mother   Sally

Paul Bunyan

Narrator: Our tall tale begins with a young boy named Paul Bunyan. Paul is no ordinary boy. You see, he is big—really, really, big. How big? Try 10 times the size of a regular two-year-old. Our story begins on Paul's second birthday.

(Mr. and Mrs. Bunyan are at home talking about how to celebrate Paul's birthday.)

Father: Two years old, and he is bigger than we are! I don't know what to do.

Mother: Still, he is awfully cute, and I know you love him.

Father: That's true. But he has a way of getting himself into giant-sized mischief.

Mother: That's just what children do.

Father: I guess you're right. (*Leaving*) I'll go get the lumber wagon.

Mother: What for?

Father: If we are going to take him for a ride, nothing else can hold him.

Narrator: Paul continued to grow bigger and bigger. He did get into mischief, as children often do.

Mother: *(walking, holding Paul by the hand)* I have some bad news. The baby walked into town today. Now the town is in ruins. He just can't help it!

Father: Let's face facts. Paul isn't like other babies. Most babies just eat one bowl of porridge. Paul eats 400!

Mother: Most babies play with toys. Paul plays with an ax. The other day he dragged his ax behind him. Now we have the Grand Canyon.

Father: When he started to walk, his footprints made the Great Lakes. *(Disappointed)* I think we need to find some place big enough for Paul, some place where he can't get into mischief.

Narrator: And so young Paul went to live in the woods, where he continued to grow bigger and bigger. He became a lumberjack. He brushed his teeth with the tops of pine trees and wrestled polar bears for fun. He whacked down 20 trees with one swing of his mighty ax. His best friend was a giant blue ox named Babe. One day, Paul got a letter.

Paul: *(holding a letter)* It says here the President wants me to chop down all the trees in North and South Dakota by spring. He wants to make room for new settlers coming in. I think that even I will need some help to do that.

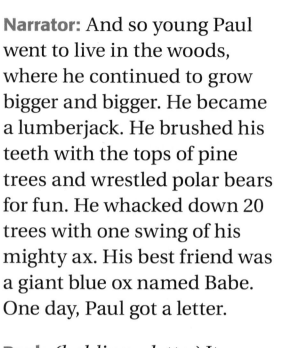

Narrator: So Paul made some new friends.

(Elmer and Sally enter)

Paul: *(shaking hands with Elmer)* Elmer, I hear you're a really good lumberjack. Is that true? And you, Sally, are the best cook west of the Mississippi River. Can you help me?

Elmer/Sally: *(together)* Sure.

Paul: Great. Let's get started. Sally, can you cook enough for 10,000 lumberjacks?

Sally: No problem. Just find me a lake and dump in all the pork and beans you can lay your hands on. Then, build a few fires to boil the lake, and I'll make you the best soup you've ever tasted.

(Sally stirs the lake of soup. Elmer and Paul chop trees furiously.)

Narrator: The lumberjacks worked all winter long, day and night. Sally's soup kept them going strong. By spring, they had finished the job.

Sally: Well, you did it. Look! There's the first wagon bringing settlers here.

Paul: I should be happy, but I'm not.

Elmer: Why?

Paul: All I can think of is how they'll never hear the wind through the trees.

Elmer: So?

Paul: Well, that's wrong. I just chopped a thousand trees. Now I'm going to plant a thousand more.

Narrator: And that's exactly what he did. Many more stories have been told about Paul Bunyan. These tall tales entertained men, women, and children all over the United States. Paul's spirit gave them courage. Paul's energy, size, and strength became a symbol for the United States.

Write About It!

Write a tall tale of your own. Use the tall tale to explain how your community came to be.

Symbols and Landmarks in Your Community 3.4.3

SAN JOSÉ

Nadia lives in San José. She learned about her community's symbols, landmarks, and city seal. Then she decided to make her own city seal. You can make a city seal for your community, too. Here is what to do:

- Go to your city hall, your local library, or on the Internet to find out about your city or town's city seal and local landmarks.

- Think about other people, places, or things which might be symbols of your community and which you could put on a city seal. What is your city known for? What animals live nearby? Were any famous people born in your community? What is produced in your area?

LOG ON
For more help in finding out about your town's landmarks and seal, visit:

http://www.macmillanmh.com/ss/ca/local

ACTIVITY

Make a City Seal

Step 1 Look at your notes and pictures. Choose one or more things you would like to put on your own city seal.

Step 2 Try out many ideas on scratch paper, until you get a design you really like. Some city seals picture just one place or thing on it. Others include three or four symbols.

Step 3 Then draw your best design on stiff paper or poster board.

Step 4 Include your city's name on your seal. You may also want to include the year it was founded, or a nickname for the city.

Step 5 Share your city seal with your classmates.

Materials
- markers, colored pencils, or crayons
- scratch paper
- stiff paper or poster board

Vocabulary Review

Copy the sentences below on a separate sheet of paper. Use the list of vocabulary words to fill in the blanks.

landmark   slavery
segregation   symbol

1. _____ is the practice of
3.4.6 keeping people against their will and forcing them to work without pay.

2. A _____ is an important
3.4.3 building, structure, or place.

3. A _____ is something that
3.4.3 stands for another thing.

4. Separating people by race is
3.4.3 called _____ .

5. Test Preparation A government
3.4.6 in which citizens choose their leaders is a _____ .

A. **symbol**   C. **democracy**
B. **hero**   D. **landmark**

Comprehension Check

6. Why did the ministers of Anne
3.4.6 Hutchinson's colony not like the way she was teaching?

7. What was the purpose of
3.4.6 writing the Declaration of Independence?

8. What are two symbols on the
3.4.3 American flag?

9. Critical Thinking Sometimes it
3.4.6 is important to fight to change laws. Why?

10. Critical Thinking Why is it
3.4.6 difficult to fight for freedoms?

For each sentence, tell whether it is a fact or an opinion.

Fact and Opinion

11. Our country's flag is very pretty.
3.4.3

12. The flag of the United States is
3.4.3 red, white, and blue.

13. The Statue of Liberty is our
3.4.3 nation's greatest symbol of freedom.

14. The Declaration of
3.4.3 Independence was signed in 1776.

15. Test Preparation Which word
3.4.3 means something that can be proved to be true?

    A. question   **C. fact**
    B. opinion   **D. decision**

16. Test Preparation Is the following
3.4.3 sentence a fact or an opinion?

    The bald eagle is a symbol of our country.

Quote

Reread page 379, to answer the questions below.

17. What did Susan B. Anthony
3.4.6 mean when she wrote "I have gone and done it"?

18. What makes Susan B. Anthony's
3.4.6 letter a primary source?

19. Make a Poster Work in a small
3.4.6 group to discuss what the
ELA
W2.0 United States stands for. Then, create a new symbol for our country. Explain how your symbol represents the United States.

20. Descriptive Think about a hero
3.4.6 you read about in this chapter.
ELA
W2.2 Write a paragraph that describes what it might be like to fight for freedom with that hero.

For help with the process of writing, visit:

www.macmillanmh.com/ss/ca/writing

Unit Review and Test Prep

Comprehension and Critical Thinking Check

Write a sentence or more to answer each question.

1. Why is **liberty** an important American belief? `3.4.3`

2. What responsibilities do states have in our **federal** system? `3.4.4`

3. What decisions does the **judicial branch** make? `3.4.4`

4. Who do the **laws** the national government makes apply to? `3.4.4`

5. What are some of the things a **city manager** does? `3.4.4`

6. Name one **symbol** of our country. What does it stand for? `3.4.3`

7. What are some things governments use **taxes** for? `3.4.4`

8. Name an American **hero**. What did he or she fight for? `3.4.6`

9. **Critical Thinking** Why is the **Bill of Rights** an important part of our country's laws? `3.4.1`

10. **Critical Thinking** Why is it important for all people to be treated equally in our **democracy**? `3.4.1`

Reading Social Studies Check

Compare and Contrast

Reread "Freedom for All" on page 378. Use the chart to compare and contrast the lives of Frederick Douglass and Harriet Tubman. `3.4.6` `ELA R2.3`

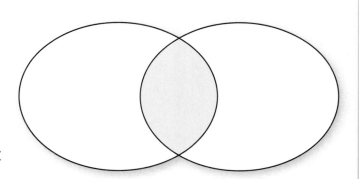

11. How were the lives of Harriet Tubman and Frederick Douglass similar? `ELA R2.3`

12. What are the different ways they fought against slavery? `ELA R2.3`

13. What makes both Harriet Tubman and Frederick Douglass heroes? `ELA R2.3`

Read the paragraphs. Then answer the questions.

Laws protect us. They help people get along. In California people come up with many ideas for new laws. How do these ideas become laws? Someone in the legislative branch shares an idea for a law. The idea is turned into a bill. Members of the legislative branch discuss the bill. Then they vote on the bill. If they approve the bill, it goes to the governor.

The governor can sign the bill into law. The governor can also say no to the bill becoming a law. However, if the bill has the support of two out of every three members of the legislature, then the bill still becomes a new law. Laws made in California are only for people in California.

14. What is a bill?

3.4.4

  A a new law

  B a vote

  C an idea for a new law

  D a way to vote for a new law

15. What happens if the governor turns down a bill?

3.4.4

  A The bill can't become a law.

  B The bill can become a law with a two-thirds vote of the legislature.

  C The governor can't turn down a bill.

  D The bill becomes a law anyway.

Write About History

16. Personal Letter Write a letter to your mayor about a change you would like to make in your community. Expain why your idea would make the community a better or safer place to live.

ELA W2.3

17. Descriptive Choose one of the rights that you learned about and write a paragraph explaining why it is important.

3.4.1 ELA W2.2

18. Descriptive Think about why the Pledge of Allegiance was written and what it means. Then write your own class pledge.

ELA W2.2

For help with the process of writing, visit:

www.macmillanmh.com/ss/ca/writing

Why do communities need government?

Write About the Big Idea 3.4.1 ELA W.2.3

Write a Formal Invitation Letter

Think about what you have learned about government. Fill in the graphic organizer with what you have learned.

Write a letter to a member of your local or state government inviting them to visit your class. Use your graphic organizer to tell what you would like to know more about.

What I Know	What I Want to Know	What I Learned
1. Police and fire departments protect our community	1. Who is responsible for police and fire departments?	1. My local government is . . .
2.	2.	2.
3.	3.	3.
4.	4.	4.

Write a Formal Invitation Letter

Writing a letter to a government official takes some planning. Review the steps to help you.

1. Plan
- Invitations you send to your friends are informal. However, one you write to a member of government will be more formal.

2. Write a First Draft
- Clearly explain your reason for writing.
- Choose several dates and times to suggest for a visit.
- Include a heading, inside address, greeting, body, and closing. Remember to sign your letter.

3. Revise and Proofread
- Check that you have all the parts of a formal letter.
- Fix errors in spelling, capitalization, and punctuation.
- Rewrite it neatly, then mail it.

Speak About the Big Idea 3.4.4 ELA SL2.3

Role Play a Government Official

Find out more about a job in your local government. Then teach your classmates about that job.

Prepare Work in pairs. Research a government job you would like to know more about. Make a list of questions. Find out who does the job and what they do.

Present Tell the class what person and job you researched. Then describe the responsibilities of the job. Dress as if you had the government job. Allow time for your classmates to ask questions and to summarize what they learned.

Parks Director
Responsibilities

• Street Landscaping
• Maintenance
• Building new parks
• Community Gardens

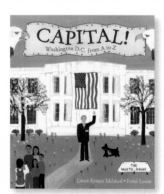

LAUNCH PAD For help with the Big Idea activity, visit:

www.macmillanmh.com/ss/ca/launchpad

Read More About the Big Idea

America Is . . .

Louise Borden This is the author's answer to the question, "What is it like to live in America?"

Capital!

Laura Krauss Melmed
Go on an alphabetic tour of our nation's capital.

Uncle Sam and Old Glory

Delno C. West and Jean M. West Learn the stories behind the country's most famous national symbols.

Reference Section

The Reference Section has many parts, each with a different type of information. Use this section to look up people, places, and events as you study.

★☆★

Holidays

Communities Celebrate Holidays

During the year people in communities around our country come together to celebrate holidays that are important to them. Holidays help us to remember and celebrate different cultures, important people, and events.

In this special section you will read about many holidays. You will see how people all across our country celebrate holidays.

Labor Day

Did you know that the Labor Day holiday is more than one hundred years old? The first Labor Day was celebrated on September 5, 1882.

Labor Day was created by labor organizations to celebrate American workers. The holiday was originally celebrated with large parades of workers. The workers would march through the streets with colorful posters and banners.

Today, most people celebrate Labor Day by spending time with their friends and families. Many communities have large picnics on Labor Day. Other people take one last vacation trip before fall comes.

ACTIVITY

Suppose you are going to be in a parade. Make a poster that celebrates jobs that workers do.

Rosh Hashanah

Rosh Hashanah (rohsh huh SHAH nuh) is a religious holiday celebrated by Jewish people all around the world. It celebrates the Jewish New Year. It lasts for two days during September or October. It is a time for people to think about how they get along with others, and to remember the year that has passed. Families gather and enjoy special foods.

People blow the shofar (SHOH fahr), or ram's horn, on this holiday. It was blown in ancient times to announce important events. Another tradition is dipping apples in honey. This symbolizes the hope for a sweet new year.

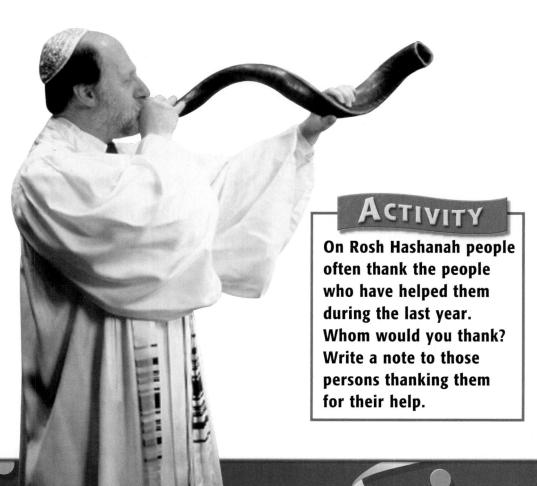

ACTIVITY

On Rosh Hashanah people often thank the people who have helped them during the last year. Whom would you thank? Write a note to those persons thanking them for their help.

Eid al-Fitr

People in Muslim communities all over the world celebrate a religious holiday called Eid al-Fitr (EED AHL FIHT er), which means the "Festival of Fast-Breaking." Eid al-Fitr takes place every year after the end of a month called Ramadan (rah mah DAHN). It usually falls in December. During Ramadan, Muslims fast, or do not eat, during the day. They do good deeds and study their holy book, the Quran.

On the first day of Eid al-Fitr families and friends celebrate with an early morning prayer. Children dress in new clothes and get presents. Families share a special meal. Sweet foods made with dates and honey are favorite treats.

ACTIVITY

The month of Ramadan begins with a new moon. What is a new moon? Other stages of the moon are the quarter, half, and full moons. Illustrate a chart with the moon's stages.

Thanksgiving

Pass the turkey, please! In 1621, there was a Thanksgiving celebration in Plymouth, Massachusetts. The Pilgrims wanted to give thanks to God for their rich harvest. They also wanted to thank the Wampanoag Indians for showing them how to grow crops and survive the harsh winter.

Today many Americans celebrate the Thanksgiving holiday with a special meal. We celebrate Thanksgiving on the fourth Thursday of November. It is a time for us to be thankful for the many good things in our lives.

ACTIVITY

In 1863 President Lincoln gave a speech asking all Americans to observe a day of giving thanks. Think of a holiday you think all Americans should celebrate, and write a speech about why we should celebrate it.

Winter Holidays

Hanukkah

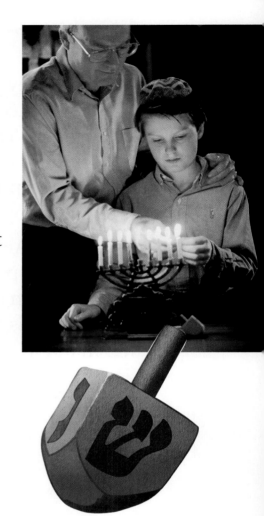

Hanukkah (HAH nah kah) is a religious holiday celebrated by Jewish people around the world. Hanukkah is eight days long and usually falls in December. It celebrates a victory of 2,000 years ago that brought religious freedom to Jews.

Lighting the menorah (muh NAWR uh), a holy lamp or candleholder, each night is an important part of Hanukkah. Today Jews light one candle for each night of Hanukkah. On the eighth night all the candles are lit.

Christmas

Christmas is a religious holiday that is celebrated by Christian people around the world. Christmas celebrates the birth of Jesus on December 25.

On Christmas Day people gather around the Christmas tree. They give each other gifts. Some people like to celebrate the holiday by singing Christmas carols.

Kwanzaa

Kwanzaa (KWAHNZ uh) is a holiday celebrated by many African Americans today. The name "Kwanzaa" comes from the African language of Swahili (swah HEE lee). It means "first fruits." During Kwanzaa, people gather to celebrate the fall crops, pride in their African background, and beliefs such as working together as a community.

Kwanzaa lasts for seven days, from December 26 to January 1. People gather each night of this week to celebrate and share food. They also light candles on the kinara (kee NAH rah), a candleholder.

ACTIVITY

Winter holidays are a time to celebrate community. Many people give thanks for the things they have and the people they know. Write a poem that celebrates your community or family.

Martin Luther King, Jr., Day

Dr. Martin Luther King, Jr., was born in Atlanta, Georgia, on January 15, 1929. During the 1950s and 1960s, he worked to make sure people of all races were treated fairly. In 1963 he made an important speech in Washington, D.C. He said, "I have a dream that my four children will one day live in a nation where they will not be judged by the color of their skin. . . ."

Dr. King was killed in 1968. His birthday became a holiday that is celebrated on the third Monday in January. Today, many people honor this day by working together for their community. In this way, they are trying to make Dr. King's dream come true.

ACTIVITY

The dream of Martin Luther King, Jr., was that one day Americans of all races could live together as friends. Write about something you wish for that would help the world.

Presidents' Day

Happy Birthday, George and Abraham! Though their birthdays are on different days of the month, we celebrate George Washington's and Abraham Lincoln's birthdays on the same day. It is the third Monday in February. This holiday is called Presidents' Day.

George Washington was our country's first President, and a general in the Revolutionary War. Abraham Lincoln was President of our country during the Civil War. He was killed in 1865. Presidents' Day is a time to remember both great men.

ACTIVITY

Do you know which famous Presidents are pictured on American coins? Make a chart showing the names of the Presidents found on the following coins: penny, nickel, dime, quarter, and half dollar.

César Chávez Day

César Chávez was born on March 31, 1927, in Yuma, Arizona. When César was a boy, he worked with his family as a migrant farm worker, traveling from farm to farm picking crops. It was a hard life, and the farm workers were usually treated badly by the owners of the farms. When Chávez grew up, he began working with farm workers to improve their lives. He organized a union to get fair treatment for farm workers.

Chávez's birthday is now a holiday. It is a time to remember someone who believed in non-violence and fought for justice.

ACTIVITY

César Chávez tried to get farm workers to work together for justice. Write about why people working together might be better than each person working alone.

Cinco de Mayo

Have you ever heard someone say "Viva la libertad!" (vee VAH LAH LEE bir tahd)? It means "Long live liberty" in Spanish. In some communities you can hear these words during a holiday called Cinco de Mayo (SEEN koh DAY MIGH yoh). This holiday celebrates a Mexican victory over a much larger French army, on May 5, 1862. The Mexicans fought because they wanted liberty, or freedom, from France.

Cinco de Mayo means "Fifth of May" in Spanish. On this day, Mexicans and Mexican Americans celebrate with parades, dancing, mariachi music, and Mexican foods.

ACTIVITY

You read that Cinco de Mayo means "Fifth of May" in Spanish. Find out how to say other numbers and months in Spanish. Can you say your birthday in Spanish?

Memorial Day

On the last Monday in May we celebrate Memorial Day. The holiday used to be called Decoration Day, because people would decorate the graves of soldiers who had lost their lives in war. Memorial Day began as a day to remember those killed during the Civil War. Today we honor all soldiers who have died for our country.

People celebrate Memorial Day in different ways. Families place flags and flowers at the graves of relatives who died in wars. Many communities remember our soldiers with a parade. Often a lone bugler will play "Taps," the song for fallen soldiers. How is Memorial Day celebrated in your community?

ACTIVITY

Design a patriotic poster celebrating Memorial Day. Hang it in your classroom to remember the Americans who have lost their lives in war.

Independence Day

Summer is a special time across our country. For many people summer fun starts only after a very well-known holiday. Independence Day marks the celebration of our country's birthday on July 4,1776. It reminds us of our country's declaration of independence from Great Britain.

How do you like to celebrate Independence Day? If your town is like many across the country, you enjoy a fireworks display!

ACTIVITY

Do you know what the colors of our flag stand for? The red stands for courage. The white stands for purity. The blue is for loyalty. If you were to make a flag for your classroom, what colors would you use? Would your classroom flag have stars? How many? What you'll need
- construction paper
- crayons
- scissors

Your flag can be of any shape and any colors.

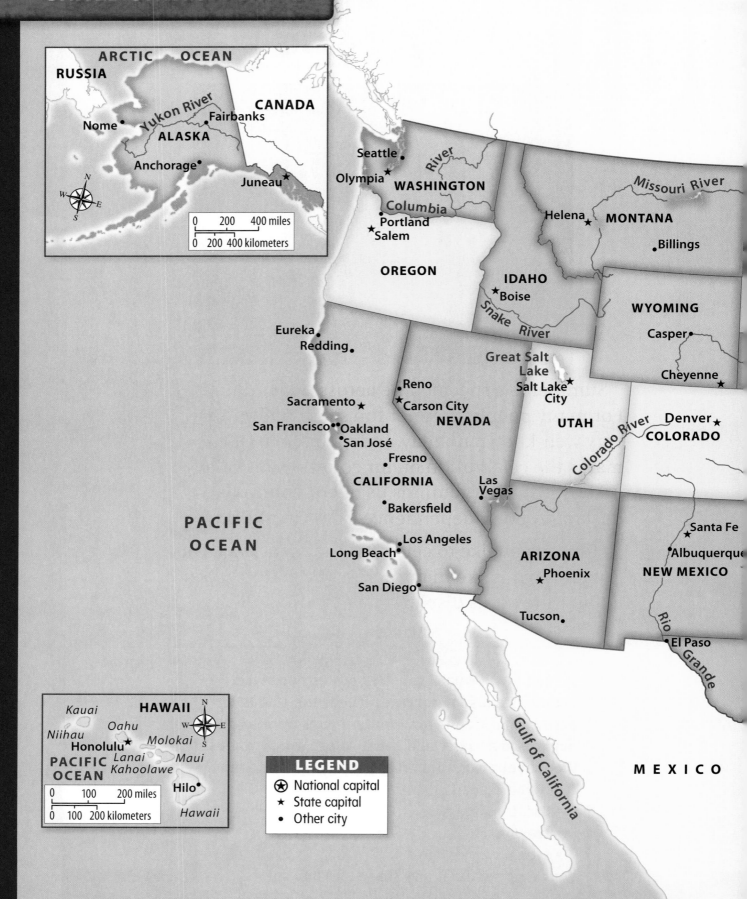

ARCTIC OCEAN

RUSSIA

Yukon River

CANADA

Nome

Fairbanks

ALASKA

Anchorage

Juneau

N
W   E
S

0   200   400 miles
0   200   400 kilometers

Seattle

Olympia   WASHINGTON

Columbia   River

Portland
Salem

OREGON

Helena   MONTANA

Billings

IDAHO
Boise

Snake   River

WYOMING

Casper

Cheyenne

Missouri River

Eureka
Redding

Great Salt
Lake

Salt Lake
City

Reno

Sacramento   Carson City

San Francisco   Oakland
San José   NEVADA

UTAH

Colorado River

Denver

COLORADO

Fresno

CALIFORNIA

Las
Vegas

Bakersfield

Santa Fe

Los Angeles

Long Beach

ARIZONA

Albuquerque

NEW MEXICO

San Diego

Phoenix

PACIFIC
OCEAN

Tucson

El Paso

Rio Grande

Gulf of California

MEXICO

HAWAII

Kauai

Oahu

N
W   E
S

Niihau

Molokai

Honolulu

Lanai   Maui

PACIFIC
OCEAN   Kahoolawe

Hilo

0   100   200 miles
0   100   200 kilometers

Hawaii

LEGEND

⊛ National capital
★ State capital
• Other city

CANADA

NORTH DAKOTA
★ Bismarck
★ Fargo

SOUTH DAKOTA
★ Pierre
★ Sioux Falls

MINNESOTA
• Duluth
St. Paul ★
• Minneapolis

Lake Superior

MICHIGAN

Lake Huron

WISCONSIN
• Milwaukee
Madison ★

Lake Michigan

Grand Rapids •
Lansing ★

• Detroit

Lake Erie

Lake Ontario

• Buffalo

NEW HAMPSHIRE
★ Concord

MAINE
★ Augusta

VERMONT
Montpelier ★

NEW YORK
Albany ★

Hartford ★

MASSACHUSETTS
★ Boston

★ Providence
RHODE ISLAND
CONNECTICUT

★ New York

NEBRASKA
• Omaha
• Lincoln

Platte River

Missouri River

IOWA
Cedar Rapids •
Des Moines ★

ILLINOIS
Springfield ★

INDIANA
Indianapolis ★

Ohio River

• Chicago

OHIO
Columbus ★

• Cleveland

• Pittsburgh

PENNSYLVANIA
Harrisburg ★

Trenton ★
NEW JERSEY
• Philadelphia
Dover ★

DELAWARE
Annapolis ★
MARYLAND

KANSAS
Topeka ★
• Wichita

Kansas City
Kansas City

St. Louis •

MISSOURI
Jefferson City ★

Arkansas River

KENTUCKY
Frankfort ★

Washington, D.C. ⊛

WEST VIRGINIA
• Charleston

• Richmond

VIRGINIA

OKLAHOMA
Oklahoma City ★
• Tulsa

Red River

ARKANSAS
Little Rock ★

Mississippi River

• Memphis

TENNESSEE
• Nashville

Tennessee River

NORTH CAROLINA
★ Raleigh
• Charlotte

SOUTH CAROLINA
• Columbia

• Charleston

TEXAS
• Dallas

Brazos River

Austin ★
• San Antonio
• Houston

• Corpus Christi

LOUISIANA
Baton Rouge ★
• New Orleans

MISSISSIPPI
Jackson ★

• Mobile

ALABAMA
Montgomery ★

GEORGIA
Atlanta ★

• Savannah

• Jacksonville

Tallahassee ★

FLORIDA
• Tampa

• Miami

ATLANTIC OCEAN

THE BAHAMAS

Gulf of Mexico

CUBA

N
W   E
S

0   200   400 miles
0   200   400 kilometers

R17

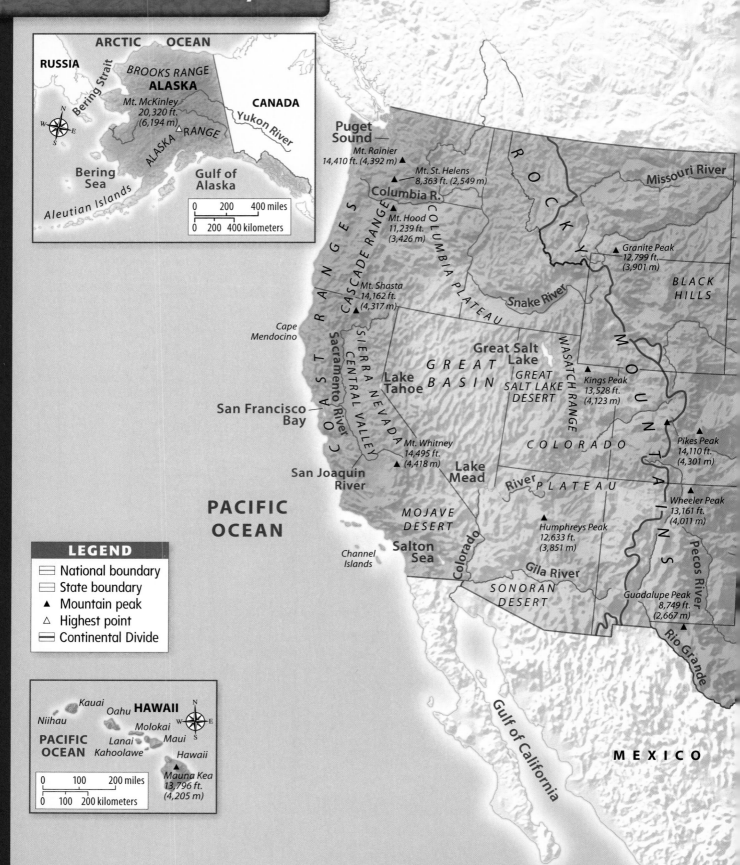

ARCTIC OCEAN

RUSSIA

BROOKS RANGE

ALASKA

Bering Strait

Mt. McKinley
20,320 ft.
(6,194 m)

CANADA

ALASKA RANGE

Yukon River

Bering
Sea

Gulf of
Alaska

Aleutian Islands

| 0 | 200 | 400 miles |
| 0 | 200 | 400 kilometers |

Puget
Sound

Mt. Rainier
14,410 ft. (4,392 m) ▲

Mt. St. Helens
8,363 ft. (2,549 m) ▲

Columbia R.

Mt. Hood
11,239 ft.
(3,426 m)

ROCKY

Missouri River

Granite Peak
12,799 ft.
(3,901 m)

BLACK
HILLS

Snake River

COLUMBIA PLATEAU

Mt. Shasta
14,162 ft.
(4,317 m) ▲

Cape
Mendocino

CASCADE RANGE

COAST RANGES

Sacramento River

SIERRA NEVADA

CENTRAL VALLEY

Great Salt
Lake

GREAT
BASIN

Lake
Tahoe

GREAT
SALT LAKE
DESERT

WASATCH RANGE

Kings Peak
13,528 ft.
(4,123 m) ▲

COLORADO

MOUNTAINS

San Francisco
Bay

Mt. Whitney
14,495 ft.
(4,418 m) ▲

Lake
Mead

River

PLATEAU

Pikes Peak
14,110 ft.
(4,301 m) ▲

San Joaquin
River

MOJAVE
DESERT

Salton
Sea

Colorado

Wheeler Peak
13,161 ft.
(4,011 m) ▲

PACIFIC
OCEAN

Channel
Islands

Humphreys Peak
12,633 ft.
(3,851 m) ▲

Gila River

Pecos River

SONORAN
DESERT

Guadalupe Peak
8,749 ft.
(2,667 m) ▲

Rio Grande

LEGEND
- National boundary
- State boundary
- ▲ Mountain peak
- △ Highest point
- Continental Divide

Gulf of California

MEXICO

Kauai
Niihau
Oahu **HAWAII**
Molokai
Lanai Maui
Kahoolawe
**PACIFIC
OCEAN**
Hawaii
Mauna Kea
13,796 ft.
(4,205 m) ▲

| 0 | 100 | 200 miles |
| 0 | 100 | 200 kilometers |

CANADA

MESABI RANGE

Lake Superior

GREAT LAKES

Mississippi River

Lake Michigan

Lake Huron

Lake Ontario

St. Lawrence River

GREEN MTS.

WHITE MTS.

Mt. Washington
6,288 ft.
(1,917 m)

ADIRONDACK MTS.

Cape Cod

Lake Erie

ALLEGHENY PLATEAU

Long Island

GREAT PLAINS

Platte River

Missouri River

CENTRAL PLAINS

Wabash River

Ohio River

ALLEGHENY MTS.

Delaware Bay

APPALACHIAN MOUNTAINS

Potomac River

PIEDMONT

Chesapeake Bay

Arkansas River

INTERIOR PLAINS

OZARK PLATEAU

Mt. Mitchell
6,684 ft.
(2,037 m)

Tennessee River

Savannah R.

Cape Hatteras

Red River

OUACHITA MOUNTAINS

Mississippi River

ATLANTIC COASTAL PLAIN

ATLANTIC OCEAN

Brazos River

Alabama River

Colorado River

EDWARDS PLATEAU

GULF COASTAL PLAIN

Mobile Bay

Mississippi River Delta

Lake Okeechobee

THE BAHAMAS

Galveston Bay

Gulf of Mexico

N W E S

Florida Keys

Straits of Florida

CUBA

THE 50 UNITED STATES

ARCTIC
Bering Sea
ALASKA
Gulf of Alaska
LEGEND
National boundary
State boundary
National capital
N
W
E
S
PACIFIC OCEAN
WASHINGTON
OREGON
NEVADA
CALIFORNIA
HAWAII
0 300 600 miles
0 300 600 kilometers

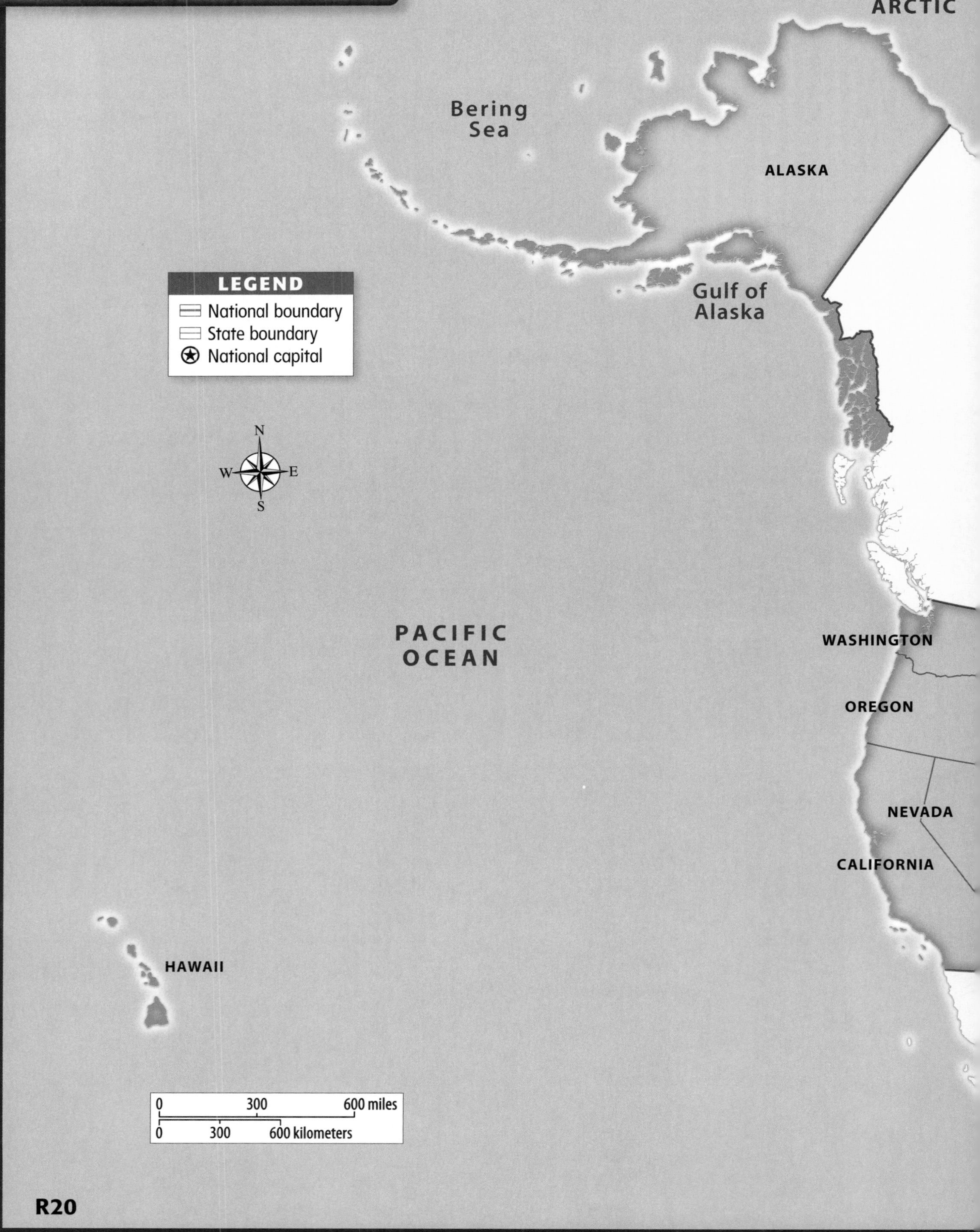

OCEAN

Greenland
(Denmark)

Labrador
Sea

Hudson
Bay

CANADA

Great
Lakes

NEW
HAMPSHIRE
VERMONT
MAINE

MASSACHUSETTS

RHODE ISLAND
CONNECTICUT
NEW JERSEY
DELAWARE
MARYLAND

MONTANA

NORTH
DAKOTA

MINNESOTA

IDAHO

SOUTH
DAKOTA

WISCONSIN

MICHIGAN

NEW
YORK

WYOMING

NEBRASKA

IOWA

PENNSYLVANIA

OHIO

UTAH

INDIANA

WEST
VIRGINIA

Washington, D.C.

COLORADO

KANSAS

ILLINOIS

VIRGINIA

MISSOURI

KENTUCKY

ARIZONA

OKLAHOMA

ARKANSAS

TENNESSEE

NORTH
CAROLINA

NEW
MEXICO

SOUTH
CAROLINA

MISSISSIPPI

GEORGIA

ATLANTIC
OCEAN

TEXAS

ALABAMA

LOUISIANA

FLORIDA

THE
BAHAMAS

MEXICO

Gulf of
Mexico

CUBA

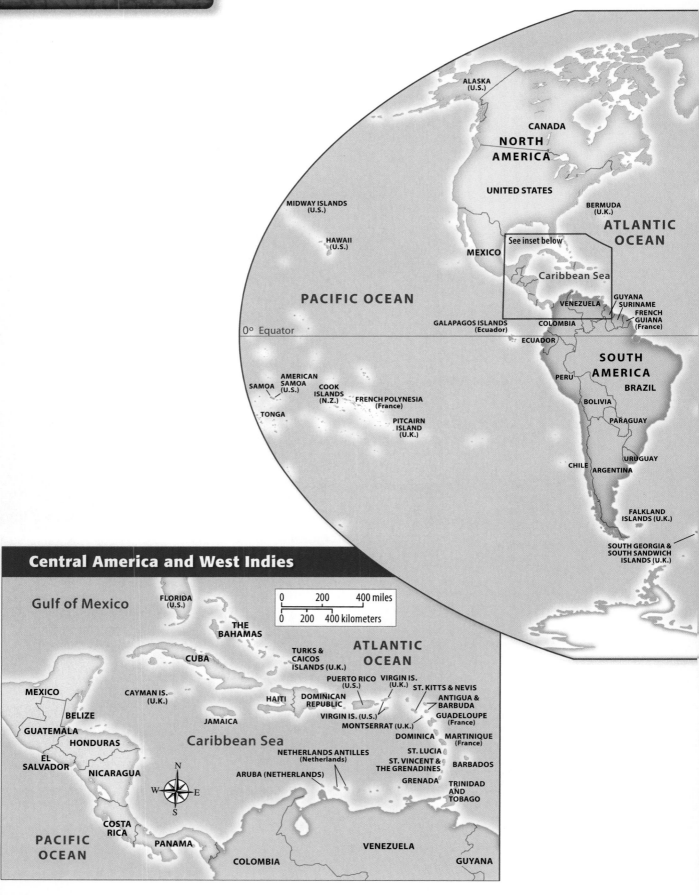

ALASKA (U.S.)

CANADA

NORTH AMERICA

UNITED STATES

MIDWAY ISLANDS (U.S.)

BERMUDA (U.K.)

ATLANTIC OCEAN

HAWAII (U.S.)

See inset below

MEXICO

Caribbean Sea

GUYANA
SURINAME
FRENCH GUIANA (France)

VENEZUELA

PACIFIC OCEAN

GALAPAGOS ISLANDS (Ecuador)

COLOMBIA

0° Equator

ECUADOR

SOUTH AMERICA

PERU

BRAZIL

AMERICAN SAMOA (U.S.)

SAMOA

COOK ISLANDS (N.Z.)

FRENCH POLYNESIA (France)

BOLIVIA

PARAGUAY

TONGA

PITCAIRN ISLAND (U.K.)

URUGUAY

CHILE

ARGENTINA

FALKLAND ISLANDS (U.K.)

SOUTH GEORGIA & SOUTH SANDWICH ISLANDS (U.K.)

Central America and West Indies

Gulf of Mexico

FLORIDA (U.S.)

0   200   400 miles
0   200   400 kilometers

THE BAHAMAS

ATLANTIC OCEAN

CUBA

TURKS & CAICOS ISLANDS (U.K.)

MEXICO

CAYMAN IS. (U.K.)

PUERTO RICO (U.S.)

VIRGIN IS. (U.K.)

ST. KITTS & NEVIS

HAITI

DOMINICAN REPUBLIC

ANTIGUA & BARBUDA

BELIZE

JAMAICA

VIRGIN IS. (U.S.)

GUADELOUPE (France)

GUATEMALA

MONTSERRAT (U.K.)

HONDURAS

Caribbean Sea

DOMINICA

MARTINIQUE (France)

EL SALVADOR

NETHERLANDS ANTILLES (Netherlands)

ST. LUCIA

NICARAGUA

ST. VINCENT & THE GRENADINES

BARBADOS

N
W   E
S

ARUBA (NETHERLANDS)

GRENADA

TRINIDAD AND TOBAGO

COSTA RICA

PACIFIC OCEAN

PANAMA

VENEZUELA

COLOMBIA

GUYANA

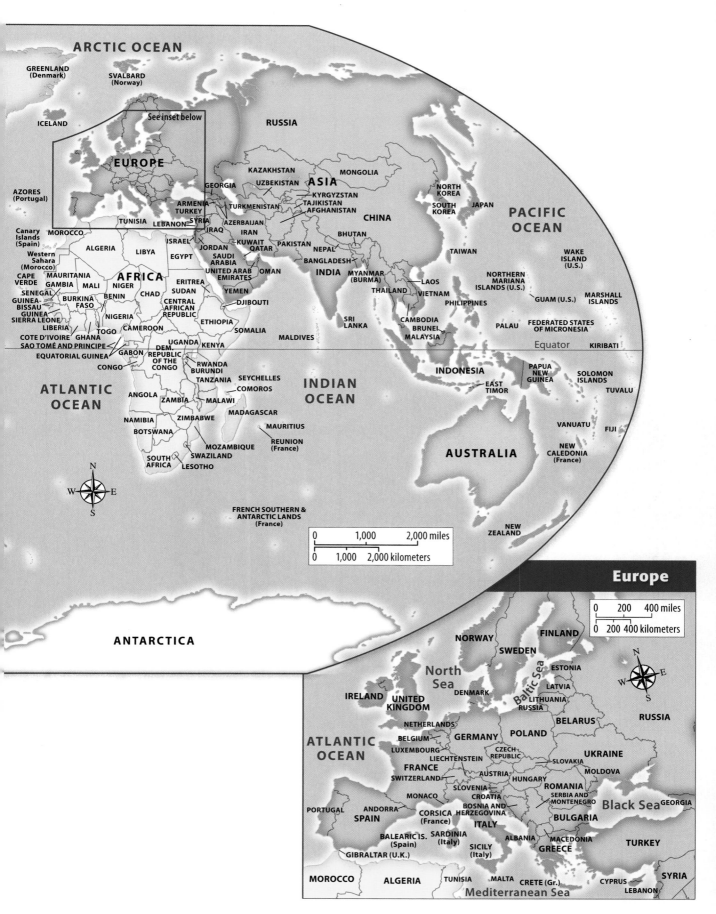

ARCTIC OCEAN

GREENLAND
(Denmark)

SVALBARD
(Norway)

ICELAND

RUSSIA

See inset below

EUROPE

AZORES
(Portugal)

GEORGIA

KAZAKHSTAN

MONGOLIA

ASIA

ARMENIA
TURKEY

UZBEKISTAN

KYRGYZSTAN
TAJIKISTAN
AFGHANISTAN

NORTH
KOREA

SOUTH
KOREA

JAPAN

PACIFIC
OCEAN

TUNISIA

LEBANON

SYRIA

TURKMENISTAN

CHINA

MOROCCO

IRAQ

AZERBAIJAN

IRAN

Canary
Islands
(Spain)

ISRAEL

ALGERIA

LIBYA

JORDAN
EGYPT

KUWAIT
QATAR

SAUDI
ARABIA

PAKISTAN

BHUTAN

NEPAL

BANGLADESH

TAIWAN

WAKE
ISLAND
(U.S.)

Western
Sahara
(Morocco)

CAPE
VERDE

MAURITANIA

GAMBIA

MALI

NIGER

BENIN

CHAD

UNITED ARAB
EMIRATES

ERITREA

SUDAN

OMAN

YEMEN

INDIA

MYANMAR
(BURMA)

THAILAND

LAOS

VIETNAM

NORTHERN
MARIANA
ISLANDS (U.S.)

GUAM (U.S.)

MARSHALL
ISLANDS

GUINEA-
BISSAU

GUINEA

SIERRA LEONE

LIBERIA

BURKINA
FASO

NIGERIA

AFRICA

CENTRAL
AFRICAN
REPUBLIC

DJIBOUTI

CAMBODIA

PHILIPPINES

PALAU

FEDERATED STATES
OF MICRONESIA

COTE D'IVOIRE

GHANA

TOGO

CAMEROON

ETHIOPIA

SOMALIA

SRI
LANKA

MALDIVES

BRUNEI
MALAYSIA

Equator

KIRIBATI

SAO TOMÉ AND PRINCIPE

EQUATORIAL GUINEA

GABON

CONGO

DEM.
REPUBLIC
OF THE
CONGO

UGANDA

RWANDA

BURUNDI

KENYA

TANZANIA

SEYCHELLES

COMOROS

INDIAN
OCEAN

INDONESIA

EAST
TIMOR

PAPUA
NEW
GUINEA

SOLOMON
ISLANDS

TUVALU

ATLANTIC
OCEAN

ANGOLA

ZAMBIA

MALAWI

NAMIBIA

ZIMBABWE

BOTSWANA

MADAGASCAR

MAURITIUS

REUNION
(France)

VANUATU

FIJI

NEW
CALEDONIA
(France)

AUSTRALIA

SOUTH
AFRICA

SWAZILAND

LESOTHO

MOZAMBIQUE

N
W   E
S

FRENCH SOUTHERN &
ANTARCTIC LANDS
(France)

0   1,000   2,000 miles

0   1,000   2,000 kilometers

NEW
ZEALAND

ANTARCTICA

Europe

0   200   400 miles

0   200 400 kilometers

NORWAY

SWEDEN

FINLAND

North
Sea

DENMARK

Baltic Sea

ESTONIA

LATVIA

N
W   E
S

IRELAND

UNITED
KINGDOM

LITHUANIA
RUSSIA

BELARUS

RUSSIA

NETHERLANDS

GERMANY

POLAND

ATLANTIC
OCEAN

BELGIUM

LUXEMBOURG

LIECHTENSTEIN

CZECH
REPUBLIC

SLOVAKIA

UKRAINE

FRANCE

AUSTRIA

HUNGARY

MOLDOVA

SWITZERLAND

SLOVENIA

ROMANIA

PORTUGAL

ANDORRA

SPAIN

MONACO

CORSICA
(France)

CROATIA

BOSNIA AND
HERZEGOVINA

SERBIA AND
MONTENEGRO

Black Sea

GEORGIA

BULGARIA

BALEARIC IS.
(Spain)

SARDINIA
(Italy)

ITALY

ALBANIA

MACEDONIA

TURKEY

GIBRALTAR (U.K.)

SICILY
(Italy)

GREECE

MOROCCO

ALGERIA

TUNISIA

MALTA

CRETE (Gr.)

CYPRUS

SYRIA

LEBANON

Mediterranean Sea

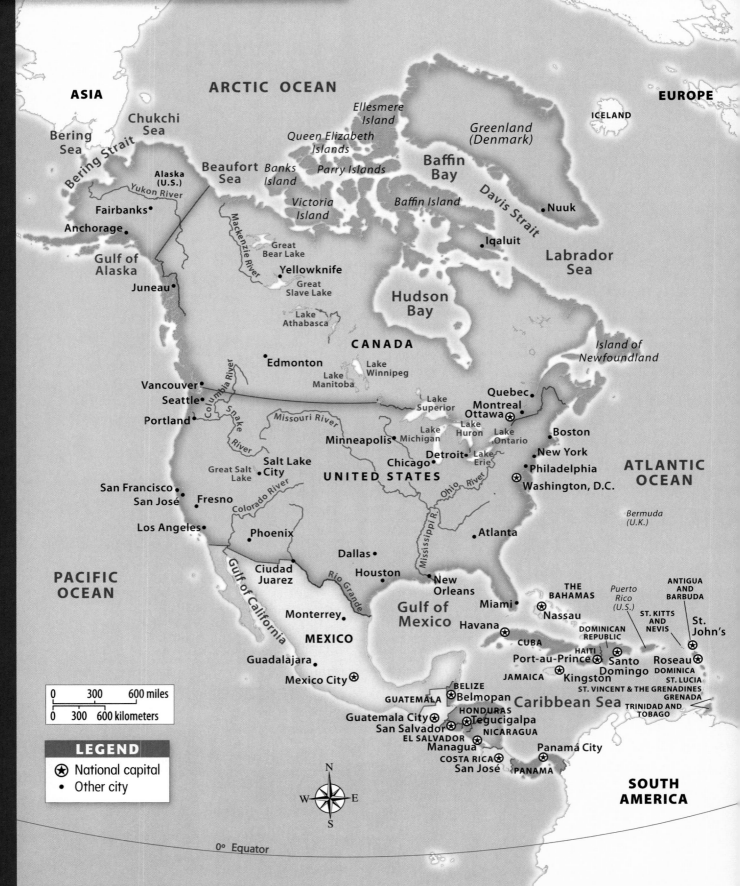

ASIA

ARCTIC OCEAN

EUROPE

Chukchi Sea

Bering Sea

Bering Strait

Ellesmere Island

Queen Elizabeth Islands

Greenland (Denmark)

ICELAND

Alaska (U.S.)

Beaufort Sea

Banks Island

Parry Islands

Baffin Bay

Yukon River

Fairbanks •

Anchorage •

Victoria Island

Baffin Island

Davis Strait

• Nuuk

Gulf of Alaska

Mackenzie River

Great Bear Lake

• Iqaluit

Labrador Sea

Juneau •

Yellowknife •

Great Slave Lake

Hudson Bay

Lake Athabasca

CANADA

Island of Newfoundland

Edmonton •

Lake Winnipeg

Columbia River

Vancouver •

Lake Manitoba

Quebec

Seattle •

Snake River

Lake Superior

Montreal

Ottawa ⊛

Portland •

Missouri River

Minneapolis •

Lake Michigan

Lake Huron

Lake Ontario

• Boston

ATLANTIC OCEAN

Salt Lake City •

Chicago •

Detroit •

Lake Erie

• New York

Great Salt Lake

UNITED STATES

• Philadelphia

San Francisco •

⊛ Washington, D.C.

San José •

Fresno •

Colorado River

Ohio River

Bermuda (U.K.)

Los Angeles •

Phoenix •

• Atlanta

Mississippi R.

Dallas •

PACIFIC OCEAN

Ciudad Juarez •

Rio Grande

Houston •

• New Orleans

THE BAHAMAS

Puerto Rico (U.S.)

ANTIGUA AND BARBUDA

Gulf of California

Miami •

⊛ Nassau

ST. KITTS AND NEVIS

St. John's ⊛

Monterrey •

Gulf of Mexico

Havana ⊛

DOMINICAN REPUBLIC

MEXICO

CUBA

HAITI

Port-au-Prince ⊛

Santo ⊛ Domingo

Roseau ⊛

DOMINICA

Guadalajara •

JAMAICA

Kingston ⊛

ST. LUCIA

Mexico City ⊛

BELIZE

Caribbean Sea

ST. VINCENT & THE GRENADINES

GUATEMALA

⊛ Belmopan

GRENADA

HONDURAS

TRINIDAD AND TOBAGO

Guatemala City ⊛

⊛ Tegucigalpa

San Salvador ⊛

NICARAGUA

EL SALVADOR

Managua ⊛

Panamá City •

COSTA RICA

San José ⊛

PANAMA

SOUTH AMERICA

N W E S

0 300 600 miles

0 300 600 kilometers

LEGEND

⊛ National capital

• Other city

0° Equator

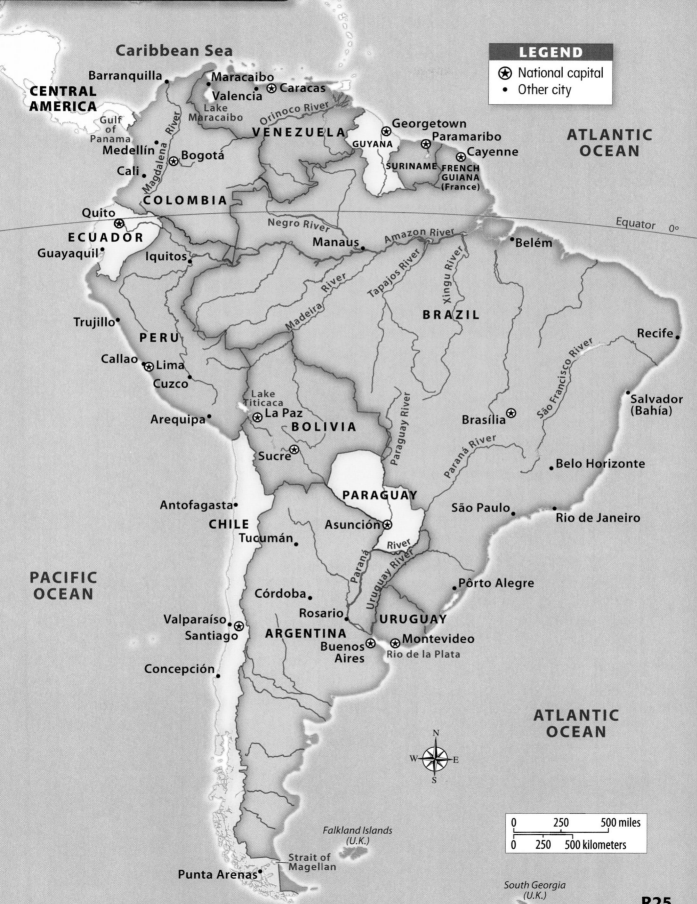

SOUTH AMERICA: Political

Caribbean Sea

CENTRAL
AMERICA

Gulf
of
Panama

Barranquilla

Maracaibo
Valencia
⊛ Caracas

Lake
Maracaibo

Orinoco River

VENEZUELA

GUYANA
⊛ Georgetown
Paramaribo ●
⊛
SURINAME
Cayenne ●
FRENCH
GUIANA
(France)

ATLANTIC
OCEAN

Medellín ●
● Bogotá

Magdalena River

Cali ●

COLOMBIA

Quito ⊛

ECUADOR

Guayaquil ●

Iquitos ●

Negro River

Manaus ●

Amazon River

Belém ●

Equator   0°

Trujillo ●

PERU

River

Madeira

Tapajos River

Xingu River

BRAZIL

Recife ●

Callao ● ⊛ Lima
Cuzco ●

Lake
Titicaca

Arequipa ●

⊛ La Paz

BOLIVIA

Sucre ⊛

São Francisco River

Brasília ⊛

Paraguay River

Salvador
(Bahía) ●

Belo Horizonte ●

Antofagasta ●

PARAGUAY

Paraná River

São Paulo ●

Rio de Janeiro ●

CHILE

Tucumán ●

Asunción ⊛

Paraná River

Uruguay River

Pôrto Alegre ●

PACIFIC
OCEAN

Córdoba ●

Rosario ●

URUGUAY

Valparaíso ●
Santiago ⊛

ARGENTINA

Buenos
Aires ⊛

⊛ Montevideo

Rio de la Plata

Concepción ●

ATLANTIC
OCEAN

LEGEND
⊛ National capital
● Other city

N
W ✦ E
S

Falkland Islands
(U.K.)

Strait of
Magellan

Punta Arenas ●

| 0 | 250 | 500 miles |
| 0 | 250 | 500 kilometers |

South Georgia
(U.K.)

R25

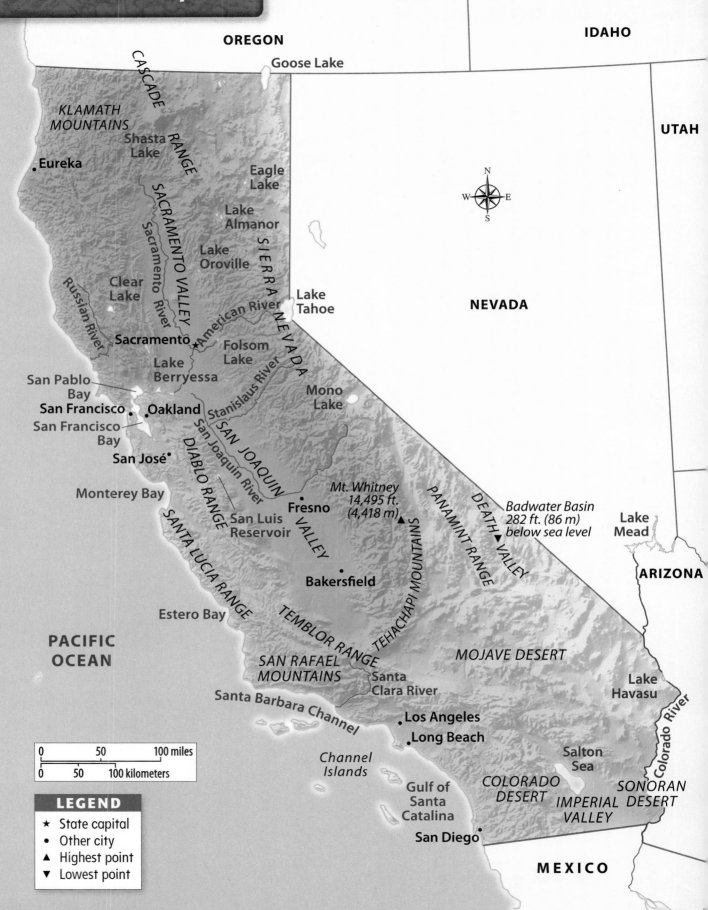

CALIFORNIA: Physical

IDAHO

OREGON

Goose Lake

UTAH

CASCADE RANGE

KLAMATH MOUNTAINS

Shasta Lake

Eureka

Eagle Lake

Lake Almanor

Lake Oroville

SACRAMENTO VALLEY

Sacramento River

Clear Lake

Russian River

SIERRA NEVADA

Lake Tahoe

NEVADA

N
W   E
S

American River

Sacramento

Folsom Lake

Lake Berryessa

Stanislaus River

Mono Lake

San Pablo Bay

San Francisco

Oakland

San Francisco Bay

San José

Monterey Bay

DIABLO RANGE

SAN JOAQUIN VALLEY

San Joaquin River

San Luis Reservoir

Fresno

Mt. Whitney 14,495 ft. (4,418 m)

PANAMINT RANGE

DEATH VALLEY

Badwater Basin 282 ft. (86 m) below sea level

Lake Mead

SANTA LUCIA RANGE

Bakersfield

TEHACHAPI MOUNTAINS

ARIZONA

Estero Bay

PACIFIC OCEAN

TEMBLOR RANGE

MOJAVE DESERT

SAN RAFAEL MOUNTAINS

Santa Clara River

Lake Havasu

Santa Barbara Channel

Los Angeles

Long Beach

Colorado River

Channel Islands

Salton Sea

Gulf of Santa Catalina

COLORADO DESERT

SONORAN DESERT

IMPERIAL VALLEY

San Diego

MEXICO

0   50   100 miles
0   50   100 kilometers

LEGEND
★ State capital
• Other city
▲ Highest point
▼ Lowest point

R26

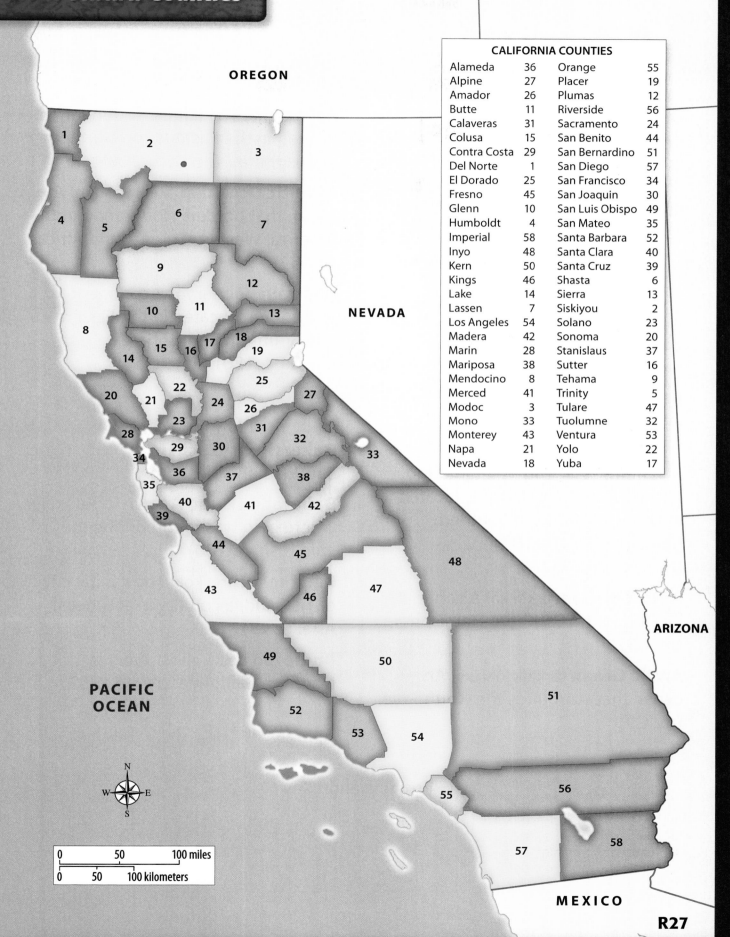

CALIFORNIA: Counties

OREGON

NEVADA

ARIZONA

PACIFIC OCEAN

MEXICO

CALIFORNIA COUNTIES

County		County	
Alameda	36	Orange	55
Alpine	27	Placer	19
Amador	26	Plumas	12
Butte	11	Riverside	56
Calaveras	31	Sacramento	24
Colusa	15	San Benito	44
Contra Costa	29	San Bernardino	51
Del Norte	1	San Diego	57
El Dorado	25	San Francisco	34
Fresno	45	San Joaquin	30
Glenn	10	San Luis Obispo	49
Humboldt	4	San Mateo	35
Imperial	58	Santa Barbara	52
Inyo	48	Santa Clara	40
Kern	50	Santa Cruz	39
Kings	46	Shasta	6
Lake	14	Sierra	13
Lassen	7	Siskiyou	2
Los Angeles	54	Solano	23
Madera	42	Sonoma	20
Marin	28	Stanislaus	37
Mariposa	38	Sutter	16
Mendocino	8	Tehama	9
Merced	41	Trinity	5
Modoc	3	Tulare	47
Mono	33	Tuolumne	32
Monterey	43	Ventura	53
Napa	21	Yolo	22
Nevada	18	Yuba	17

0   50   100 miles
0   50   100 kilometers

N
W   E
S

Gazetteer

This Gazetteer is a geographical dictionary that will help you to pronounce and locate the places discussed in this book. The letters and numbers tell you where each place first appears on a map (m.) or in the text (t.).

A

Africa (af'ri kə) A continent south of Europe, between the Atlantic and Indian oceans. (m. G9)

American River (ə mer'i kən riv'ər) A river in Northern California. (m. R26, t. 22)

Anaheim (an'ə hīm) The tenth most populous city in California, located in Orange County, in Southern California. 34°N, 118°W. (m. 123, t. 259)

Antarctica (ant ärk'ti kə) A continent located in the Southern Hemisphere. (m. G9)

Arctic Ocean (ärk'tik ō'shən) An ocean that surrounds the North Pole. (m. G9)

Asia (ā'zhə) The largest continent, located in the Eastern and Northern hemispheres. (m. G9, t. 108)

Atlantic Ocean (at lan'tik ō'shən) An ocean that borders North and South America, Western Europe, and Africa. (m. G9)

Australia (ôs trāl'yə) A continent and country located in the Eastern and Southern hemispheres. (m. G9, t. 180)

B

Bakersfield (bā'kərs fēld) A city in the San Joaquin Valley. (m. 9, t. 282)

Ballarat (bal'ə rat) A town in Australia where gold was found during the gold rush. (t. 180)

Bangkok (bang'kok) The capital city of Thailand, a country in southeast Asia. (t. 23)

Bodie (bō'dē) A ghost town in Northern California. (m. 35, t. 52)

Pronunciation Key

a	at	ē	me	ō	old	ū	use	ng	song
ā	ape	i	it	ô	fork	ü	rule	th	thin
ä	far	ī	ice	oi	oil	u̇	pull	th	this
âr	care	îr	pierce	ou	out	ûr	turn	zh	measure
e	end	o	hot	u	up	hw	white	ə	about, taken, pencil, lemon, circus

C

California (kal əfôr'nyə) One of the Pacific states of the West region, it is the most populous state in the United States. (m. G10, t. 11)

Canada (kan'ədə) A country in North America, north of the United States. (m. R20, t. 306)

Central Valley (sen'trəl val'ē) A large valley in California between the Coast Ranges and the Sierra Nevada. (m. 47, t. 38)

Chicago (shi kä'gō) A large city in the state of Illinois. (m. 205, t. 204)

China (chī'nə) A country in eastern Asia. (m. R22, t. 315)

Chinatown (chī'nətoun) A neighborhood in San Francisco that is home to a large number of Chinese Americans. (t. 232)

Columbia State Historic Park (kəlum'bē ə stāt his tôr'ik pärk) A former goldmining town in central California, now a state park where people can learn about the Gold Rush. (m. 182, t. 182)

Costa Mesa (kōs'tə mā'sə) A town in Southern California located in Orange County. (t. 109)

E

Eastern Hemisphere (ēs'tûrn hem'is fîr) The half of Earth east of the prime meridian. (m. 225, t. 224)

Ecuador (e'kwədôr) A country in western South America, home to the Secoya Indians. (m. R22, t. 145)

Eureka (yû rē'kə) A city in Northern California. (m. 9, t. 110)

Europe (yur'əp) One of Earth's seven continents, between Asia and the Atlantic Ocean. (m. G9)

F

Fremont (frē'mont) A city in Alameda County, between Oakland and San José. (t. 345)

Fresno (frez'nō) A city in California's San Joaquin Valley; 36° 119°W. (m. 9, t. 282)

Fresno County (frez'nō koun'tē) A county in central California. (m. R27, t. 292)

G

Glendale (glen'dāl) A city in Southern California. (m. 197, t. 390)

I

India (in'dē ə) A country in southwest Asia. (m. R23, t. 214)

Indian Ocean (in′dē ən ō′shən) An ocean between Africa, southern Asia, and Australia. (m. G9)

Ione (ī ō′nē) A town in central California. (t. 148)

Japan (jəpan′) A country of many islands, off the eastern coast of Asia in the Pacific Ocean. It is one of California's leading trading partners. (m. R23, t. 214)

Klamath River (klaʹməth rivʹər) A river in northwestern California that begins in the Klamath Mountains and flows into the Pacific Ocean. (m. 9, t. 110)

Lake Erie (lāk îr′ē) The most southern of the five Great Lakes. It is located on the border between the United States and Canada. (m. 47)

Lake Huron (lāk hyur′ən) The second-largest of the five Great Lakes. It is located on the border between the United States and Canada. (m. 47)

Lake Michigan (lāk mish′i gən) The third-largest of the five Great Lakes. It lies between the states of Michigan and Wisconsin. (m. 47)

Lake Ontario (lāk on târ′ē ō) The smallest of the five Great Lakes. It is located on the border between the United States and Canada. (m. 47)

Lake Superior (lāk səpîr′ē ər) The largest of the five Great Lakes. It is located on the border between the United States and Canada. (m. 47)

Lakewood (lāk′wüd) A suburb of Los Angeles that was one of the first large planned communities. (m. 167, t. 189)

Laos (lous) A country in southeast Asia. (m. R23, t. 290)

Latin America (lat′ən əmer′i kə) The part of the Western Hemisphere south of the United States, including Mexico, Central America, and South America. (t. 192)

Long Beach (lông bēch) The fifth most populous city in California, located in Los Angeles County and known for its large port. (m. 9, t.11)

Los Angeles (lôs an′jələs) California's most populous city, located in Southern California. (m. 9, t. 21)

Los Angeles County (lôs an′jələs koun′tē) A county in Southern California. (m. R27, t. 190).

Los Angeles River (lôs an′jələs riv′ər) A river that runs through the city of Los Angeles. (m. 14)

M

Mexico (meks′i kō) A country in North America, south of and bordering the southwestern United States. (m. R22, t. 125)

Mississippi River (mis əsip′ē riv′ər) One of the longest rivers in North America. It flows south from northern Minnesota into the Gulf of Mexico. (m. 47)

Mojave Desert (mō hä′vē dez′ərt) A desert in southeastern California. (m. 46, t. 98)

N

Nakhodka (nəkōd′kə) A port city in Russia on the Pacific coast. It is a sister city of Oakland, California. (m. 318, t. 318)

North America (nôrth əmer′i kə) A continent in the Northern and Western hemispheres. (m. G9)

Northern Hemisphere (nôr′thərn hem′is fîr) The half of Earth north of the equator. (m. 225, t. 224)

O

Oakland (ōk′lənd) A city on the east side of San Francisco Bay, a major West Coast shipping port, and California's eighth-largest city. (m. 9, t. 16)

Owens River (ō′ənz riv′ər) A river in the Owens Valley. Its flow is diverted for some of Los Angeles's drinking water. (m. 69, t. 68)

Owens Valley (ō′ənz val′ē) A high mountain valley, 200 miles northeast of Los Angeles. (m. 69, t. 68)

Oxnard (ox′närd) A town in Southern California. (t. 368)

P

Pacific Ocean (pəsif′ik ō′shən) An ocean that borders western North and South America and eastern Asia. (m. G9)

Philadelphia (fil ədel′fē ə) A city in Pennsylvania where the Declaration of Independence was signed. (m. G12, t. 343)

Placerville (plas′ər vil) A town near the Sierra Nevada in California where gold was found. (m. 167, t. 177)

R

Redwood National Park (red'wu̇d nash'ə nəl pärk) A national park in the Coast Ranges of California. (m. 56 , t. 56)

Riverside (riv'ər sīd) A large city in Southern California once known for its many orange groves. (t. 74)

Rocklin (rok'lən) A suburb of Sacramento, California, in the central part of the state. (m. 9, t. 24)

Russia (rush'ə) A country in northern Europe and Asia. (m . R 23, t. 318)

S

Sacramento (sakrə men'tō) The capital of California, it is located in the central part of the state. (m. 9, t. 22)

Sacramento River (sakrə men'tō riv'ər) A river that flows 382 miles, from the Cascade Mountains through Northern California into San Francisco Bay. (m. 9, t. 22)

Salinas (sə lē'nəs) A city in the Salinas Valley. It was the hometown of writer John Steinbeck. (m. G13)

San Bernardino (san ber'nə dē nō) A city in Southern California. (m. 199, t. 201)

San Diego (san dē ā'gō) The second most populous city in California, located in Southern California, near the border with Mexico. (m. G14, t. 125)

San Francisco (san frən sis'kō) The fourth most populous city in California, located in Northern California, on the Pacific Ocean. (m. 9, t. 110)

San Francisco Bay (san frən sis'kō bā) A bay off the Pacific Ocean on the California coastline at the city of San Francisco. (m. 9, t. 228)

San Joaquin River (san wä kēn' riv´ər) A river that flows 350 miles from the Sierra Nevada through central California into San Francisco Bay. (m. 9)

San José (san hō zā') The third most populous city in California, located in Northern California. (m. 9, t. 211)

Santa Ana (san'tə a'nə) The ninth most populous city in California, located in Orange County. (m. 35, t. 238)

Santa Barbara (san'tə bär'bər ə) A city in Southern California. (m. 167, t. 170)

Santa Barbara Channel (san'tə bär'bər ə chan'əl) A body of water that lies between the Pacific Coast and the Channel Islands. (m. R26, t. 170)

Santa Clara County (san'tə kler'ə koun'tē) A county in the San Francisco Bay area. (m. R27, t. 213)

Santa Cruz (san'tə krūz) A town in Northern California, on the Pacific Ocean. (m. 287 t. 304)

Shasta County (shas'tə coun'tē) A county in Northern California. (m. 51, t.67)

Shasta Lake (shas'tə lāk) A lake formed by a dam on the Sacramento River. (m. R26, t. 67)

Sierra Nevada (sē er'ə nəvad'ə) A mountain range in eastern California. (m. R26, t. 41)

South Africa (south af'ri kə) A country in Africa. (m. R23, t. 380)

South America (south əmer'i kə) A continent in the Southern and Western hemispheres. (m. G9)

Southern Hemisphere (suth'ərn hem is fîr) The half of Earth south of the equator. (m. 225, t. 224)

Spain (spān) A country in southwestern Europe. (m. R23, t. 143)

Stockton (stok'tən) A town located in California's Central Valley. (m. 187, t. 361)

Tehachapi Mountains (te hä'chä pē mount'ənz) A mountain range in Southern California. (m. R26, t. 98)

Texas (teks'əs) A state in the southwestern United States, on the border with Mexico. (m. G10, t. 278)

Thailand (tī'land) A country in southeast Asia. (m. R23, t. 23)

Trinity River (trin'i tē riv'ər) A river in Northern California that runs into the Klamath River. (t. 100)

Vietnam (vē et näm') A country in southeast Asia. (m. R23, t. 213)

Washington, D.C. (wô'shing tən dē sē) The capital of the United States. It is the home of our country's national government. (m. G11, t. 351)

Western Hemisphere (wes'tərn hem is fîr) The half of Earth west of the prime meridian. (m. 225, t. 224)

Wheatland (hwēt'lənd) A small town northeast of Sacramento, California. (m. 9, t. 24)

Biographical Dictionary

The Biographical Dictionary lists the people you have learned about in this book.
The Pronunciation Key tells you how to say their names.
The page numbers let you see where each person first appears in the text.

Anthony, Susan B. (anth'ə nē) 1820–1906 A teacher and reformer, she fought to give women the right to vote. (p. 379)

Boyar, Louis (boi'ər) 1888–1976 Entrepreneur who was one of the founders of Lakewood, California. (p. 190)

Brown, Grafton Tyler (broun) 1841–1914 African American cartographer and artist. (p. 41)

Bush, George W. 1946– The forty-third President of the United States. (p. 351)

Cabrillo, Juan Rodriguez (kə brē'yo) 1498?–1543 Spanish explorer who led the first voyage along the coast of what is now California in 1542. (p. 170)

Chávez, César (chä'vez) 1927–1993 Mexican American leader who founded the farm workers union. (p. 293)

Columbus, Christopher (kə lum'bəs) 1451–1506 Italian sea captain and explorer who reached the Americas in 1492. (p. 107)

Douglass, Frederick (dug'ləs) 1818?–1895 Former enslaved African who became a famous abolitionist. (p. 378)

Figueroa, Liz (fē gä rō'a) 1951– State Senator, the first Latina Senator from Northern California. (p. 345)

Franklin, Benjamin (fran'klən) 1706–1790 American colonial leader, writer, scientist, and abolitionist. (p. 262)

pronunciation key				
a at	ē me	ō old	ū use	ng song
ā ape	i it	ô fork	ü rule	th thin
ä far	ī ice	oi oil	u̇ pull	th this
âr care	îr pierce	ou out	ûr turn	zh measure
e end	o hot	u up	hw white	ə about, taken, pencil, lemon, circus

H

Huerta, Dolores (wer'tä) 1930– With César Chávez, she co-founded the National Farm Workers Association, a union for farm workers, in 1962. (p. 297)

Hutchinson, Anne (huch'ən sən) 1591–1643 Woman who fought for religious freedom in America. (p. 376))

J

Jefferson, Thomas (jef'ər sən) 1743–1826 The third President of the United States, 1801–1809. He helped write the Declaration of Independence. (p. 337)

K

King, Martin Luther, Jr. 1929–1968 African American leader who worked to make laws fair for all. (p. 380)

L

Lincoln, Abraham (ling'kən) 1809–1865 The sixteenth President of the United States, 1861–1865. He led the north during the Civil War and wanted to end slavery. (p. 378)

M

Mandela, Nelson (man del'ə) 1918– After spending 27 years in prison for fighting to change unfair laws in South Africa, he became the country's president in 1994. (p. 380)

Marshall, James (mär'shal) 1810–1885 His discovery of gold at the American River began the California Gold Rush in 1848. (p. 177)

Mineta, Norm (mi net'ə) 1931– The first Asian American mayor of a major city, and Secretary of Transportation under President George W. Bush. (p. 216)

Mulholland, William (mul hol'ənd) 1855–1935 The chief engineer for Los Angeles, he built the aqueduct that brought water to the city. (p. 68)

R

Robinson, David Laughing Horse (rob'in sən) 1955– A Kawaiisu Native American artist and elder. (p. 99)

Rudd, Justin 1969– A citizen who organized a cleanup of the beach in Long Beach, California. (p. 14)

Schwarzenegger, Arnold (shwôrtz'ə neg ər) 1947– Movie actor who became the 38th governor of California in 2003. (p. 353)

Serra, Junípero (ser'ə, hū nē'pe rō) 1713–1784 A priest born in Spain. He started the first Spanish mission in California, San Diego de Alcalá. (p. 141)

Stanton, Elizabeth Cady (stan'tən) 1815–1902 A leader who fought for women's rights. (p. 379)

Steinbeck, John (stīn'bek) 1902–1968 Author born in Salinas, California, who wrote *The Grapes of Wrath*, about poor farm workers. He won the Nobel Prize for Literature in 1962. (p. 204)

T

Taper, Mark (tā'pər) 1901–1994 Entrepreneur who was one of the founders of Lakewood, California. (p. 190)

Tubman, Harriet (təb'mən) 1820–1913 Famous abolitionist and "conductor" on the Underground Railroad. (p. 378)

Vizcaíno, Sebastián (viz kī ē'nō) 1550?–1615 Spanish sea captain who explored California's coast in 1602. (p. 170)

Washington, George (wô'shing tən) 1732–1799 The first President of the United States. He led Continental Army during the War for Independence. (p. 343)

Weingart, Ben (wīn'gärt) 1888–1980 Entrepreneur who was one of the founders of Lakewood, California. (p. 190)

Youngblood, Mary (yung'blud) 1958– Award-winning Native American musician. (p. 109)

GLOSSARY

This Glossary will help you to pronounce and understand the meanings of the vocabulary terms in this book. The page number at the end of the definition tells where the term first appears.

A

adapt (ə dapt′) To change the way you live. (p. 42)

adobe (ə dō′bē) A kind of brick made from clay and straw. (p. 172)

agriculture (ag′ri kul chər) Growing food and raising or attracting animals for food. (p. 128)

aqueduct (ak′wi dukt) A large pipe or other channel that carries water over a long distance. (p. 68)

artifact (är′ti fakt) Something that was made or used by people in the past. (p. 138)

assembly line (ə sem′blē līn) A line of people and machines that work together to make a product. (p. 312)

astronomy (ə stron′ə mē) The science that deals with the sun, moon, stars, and planets. (p. 136)

B

bar graph (bär graf) A graph that uses bars to show and compare information. (p. 208)

benefit (ben′ə fit) Something that helps a person. (p. 268)

Bill of Rights (bil əv rīts) The part of the United States Constitution that makes sure our most important rights are protected by law. (p. 346)

boundary (bound′ə rē) A line that marks the limits of a country, state, or other area. (p. 228)

budget (buj′it) A plan for using money. (p. 261)

byline (bī′līn) Words that tell who wrote a newspaper story. (p. 184)

C

cable car (kā′bəl kär) A kind of streetcar that is pulled by a cable. (p. 229)

capital (kap′i təl) A city where a nation or a state has its government. (p. 22)

Pronunciation Key									
a	at	ē	me	ō	old	ū	use	ng	song
ā	ape	i	it	ô	fork	ü	rule	th	thin
ä	far	ī	ice	oi	oil	ù	pull	th	this
âr	care	îr	pierce	ou	out	ûr	turn	zh	measure
e	end	o	hot	u	up	hw	white	ə	about, taken, pencil, lemon, circus

capital resources (kap′i təl rē′sôrs es) The tools and machines people use to produce goods. (p. 291)

cardinal directions (kär′də nal di rek′shəns) The directions north, east, south, and west. (p. 130)

century (sen′chə rē) One hundred years. (p.174)

ceremony (ser′ə mō nē) A special way of doing something to mark an important time. (p. 134)

citizen (sit′ə zən) A person who lives in a community and has certain rights and duties. (p. 144)

city council (sit′ē koun′səl) The legislative branch of local government. (p. 362)

city manager (sit′ē man′i jər) In some cities, the head of the city's executive branch. (p. 362)

claim (klām) A legal right to mine on certain land. (p. 179)

climate (klī′mət) The average weather in a place over a long period of time. (p. 40)

coast (kōst) Land next to an ocean. (p. 11)

common good (kom′ən gùd) What is best for everyone. (p. 344)

community (kə mū′ni tē) A place where people live, work, and play. (p. 11)

commute (kə mūt′) To travel regularly to and from work or school over a distance. (p. 24)

compass rose (kum′pəs rōs) A symbol that shows where north, south, east, and west are on a map. (p. 46)

competition (kom pi tish′ən) Trying to win or gain something from others. (p. 279)

consequence (kon′si kwəns) The result of a choice. (p. 58)

conserve (kən sûrv′) Protecting and using less of forests, rivers, and other natural resources. (p. 70)

constitution (kən sti tü′shən) The basic principles used to govern a state, country, or organization; a written plan of government. (p. 145)

consumer (kən sü′mər) A person who buys and uses things. (p. 259)

container (kən tā′nər) A box, can, or jar that holds something; a steel box as big as a railroad car used to carry and ship goods. (p. 314)

cost (kôst) An amount of money paid or charged for something. (p. 268)

council (koun′səl) A group of people who work with a leader to make decisions. (p. 134)

county (koun′tē) One of the sections into which a state or country is divided. (p. 51)

culture (kul′chər) A way of life a group of people share. (p. 95)

cutaway diagram (kut′ə wā dī′ə gram) A drawing that shows the inside and outside of an object at the same time. (p. 382)

D

dam (dam) A wall built across a stream or river that holds back and controls the water. (p. 67)

decision (di sizh′ən) A choice about what to do. (p. 264)

demand (di mand′) The desire for something, or the number of people who want certain goods. (p. 290)

democracy (di mok′rə sē) A form of government that is run by the people who live under it. (p. 389)

development (di vel′əp mənt) A group of houses or buildings planned and built together. (p.190)

dictionary (dik′shən er ē) A book that has words and their meanings, arranged in alphabetical order. (p. 348)

dock (dok) A flat surface where boats and ships are tied up. (p. 12)

economy (i kon′ə mē) The way a country uses its money, goods, natural resources, and services. (p. 212)

employee (em ploi′ē) A person who works for some person or business for pay. (p. 277)

encyclopedia (en sī klə pē′dē ə) A CD, book, or set of books, that has a great deal of information about many topics. (p. 348)

entrepreneur (äntrə prə nûr′) A person who starts and runs his or her own business. (p. 190)

environment (en vī′rən mənt) The air, water, land, and all the living things around us. (p. 50)

equator (i kwā′tər) An imaginary line that divides Earth into the Northern and Southern hemispheres. (p. 224)

executive (eg zek′yə tiv) The part of government that makes sure the laws are followed. (p. 351)

expenses (ek spen′səz) Things that money is spent on. (p. 261)

explorer (ek splôr′ər) A person who goes to a place that is new to them to find out about it. (p.107)

export (ek'spôrt) To send goods out of a country to be sold. (p. 313)

fact (fakt) A statement that can be proven to be true. (p. 392)

factory (fak'tərē) A place where things are manufactured. (p. 303)

federal (fed'ər əl) A system of government that shares power between local and national governments. (p. 352)

festival (fes'təvəl) A celebration. (p. 13)

flow chart (flō chärt) Pictures that show the steps necessary to complete an activity. (p. 300)

food processing (füd pros'es ing) Taking a crop and changing it by cooking, drying, or preserving it. (p. 292)

free enterprise (frē' en'tər prīz) The freedom to buy what you choose to buy from whomever you want. (p. 275)

freeway (frē'wā) A highway with more than two lanes and no intersections or stoplights. (p. 204)

geography (jē og'rəfē) The study of land and water and the way people, plants, and animals live on them. (p. 37)

glossary (glos'ərē) An alphabetical list of important words, meanings, and pronunciations, found in the back of a book. (p. 104)

government (guv'ərn ment) A group of people in charge of leading a community, state, or nation. (p.133)

governor (guv'ər nər) The person who is elected to be in charge of the state government. (p. 353)

graph (graf) A special kind of picture that shows information in a way that is easy to understand. (p. 208)

grid map (grid map) A map that has a grid, or set of lines that cross to form boxes. (p. 358)

guide words (gīd wûrds) Words that appear at the top of each page of a dictionary. They are the first and last words on each page. (p. 348)

headline (hed'līn) Words printed in large letters at the top of a story that sum up its main idea. (p. 184)

hemisphere (hem' is fîr) One half of Earth or another sphere. (p. 224)

heritage (her'i tij) Something handed down from earlier generations or from the past, such as a special way of doing things. (p. 169)

hero (hē'rō) A person you look up to because of his or her personal qualities or achievements. (p. 375)

homeland (hōm'land) A country where a person was born or has a home. (p. 98)

hub (hub) A transportation center. (p. 203)

human resources (hū'mən rē'sôr səs) The people who work for a business or person, and their ideas. (p. 277)

immigrant (im'i grənt) A person who leaves one country to live in another country. (p. 211)

import (im'pôrt) To bring in goods made or grown in another country to be sold here. (p. 313)

income (in'kum) Money received for working. (p. 260)

index (in'deks) An alphabetical list of subjects that are mentioned in a book, with page numbers. (p. 104)

interest (in'trist) An amount of money that a bank pays you for borrowing your money, or you pay a bank if you borrow money. (p. 262)

intermediate direction (in tər mēd'dē it di rek'shən) A direction halfway between two cardinal directions. (p. 130)

interstate highway (in'tər stāt hī'wā) A road that connects cities in two or more states with at least two lanes of traffic in each direction. (p. 186)

invention (in ven'chən) Something that has been made for the first time. (p. 201)

judicial (jü dish'əl) The part of government that decides what the laws mean and whether the laws follow the Constitution. (p. 351)

keyword (kē' wûrd) Words that you enter into a search engine to find other information. (p. 28)

landfill (land'fil) Dry land that people have made by filling in watery areas. (p. 228)

landform (land'fôrm) The shape of the surface of the land. (p. 38)

landform map (land'fôrm map) A map that uses different colors to show where different kinds of landforms are found. (p. 46)

landmark (land'märk) An important building, structure, or place. (p. 389)

law (lô) A rule made by the government for people in a community. (p. 343)

leader line (lēd′ər līn) Lines that lead your eye to the part of a diagram that is labeled. (p. 382)

legislative (lej′is lā tiv) Having to do with making laws. (p. 351)

liberty (lib′ər tē) Freedom from the control of another. (p. 387)

ligament (lig′ə mənt) A band of strong tissue that connects bones or holds an organ of the body in place. (p. 126)

line graph (līn graf) A graph that shows how something changes over time. (p. 310)

link (lingk) Something that joins or connects; a connection to another Web site. (p. 28)

location (lō kā′shən) The place where something is. (p. 12)

manufacturing (man yə fak′chər ing) The business of making or processing something. (p. 303)

mass transit (mas trans′it) Public transportation that moves a lot of people. (p. 206)

mayor (mā′ər) The head of a city council usually elected by the community. (p. 362)

migrant (mī′grənt) A person who moves from place to place. (p. 300)

migrate (mī′grāt) To move from one part of the country to another. (p. 190)

mine (mīn) An area where minerals are dug out of the ground. (p. 177)

mission (mish′ən) A church or settlement built around a church. (p. 141)

motto (mot′ō) A short sentence that says what someone or a group believes in. (p. 337)

mural (mür′əl) A large picture that is painted on a wall or ceiling. (p. 231)

natural resource (nach′ər əl rē′sôrs) Something found in nature that people use. (p. 39)

nonrenewable resource (non ri nü′ə bəl rē′sôrs) A natural resource that cannot be replaced. (p. 49)

O

opinion (ə pin′yən) What someone believes or feels. (p. 392)

opportunity (op ôr tün′i tē) A good chance to do something, such as go to school or get a better job. (p. 211)

opportunity cost (op ôr tūn′i tē kôst) The value of the next best choice when you choose one thing instead of another. (p. 269)

option (op′shən) A possible choice to solve a problem. (p. 58)

petroglyph (pet′rō glif) Carvings on rock. (p.99)

plain (plān) A large area of flat land. (p. 41)

population (pop ū lā′shən) The number of people who live in a place. (p. 22)

port (pôrt) A place where boats can dock, load, and unload safely. (p. 12)

powwow (pou′wou) A Native American festival where people share drumming, costumes, dances, and crafts. (p. 109)

preservation (prez ər vā′shən) Protection from loss, damage, or decay. (p. 229)

prime meridian (prīm mə rid′ē ən) An imaginary line that divides Earth into the Western and Eastern hemispheres. (p. 224)

private property (prī′vit prop′ər tē) Property that belongs to individual people or businesses, not the government or church. (p. 171)

producer (prə dü′sər) A person or business that makes or creates and sells a product. (p. 275)

profit (prof′it) The amount of money left after all the costs of operating a business have been paid. (p. 276)

rancho (ranch′ō) Cattle ranch. (p.171)

real estate (rēl′ es tāt′) Land together with all buildings and plants on it. (p. 212)

reference source (ref′ər əns sôrs) A book, CD, or Web site that has facts about many subjects, arranged so that you can look them up. (p. 348)

region (rē′jun) An area with common features that set it apart from other areas. (p. 41)

renewable resource (ri nü′ə bəl rē′sôrs) A natural resource that can be replaced. (p. 49)

reservation (res ûr vā′shən) Land set aside for Native Americans. (p. 108)

reservoir (rez′ər vwär) A place to store water. (p. 67)

responsibility (ri spon sə bil′i tē) A duty or job. (p. 338)

right (rīt) Something that everyone deserves. (p. 338)

road map (rōd map) A map that shows roads. (p. 186)

rural (rûr′əl) A place of farms or open land. (p. 25)

S

savings account (sā′vingz ə kount′) Money that a person keeps in a bank. (p. 262)

scale (skāl) The size of a plan, map, or model compared with the actual size of the area on Earth. (p. 16)

search engine (sûrch en′jən) A computer program that looks for information on the Internet. (p. 28)

segregation (seg ri gā′shən) The separation of people by race or color of their skin. (p. 380)

shaman (shä′mən) A person who is a religious leader and a healer. (p. 135)

slavery (slā′və rē) Keeping people against their will and forcing them to work without pay. (p. 377)

snare (snâr) A trap for small animals. (p. 126)

solution (sə lü′shən) An answer to a problem that solves it. (p. 58)

sovereign (sov′rən) Not controlled by others; independent. (p. 144)

sphere (sfîr) A round object like a ball. (p. 224)

state highway (stāt hī′wā) A highway that begins and finishes inside a state. (p. 186)

suburb (sub′ûrb) A community that is near a city. (p. 24)

supply (sə plī′) Amount of something available at any time. (p. 291)

symbol (sim′bəl) Something that represents something else. (p. 387)

T

table of contents (tā′bəl əv kon′tents) A list in the front of a book of the chapters and other parts of the book. (p. 104)

tax (taks) Money that people pay to support the government. (p. 353)

technology (tek nol′ə jē) The use of skills, ideas, and tools to meet peoples' needs. (p. 95)

thesaurus (thə sôr′əs) A book that lists synonyms, or words that have similar meanings. (p. 348)

timber (tim′bər) Wood that is used in building things. (p. 50)

time line (tīm līn) A list that shows the order of important events. (p. 174)

tourist (tùr′ist) A person who visits a place for fun. (p. 180)

trade off (trād ôf) An exchange of one thing you want in return for another. (p. 269)

tradition (trə dish′ən) A belief or custom handed down from the past, such as from parents to children. (p. 109)

Underground Railroad
(un′dər ground rāl′rōd) A system of secret routes and hiding places used by escaping enslaved Africans to reach freedom in the North or Canada. (p. 378)

union (ūn′yən) A group of workers who join together to improve their working conditions. (p. 293)

urban (ûr′bən) A city and its surrounding communities. (p. 22)

vegetation (vej i tā′shən) Plant life. (p. 126)

volunteer (vol ən tîr′) A person who chooses to do something without getting paid. (p. 344)

Index

This index lists many topics that appear in the book, along with the pages on which they are found. Page numbers after a *c* refer you to a chart, after an *m* refer you to a map, after a *p* refer you to photographs or artwork.

CREDITS

Photography Credits: All photographs are by Macmillan/McGraw-Hill (MMH) and Ken Karp for MMH, Michael Groen for MMH, except as noted below:

Cover Photos: (b) Frazer Harrison/Getty Images; (t) Robert Holmes/CORBIS; (inset) Ed Young/CORBIS; (bkgd) M. Angelo/CORBIS. G2: (bkgd) CORBIS; (t) Courtesy Steve Cunha. G4: (t) Richard Cummins/CORBIS; (b) Susan Ragan/AP-Wide World. G5: (t) Getty Images; (c) Getty Images; (b) Richard Glover; Ecoscene/CORBIS. IV: Thomas Hallstein/Outsight Photography. V: Ron Austing; Frank Lane Picture Agency/CORBIS. VI: AP/Wide World Photos. VII: From "The Lakewood Story." IX: Joe Sohm/Alamy Images.

Unit 1

2-3: (b) Nik Wheeler/CORBIS. 8: Dean Conger/CORBIS. 9: Tom Myers Photography. 10-11: Reed Saxon/AP Photo. 11: (tr) Dean Conger/CORBIS. 12: Tim Rue/CORBIS. 13: (b) Chris Carlson/AP Photo; (t) Juanito Holandez/AP Photo/Press -Telegram. 14: (tl) Justin Rudd; (tr) Stuart Westmorland/CORBIS; (cl) Femorale. 15: Taxi/Getty Images. 18: Gary Ballard. 19: Library of Congress. 20: Alamy Images. 21: (cr) Ric Francis/AP Photo; (tr) Joseph Sohm/CORBIS. 22: (t) Tom Myers Photography; (cr) Tom Myers Photography. 23: CORBIS. 24: (tr) Gary Jones/TheWinningShot.com; (bl) Francesc Muntada/CORBIS. 25: (tr) Rich Pedroncelli/AP Photo; (b) Robert W. Ginn/Photo Edit. 26: Mark E. Gibson/CORBIS. 27: Peter Beck/CORBIS. 30: (tl) Getty Images. 31: Getty Images. 34: (l) Bill Ross/CORBIS; (r) Claver Carroll /Photolibrary/age footstock. 35: Courtesy of The Department of Water and Power. 36: (b) Bill Ross/CORBIS. 37: (t) Ron Austing; Frank Lane Picture Agency/CORBIS; (b) Thomas Hallstein/Outsight Photography. 38: Thomas Hallstein/Outsight Photography. 39: (b) Nick Ut/AP Photos; (t) Neil Rabinowitz/CORBIS. 40: (b) Barrie Rokeach/Aerial Terrestrial Photography; (t) CORBIS; (inset) Elk Photography. 41: The Granger Collection. 42: Index Stock Imagery. 43: Annie Griffiths-Belt/CORBIS. 44: British Columbia Archives Collection. 45: (r) Courtesy of the Bancroft Library, University of California, Berkeley; (t) Museum of the African Diaspora. 48: Getty Images. 49: (b) Getty Images; (t) Foodpix. 50: (t) W. Cody/CORBIS; (b) Catherine Karnow/CORBIS. 52: (b) Claver Carroll/Photolibrary/age footstock; (inset) Gregory H. Bock. 53: (t) Craig Cozart/Stock Connection; (b) Getty Images News and Archives. 55: Getty Images. 56: (tl) Lester Lefkowitz/CORBIS; (cr) Grant Faint/Getty Images; (bl) Ron Watts/CORBIS. 57: (tl) Carol Cohen/CORBIS; (cr) Q T Luong/Terra Galleria Photography. 59: Jeff Greenberg/Photo Edit. 60: (bkgd) Greg Pease/Getty Images. 61: (bkgd) Getty Images 62-63: (bkgd) Getty Images. 66: CORBIS. 67: (t) Photodisc/Getty; (b) Lester Lefkowitz/Getty Images. 68: Courtesy of The Department of Water and Power. 69: Jim Wark/AirPhoto. 70: Jeff Becerra. 71: Gibson Stock Photography. 72-73: (bkgd) Craig Aurness/CORBIS. 74: (t) Mark E. Gibson/CORBIS. 77: CORBIS. 83: (b) George Ancona.

Unit 2

84: Courtesy of Viejas Enterprises; (bkgd) Craig Aurness/CORBIS. 90: The Field Museum, CSA10372, Photographer John Hudson. 92: (l) Denver Art Museum Collection: gift of Mrs. D. Bromfield; (r) Dugan Aguilar. 94: Lawrence Migdale/Photopix. 95: (tr) Denver Art Museum Collection: gift of Mrs. D. Bromfield; (br) A.W. Ericson/National Museum of the American Indian. 96: (tr) Phoebe A. Hearst Museum of Anthropology; (br) Raymond Bial/First Light Phtography. 98: (b) Native Stock Pictures. 99: (bl) David Laughing Horse; (tr) Evvie and Don Austin. 100: (b) Native Stock Pictures; (tl) The Oakland Museum. 101: Catherine Karnow/CORBIS. 102: (c) University of Southern California; (br) Lawrence Migdale/Stock Boston. 103: (b) PictureQuest; (tl), (tr) Phoebe A. Hearst Museum of Anthropology. 105: Catalog # 50/2149 Courtesy, American Museum of Natural History, Division of Anthropology. 106: Santa Barbara Mission Archive Library. 107: The Granger Collection. 108: (t) Phoebe A. Hearst Museum of Anthropology; (b) Ed Kashi/CORBIS. 109: Dugan Aguilar. 110: (inset) Bob Rowan/Progressive Image/CORBIS; (bkgd) Carol Cohen/CORBIS. 111: (b), (t) Allyson McCovey-Bunch. 112: David Young-Wolff/Photo Edit. 113: A. Ramey/PhotoEdit, Inc. 114: Courtesy of Mary Youngblood. 115: Courtesy of Mary Youngblood. 116-117: (bkgd) Pete Stone/CORBIS. 118: (tl) Michael T. Sedam/CORBIS. 122: (l) Roberta Labastida; (r) Edward H. Davis/The Constance DuBois Collection, San Diego Museum of Man. 123: Courtesy of the Viejas Tribe. 124: Roberta Labastida. 125: Brother Alfred Brousseau, Saint Mary's College. 126: (br) American Museum of Natural History; (tr) Darrell Gulin/CORBIS; (bl) Botanica/PictureArts. 127: (tr) California Academy of Science; (cr) J.W. Wall; (b) Norbert Wu/Alamy Images. 128: Richard Cummins/CORBIS. 132: Terry W. Eggers/CORBIS. 133: (br) San Diego Historical Society, Davis Collection; (tr) Phoebe A. Hearst Museum of Anthropology. 134: (t) National Museum of the American Indian/Smithsonian Institution; (b) Edward H. Davis/The Constance DuBois Collection, San Diego Museum of Man. 135: (tr) AP/Wide World Photos; (bl) Gary Ballard. 136: Phoebe A. Hearst Museum of Anthropology. 137: Jerry Schad/Photo Researchers. 140: Gary Ballard. 141: (br) Alamy Images; (tr) Jason T. Reyes. 142: Library of Congress. 143: (cr) Courtesy of the Bancroft Library, University of California, Berkeley; (tr) The Art Archive/Bill Manns. 144-145: Courtesy of Viejas Enterprises. 145: Benjamin Chambers/Reuters. 146: Gary Ballard. 147: Courtesy of Viejas Enterprises. 148: (tl) Emily Riddell/Lonely Planet Images. 155: (bl) George Ancona; (br) Dugan Aguilar.

Unit 3

156-157: Index Stock. 164: Smithsonian Inst. American Art Museum, Washington, D.C./Art Resource. 166: (l) Craig Aurness/CORBIS; (r) The Granger Collection. 167: Courtesy of City of Lakewood, California. 168: Courtesy of the Bancroft Library, University of California, Berkeley. 169: (t) Richard Cummins/CORBIS; (b) Nik Wheeler. 170: Craig Aurness/CORBIS. 171: (tl) Chuck Place Photography; (tr) CORBIS. 172: (inset) CORBIS. 173: Chuck Place Photography. 176: Bridgeman Art Library. 177: (br) The Granger Collection; (tr) Neal Mishler/Getty Images. 178: Courtesy of www.historichwy49.com. 179: (br) Historical Society of Seattle & King County/CORBIS; (t) Bettmann/CORBIS. 180: Jerry Dennis/Art Director & Trip Photo Library. 181: Gibson Stock Photography. 182: (bl) Betty Sederquist; (br) Robert Holmes Photography; (tl) Gibson Stock Photography. 183: (b) Gibson Stock Photography; (cr) Gibson Stock Photography. 184: Getty Images. 185: L.O.C./The Beinecke Rare Book and Manuscript Library, Yale University. 188: Jeff Gritchen. 189: (tr) "The Lakewood Story"; (br) Courtesy of City of Lakewood, California. 190: (l, c, r) Bettmann/CORBIS. 191: J.R. Eyerman/Time-Life Pictures/Getty Images. 192: Courtesy of City of Lakewood, California. 193: Jeff Gritchen. 194: (tl) Bob Galbraith/AP-Wide World. 198: (l) Lake County Museum/CORBIS; (r) Seema Handu. 199: Charles O'Rear/CORBIS. 200: Courtesy of Steve Lech. 201: Gunnar Kullenberg/EuroStyle Graphics/photographersdirect.com. 202: Courtesy of the Bancroft Library, University of California, Berkeley. 203: (bl) San Bernardino County Museum; (tr) Lake County Museum/CORBIS; (bl) California State Railroad Museum Library. 204: (bl) Douglas Kirkland/CORBIS; (tr) Coolstock Stock Photography. 206: Carl Morrison. 207: Carl Morrison. 209: John Sohm/Alamy Images. 210: Joseph Sohm/Alamy. 211: Larry Downing/Reuters/CORBIS. 212: (tr) Courtesy Alfredo Barajas; (b) Lawrence Migdale/Photo Researchers. 213: (tr) Lawrence Migdale; (br) Photo Edit. 214: Courtesy Seema Handu. 215: Tony Freeman/Photo Edit. 216: Alex Wong/Getty Images News and Archives. 217: (t) Bettman/CORBIS; (b) CORBIS Sygma. 218: (bkgd) CORBIS. 221: (bkgd) CORBIS. 222: (bkgd) Ramin Talaie/CORBIS. 226: Charles O'Rear/CORBIS. 227: Courtesy of Warren Whited. 228: Courtesy of the Bancroft Library, University of California, Berkeley. 230: (inset) Courtesy of the Bancroft Library, University of California, Berkeley; (bl) Robert Holmes Photography; (tl) Elk Photography. 231: Spencer Grant/Photo Edit. 232-233: Courtesy of the Choys. 234: (tr) Pete Saloutos/CORBIS; (br) Robert Landau/CORBIS; (tl) Nik Wheeler/CORBIS. 235: (cr) Chuck Place; (t) Rufus F. Folkks/CORBIS. 237: (bkgd) Joseph Sohm; ChromoSohm Inc./CORBIS. 238 (tl) Robert Landau/CORBIS.

Unit 4

246-247: Eric Risberg/AP-Wide World. 254: David Young-Wolff/PhotoEdit. 256: (l) CORBIS. 257: El Dorado Co. Photo Archives. 258: D. Boone/CORBIS. 259: CORBIS. 260: (r) David Young-Wolff/Photo Edit; (l) Jonathan Nourok/PhotoEdit. 262: Christie's Images, Inc. 263: (bkgd) Matthias Kulka/CORBIS. 264: (l) Sky Bonillo/Photo Edit; (c, r) Photoedit. 265: (b) Michael Newman/Photo Edit. 267: ©2000 Duke University Rare Book, Manuscript, and Special Collections Library Copyright: (courtesy of Library of Congress/American Memory). 270: (r) The San Diego Public Library; (l) Gary Conner/PhotoEdit. 271: Index Stock. 273-274: Index Stock Imagery. 274: S.Lingren/inStock. 275: Photodisc. 276: (r), (l) S.Lindgren/inStock. 277: (r), (bl) S.Lindgren/inStock. 278: (l) Lowell Georgia/Photo Researchers; (c) Courtesy of El Dorado Company Photo Archives; (r) S. Lindgren/inStock. 279: (l), (r) S. Lindgren/inStock. 280: Courtesy of El Dorado Company Photo Archives. 281: Foodpix. 282: (tl) Courtesy of Bakersfieldchamber.org. 283: (l, c) GettyImages; (cl, cr, r) CORBIS. 286: (l) Renee Knoeber/AP-Wide World; (r) Tim Rue/CORBIS. 287: (b) Ric Francis/AP-Wide World. 288: Ed Young/CORBIS. 289: (t) AGStockUSA, Inc./Alamy Images; (b) Sierra Nature Prints. 290: (r, bl) George Wright. 291: Renee Knoeber/AP-Wide World. 292: Gary Kazanjian/AP-Wide World; (t) Courtesy of University of California DANR. 293: Noella Ballenger/Alamy Images. 294: (l) DK Images; (cr) Foodfolio/Alamy Images; (bl) Natural Visions. 295: Martin Siepmann/Alamy Images. 296: (bl) Arthur Schatz/Getty Images News and Archives; (tl) Joe Raedle/Getty Images. 297: (b) Sakuma/AP-Wide World; (tr) Bettmann/CORBIS. 298: (bl) Complimentary of Kings County Library; (c) Photodisc; (tr) The Image Works. 299: (cr) Library of Congress; (bl) Michael T. Sedam/CORBIS; (tr) Tom Bean/CORBIS. 302: Getty Images. 303: (br) First Light Associated Photographers; (tr) Getty Images. 304: (b) Tim Rue/CORBIS; (tl), (tr) Rib Lake Plywood. 305: (tl), (tr) Rib Lake Plywood, Inc.; (cr) NHS Inc. 306: David A. Dobbs. 307: Garry Black/Masterfile. 308: Neil Rabinowitz/CORBIS. 309: (l) Library of Congress; (b) aviationshoppe.com. 310-311: Mark Richards/PhotoEdit. 312: Gibson Stock Photography. 313: Courtesy of Port of Oakland. 314: James L. Amos/CORBIS. 315: (tr) Ric Francis/AP-Wide World; (bl) Port of Oakland. 317: PU from CA 2000. 318: Courtesy Bill Emerson Oakland Nadhodka Sister City Association. 319: Courtesy of Oakland Nadhodka Sister City Association. 320: (tl) Ron Watts/CORBIS. 327: (My First Book) Football Courtesy of Wilson Sporting Goods Co.; Crayons Courtesy of Binney & Smith; Orange juice Courtesy of Florida Department of Citrus; Guitar Courtesy of Martin Guitar Company; Jelly Courtesy of Grafton Smith.

Unit 5

328: Photodisc/Getty. 332: Photodisc/Getty. 334: (l) Michael Ventura/Photo Edit; (r) AP-Wide World. 335: (l) Stephan Savoia/AP- Wide World; (r) City of Stockton. 336: LWA-Dann Tardiff/CORBIS. 337: Granger Collection LTD. 338: Joseph Sohm; Visions of America/CORBIS. 339: Michael Ventura/Photo Edit. 340: (l) The Granger Collection; (b) Courtesy of Monticello/Thomas Jefferson Foundation, Inc./University of Virginia. 341: Library of Congress. 342: GK photography/Alamy Images. 343: (tr) Dennis Degnan/CORBIS; (br) Photo Edit. 344: Lee Celano/AP-Wide World. 345: (b) Tony Freeman/Photo Edit; (t) RICH Pedroncelli/AP-Wide World. 346: AP-Wide World.

Acknowledgments

The Lakewood Story, by the City of Lakewood, California. Copyright © 2004 by the City of Lakewood. Used by permission.

The Grapes of Wrath, by John Steinbeck. Copyright © 1939 by John Steinbeck. Copyright © Renewed 1967 by John Steinbeck. Published by Penguin Books. All Rights Reserved. Used by Permission.

Linh Hoang, from article by Jesse Mangaliman. The San Jose Mercury News, February 18, 2003. Copyright © 2003 by Knight Ridder. All Rights Reserved. Used by Permission.

Cover permission for **Boom Town**, Text by Sonia Levitin. Illustrations by Cat Bowman Smith. Text Copyright © 1998 by Sonia Levitin. Illustrations Copyright © 1998 by Cat Bowman Smith. Published by Scholastic, Inc. All Rights Reserved.

Cover permission for **Picture in the Past: Life in San Francisco's Chinatown**, by Sally Senzell Isaacs. Copyright © 2003 by Reed Educational & Professional Publishing. Published by Heinemann Library. All Rights Reserved.

Cover permission for **A Mission For the People: The Story of La Purisima**, by Mary Ann Fraser. Copyright © 1997 by Mary Ann Fraser. Published by Henry Holt and Company, Inc. All Rights Reserved.

Max Malone Makes A Million, Text by Charlotte Herman. Illustrations by Cat Bowman Smith. Text © 1991 by Charlotte Herman. Illustrations © 1991 by Cat Bowman Smith. Published by Henry Holt and Company, LLC. All Rights Reserved. Used by permission.

Julia Morgan, from ThinkExist website: http://en.thinkexist.com/keyword/turn_down/ Used by Permission.

Cesar Chavez, from California Department of Education: <http://chavez.cde.ca.gov/ModelCurriculum/Teachers/Lessons/Resources/Biographies/Biographical_Sketch_4thGrd.aspx> Used by Permission.

Cover permission for **My First Book of How Things Are Made**, by George Jones. Copyright © 1995 by Pond Press. Published by Scholastic, Inc. All Rights Reserved.

Cover permission for **Great-Grandma Tells of Threshing Day**, Text by Verda Cross. Illustrations by Gail Owens. Text Copyright © 1992 by Verda Cross. Illustrations Copyright © 1992 by Gail Owens. Published by Albert Whitman & Company. All Rights Reserved.

Cover permission for **If You Made A Million**, Text by David M. Schwartz. Pictures by Steven Kellogg. Text Copyright © 1989 by David M. Schwartz. Illustrations Copyright © 1989 by Steven Kellogg. Published by HarperCollins Publishers. All Rights Reserved.

Cover permission for **America Is …**, Text by Louise Borden. Illustrated by Stacey Schuett. Text Copyright © 2002 by Louise Borden. Illustrations Copyright © 2002 by Stacey Schuett. Published by Margaret K. McElderry Books, An Imprint of Simon & Schuster Children's Publishing Division. All Rights Reserved.

Cover permission for **Capital! Washington D.C. from A to Z**, Text by Laura Kraus Melmed. Illustrated by Frané Lessac. Text Copyright © 2003 by Laura Kraus Melmed. Illustrations Copyright © 2003 Frané Lessac. Published by HarperCollins Publishers. All Rights Reserved.

Cover permission for **Uncle Sam and Old Glory: Symbols of America**, Text by Delno C. West and Jean M. West. Woodcuts by Christopher Manson. Text Copyright © 2000 by Delno C. West and Jean M. West. Illustrations Copyright © 2000 by Christopher Manson. Published by Atheneum Books for Young Readers. All Rights Reserved.

The Autobiography of Martin Luther King, Jr., Edited by Clayborne Carson, Copyright © 1998 by the Heirs to the Estate of Martin Luther King, Jr. Published by Warner Books. Used by Permission.

CALIFORNIA FRAMEWORK

Historical and Social Sciences Analysis Skills

Chronological and Spatial Thinking

1. Students place key events and people of the historical era they are studying in a chronological sequence and within a spatial context; they interpret time lines.

2. Students correctly apply terms related to time, including *past, present, future, decade, century,* and *generation.*

3. Students explain how the present is connected to the past, identifying both similarities and differences between the two, and how some things change over time and some things stay the same.

4. Students use map and globe skills to determine the absolute locations of places and interpret information available through a map's or globe's legend, scale, and symbolic representations.

5. Students judge the significance of the relative location of a place (e.g., proximity to a harbor, on trade routes) and analyze how relative advantages or disadvantages can change over time.

Research, Evidence, and Point of View

1. Students differentiate between primary and secondary sources.

2. Students pose relevant questions about events they encounter in historical documents, eyewitness accounts, oral histories, letters, diaries, artifacts, photographs, maps, artworks, and architecture.

3. Students distinguish fact from fiction by comparing documentary sources on historical figures and events with fictionalized characters and events.

Historical Interpretation

1. Students summarize the key events of the era they are studying and explain the historical contexts of those events.

2. Students identify the human and physical characteristics of the places they are studying and explain how those features form the unique character of those places.

3. Students identify and interpret the multiple causes and effects of historical events.

4. Students conduct cost-benefit analyses of historical and current events.

History—Social Science Content Standards
Grade 3 Continuity and Change

3.1 **Students describe the physical and human geography and use maps, tables, graphs, photographs, and charts to organize information about people, places, and environments in a spatial context.**

1. Identify geographical features in their local region (e.g., deserts, mountains, valleys, hills, coastal areas, oceans, lakes).

2. Trace the ways in which people have used the resources of the local region and modified the physical environment (e.g., a dam constructed upstream changed a river or coastline).

3.2 **Students describe the American Indian nations in their local region long ago and in the recent past.**

1. Describe national identities, religious beliefs, customs, and various folklore traditions.

2. Discuss the ways in which physical geography, including climate, influenced how the local Indian nations adapted to their natural environment (e.g., how they obtained food, clothing, tools).

3. Describe the economy and systems of government, particularly those with tribal constitutions, and their relationship to federal and state governments.

4. Discuss the interaction of new settlers with the already established Indians of the region.

3.3 **Students draw from historical and community resources to organize the sequence of local historical events and describe how each period of settlement left its mark on the land.**

1. Research the explorers who visited here, the newcomers who settled here, and the people who continue to come to the region, including their cultural and religious traditions and contributions.

2. Describe the economies established by settlers and their influence on the present-day economy, with emphasis on the importance of private property and entrepreneurship.

3. Trace why their community was established, how individuals and families contributed to its founding and development, and how the community has changed over time, drawing on maps, photographs, oral histories, letters, newspapers, and other primary sources.

3.4 **Students understand the role of rules and laws in our daily lives and the basic structure of the U.S. government.**

1. Determine the reasons for rules, laws, and the U.S. Constitution; the role of citizenship in the promotion of rules and laws; and the consequences for people who violate rules and laws.

2. Discuss the importance of public virtue and the role of citizens, including how to participate in a classroom, in the community, and in civic life.

3. Know the histories of important local and national landmarks, symbols, and essential documents that create a sense of community among citizens and exemplify cherished ideals (e.g., the U.S. flag, the bald eagle, the Statue of Liberty, the U.S. Constitution, the Declaration of Independence, the U.S. Capitol).

4. Understand the three branches of government, with an emphasis on local government.

5. Describe the ways in which California, the other states, and sovereign American Indian tribes contribute to the making of our nation and participate in the federal system of government.

6. Describe the lives of American heroes who took risks to secure our freedoms (e.g., Anne Hutchinson, Benjamin Franklin, Thomas Jefferson, Abraham Lincoln, Frederick Douglass, Harriet Tubman, Martin Luther King, Jr.).

3.5 **Students demonstrate basic economic reasoning skills and an understanding of the economy of the local region.**

1. Describe the ways in which local producers have used and are using natural resources, human resources, and capital resources to produce goods and services in the past and the present.

2. Understand that some goods are made locally, some elsewhere in the United States, and some abroad.

3. Understand that individual economic choices involve trade-offs and the evaluation of benefits and costs.

4. Discuss the relationship of students' "work" in school and their personal human capital.